CHASING US

KAT T. MASEN

Kat T. Masen

Chasing Us

A Second Chance Love Triangle
The Dark Love Series Book 2

ISBN: 979-8691790140
ISBN: 979-8755766654

Editing by Nicki at Swish Design & Editing
Proofing by Kay at Swish Design & Editing
Cover Image Copyright 2020
Second Edition 2020
All Rights Reserved

ONE

ALEX

Nine Years Ago

"Alex, you're finally home."

Samantha appeared out of the living room, standing inside the hallway with her arms crossed over her chest. I looked at my watch, only noticing now it was after seven. I'm not surprised she's angry since I told her I'd be home for dinner.

This had become a regular occurrence lately, and I knew I had to start being more careful. *Soon,* I kept telling myself, *soon*.

"Sorry, I got caught up at the hospital with Dad," I lied.

"Well, you're here now, I guess. I have some news to tell you." Her face brightened as she bounced around me. "Come, sit down."

I followed her to the living room. She patted the couch where I reluctantly took a seat next to her, exhausted from the double life I was living. Samantha continued to smile, something I hadn't seen in a while. She's a beautiful woman. Her long golden blonde hair flowed down her back, her eyes sparkling as she spoke. I remembered a time when I couldn't get enough of her. *But that was before...*

"Alex, I'm pregnant."

She was what?

Each word was like dynamite exploding one after another. Jerking my head back, my brain couldn't comprehend, and I blurted out the first words that came to mind. "How did this happen? I haven't fucked you in three months!"

I began to tremble with rage, my angered gaze slicing through her as I distanced myself from where she sat. Every scenario ran through my mind, but all I could come up with was nothing. I had no recollection of touching her, let alone sticking my dick inside of her long enough to get her pregnant.

Her demeanor changed with the cut of my words. The beautiful smile disappeared, her face turned red, the veins on her forehead were ready to burst at any given moment. She folded her arms, her chest rising and falling at a fast pace. I braced myself knowing the storm was about to hit, and I was standing in its path.

"That's nice, Alex. You can't even remember fucking your wife," she shot back. Animosity lingered in her words, and unable to look at her, I paced the area near the couch. "It was that night you came home drunk a month ago. I remember it because you couldn't get enough of me, fucking me for hours telling me how much you loved me." Lost in thought, she paused, the smirk of satisfaction subsiding as if she realized the enormity of this situation.

I remembered the night. It was the night Charlotte and I were doing tequila shots behind the bleachers at school. She had dared me to take shots from her belly, but I thought it was more interesting for her to hold the shot glass between her thighs. We fucked twice on the cold, dirty ground, and all I can remember was dragging myself home completely inebriated and passing out in our bed.

How could you let this happen?

The temperature was rising in the room. Suddenly, my chest tightened, unable to swallow, unable to breathe, my hands shaking uncontrollably.

I knew the signs.

I was having a panic attack.

"You took advantage of me?" I yelled as my panic morphed into anger.

Her stare was cold and uninviting. She was no longer the sweet girl I married in college, but I knew that was my fault, I brought this out of her. I felt a pang of guilt. I screwed this up big time. Fuck, what will my mom and dad say? What the hell will Adriana say? It occurred to me at this moment that I actually didn't give a shit what they thought. It was Charlotte plaguing me, and the hurt this would cause.

I eyed the vase sitting on the table, and with a lapse in judgment, I whacked the fucking ugly piece of shit, watching it smash against the wall into a million pieces, the flowers and water scattering all across the room.

Samantha jumped in shock followed by a small whimper. "Took advantage of you?" she cried, throwing her arms in the air. *"You are my husband, not hers!"*

I froze.

Not even a *flinch.*

I knew she had suspected something. I just didn't know how much she knew. My tongue was tied, there were no words I could say right now that could erase this moment.

This was it—she knew.

No turning back.

No denying the truth.

The moment I had dreaded since the day I fell in love with Charlotte had come, but this wasn't how it was supposed to happen. There wasn't supposed to be a baby involved. The room remained silent. I buried my head in my hands unable to cope with the magnitude of the situation.

"Samantha..." I didn't know how to respond, unable to rid myself of the dullness in my chest, the heaviness of my actions crippling my ability to think straight.

What would Charlotte think when she found out? I promised her I hadn't touched Samantha since we began our affair. My stomach churned—I couldn't lose her. No way could I lose Charlotte. I wouldn't know how to live without her. The pain in my chest deepened as the possibility weighed heavily on my mind that Charlotte would walk out of my life for good.

"Anyway, I'm sure your little girlfriend will find out soon. Kaley Wilson was at the doctor's office when I found out. We had a nice little chat," she gloated.

Kaley Wilson, the little bitch, had made life hell for Charlotte. She was probably knocking on Charlotte's door right now spreading the news. I needed to get out, I needed a chance to explain all this to Charlotte. She needed to know how sorry I was, but more importantly, that I didn't mean to hurt her. My poor Charlotte, my heart sank knowing what was coming. The urge to protect her from the pain was the only thing I was determined to do.

The doorbell rang much to my surprise as we weren't expecting anyone. Samantha walked over to open the door, and I heard the voices, recognizing them immediately. It was my parents and sister. I prepared myself for what was about to come.

"Hi, son. Samantha called us over saying you had some news."

My mother leaned in and kissed me on the cheek. Her face excited, I knew she had suspected something, her lifelong dream of being a grandmother finally being fulfilled. I couldn't keep up the charade, the anger I felt right now was overwhelming.

"Please, Andrew and Emily, sit down." Samantha led them to the living room, my sister grabbing Samantha's hand, jumping up and down.

"Would anyone like a drink?" Samantha asked.

"We're fine, sweetheart. Please, what's the big news?"

"Well, I might as well get straight to the point. Alex and I are expecting a baby!" she squealed.

Adriana started jumping up and down, hugging Samantha, careful not to squeeze her. My mother, already crying, also stood to hug Samantha.

My father remained still, pressing his lips tightly, not saying a single word. Unlike the women around me elated over the news, he didn't express any emotion besides an expression of disappointment.

"A bit young, don't you think?" he questioned with a bitter smile.

Yes, Dad. Fucking young and a massive fail on my behalf, I wanted to yell at him.

"Andrew, please," my mother scolded. "A child is a blessing."

"Emily, he has a career to focus on with years of studying to become a doctor, and now what?"

Despite my anger toward this outcome, I didn't appreciate being spoken about like I wasn't standing here. But what could I say? I didn't want this baby. I wasn't ready to become a father.

"You're right, Dad," I agreed, biting my tongue to stop the malice teetering on the edge. "It all seems like a waste, but you did it with Mom, same age. So, what's stopping me?"

"Because I wanted more for you!" he barked, my mother clasping her hand against her chest at his outburst. "This wasn't the plan."

"Right." I laughed, nodding. "I forgot this was *your* life... not mine."

I wanted to go to Charlotte, more than anything I had ever wanted in my life, the urge to close my eyes and make this disappear lingering in my thoughts. This was all too much—the baby and my father's disappointment in being unable to control *my* life.

"I need... I need to go for a run."

I walked into my bedroom and put on my trainers. I left the house with the women still basking in the news, and my father sulking in disappointment.

With my headphones on, I searched my playlist needing something that reminded me of a happier time. I ran hard along the hiking trails, not letting my mind think about the baby.

I stood against a tree, trying to catch my breath.

The dream was falling apart.

I was going to shatter this for us.

I needed her right now.

I needed to feel her one more time before our delusional bubble burst. The song quickly changed, and I decided to do what I had done nearly every night when we were apart—I stood in the dark watching her room.

My focus moved to her bedroom window—the lights were out—she must have been sleeping. I wanted to crawl into her bed, hold her tight, and promise Charlotte we would get through this somehow.

We could run away, leave everyone and everything behind. I'd do that for her if she asked me. I would do anything as long as it meant she stayed in my life.

We slept in separate rooms that night, but I didn't sleep. Samantha chose not to talk to me, nor did she bring up Charlotte again. I lay awake thinking of ways to get out of this. How could I have let this happen? I didn't recall having sex with her, but then again, I'd been so intoxicated.

I had to see Charlotte, just one more time. I still didn't know what I was going to do. Tomorrow, I thought, I would tell her before someone else did.

Tomorrow arrived quicker than I anticipated, and with my gut in wrenching pain all day, I decided tequila would solve the problem. So maybe I drank more than I should have, but it eased the pain and hid that hollow feeling that seeped into every crevice.

On top of the cliff, at our special place, she sensed it straight away and called me out on it. What I didn't expect was for her to think I was telling her that it was over. The pain stabbed me, not tiny daggers but samurai swords, deep cuts bound to leave permanent scars. One by one I felt them strike as I watched her expression. The sword was pulled out of my heart for a moment, so I could say the words which echoed in my head—I couldn't breathe without her.

"Ride or die, 'til death us do part."

I left Charlotte that day promising her I'd find a way for us to be together. Somehow, there had to be an answer to solve this massive fucking mess I created.

It bought me more time to figure something out.

Once I sobered up, I planned it out. I was going to tell Samantha I'd support her and the baby, but I couldn't go on with our marriage. I didn't love her. My heart belonged to Charlotte, it always would.

As I drove into my driveway, I noticed my parents' car parked behind ours. Oh, for fuck's sake, more baby talk. Taking in deep breaths, I prepared myself for the overjoyed baby talk about to fall all over me.

The moment I stepped inside the house, I heard sobbing. It was coming from the living room. I walked down the hallway to find Samantha buried into my mother's arms, my father looking furious, and Adriana, well, she sat there staring at the floor.

"What's going on?" I asked, hesitating as the ambiance in the room was morbid.

"How could you do this to Samantha, Alex?"

"Mom, what are you talking about? Do what?"

"*Charlie.*" My father strained as he spoke.

Oh fuck.

My shoulders crumpled as my eyes fell to the floor, unable to come up with anything worthy.

I knew one day it would come out, but I didn't think it would be in front of my parents like this. I searched my brain for an explanation, but nothing I said or did would ease this moment.

"Dad, I just—"

"You have screwed up big time, Alexander!" His voice echoed, bouncing off the walls with a loud aftershock startling everyone inside the room. "Your wife went into the hospital today with pains after she found emails between you and Charlie. Not only have you dishonored your marriage, but you have put your child's life at risk. What the hell were you thinking? She's eighteen!"

There were no words to explain how much I loved Charlotte, that she was everything to me. I looked at Adriana, who still refused to look my way. She'd felt betrayed by her best friend, surely. It shouldn't be this way. She knew Charlotte better than anyone else. Why couldn't she understand why I did this? I walked over to Adriana placing my hand on her shoulder only to be met by a cold stare.

"It has been decided that you and Samantha will leave for San Francisco tonight. Her sister's apartment has been vacant for months, so you'll be staying there. I'll have all your things sent to you in the next few days. You are not to contact Charlie—"

The guilt I had been feeling is suddenly overridden by anger. I walked toward where my father stood, standing eye to eye meeting his stance and interrupted his tirade, "Dad, since when can you dictate what I do with my life? You have no idea what happened!"

"You listen to me real good, son. If anything happens to that baby, you'll be held responsible for the rest of your life, you understand? You *will* make this marriage work. You made vows in a church in front of God that you would love and honor her for as long as you both shall live," he warned, his finger pointing straight at my face. "Your immaturity has landed you in this mess, but you're an *Edwards,* and you'll rectify this immediately. You are to leave this town and never return. When Mark Mason gets wind of this, you are going to wish you were long gone. As usual, I'll deal with the aftermath of your mistakes. Do not embarrass our family any further."

The doorbell rang. It was the car service. My mother ushered Samantha to the car taking along her suitcase, my father taking the other which I could only assume was mine.

I don't remember walking to the car and getting in, my mind not comprehending what just happened or what was going to happen. In my zombie-like state, my emotions and physical movement were not communicating. My father closed the door behind me.

I open the window slightly, desperately needing to speak to my sister. "Adriana, I'm sorry. Please... believe me." It was all I could manage.

She stood at the doorway not making eye contact with me, a tear falling down her cheek before she walked back into the house. I watched as my mother bowed her head, disappointed that this glorious moment was taken away from her because of my infidelity. My father stood there, his face stern. I had never in my life seen my father this way. It was a side of him that frightened me. I don't know why since I was fucking twenty-five—an adult.

I knew I was to blame for this whole situation. And if something happened to this baby, I'd never be able to live with the fact that it was because of me.

The car drove off through town and onto the interstate. I started to panic, the reality setting in that I would no longer see Charlie, no longer kiss her beautiful lips or hold her in my arms. Samantha must have sensed the anxiety I was feeling as she laughed to herself causing me to turn my head and face her.

"Don't even think about using your phone. Your father disconnected it an hour ago."

Was this her plan all along?

Trap me in our marriage by falling pregnant?

Closing my eyes, I replayed what my father had said. This baby didn't deserve to suffer because of me. I knew that, but how could I ignore the gut-wrenching pain I felt knowing I'd never see Charlotte again?

This wasn't the path I chose, but as long as Samantha was carrying my baby, I had no choice.

TWO

NIKKI

Present

"Right there... right there... who's your daddy?" Rocky hisses breathlessly.

It has been our morning ritual of late—blow jobs before breakfast. It's always quick, and Rocky never lasts long, which only means I give great head —obviously.

I pull his boxers up, satisfied with myself for getting the job done in under two minutes. Now, I have peace and quiet for the next half hour before we have to pack and head back home to the city.

The Hamptons is a great place to relax and unwind, but I miss the pressure of work. I definitely miss bossing people around and telling them to shove their million-dollar lawsuits up their asses.

But I never call myself a workaholic.

I'm not Charlie.

If there's one word to describe Charlie, it would be 'determined.' Most of the time, she knows what she wants and is unstoppable. In college, she'd cram in studying every second of the day she had free, which worked to my advantage because, let's face it, I was too busy fucking Rocky to be cramming like her. It explains why I'm a mom to a seven-year-old at the ripe old age of twenty-seven.

Charlie aced college, graduated almost top of the class, and without her, we wouldn't have started Mason & Romano. She's steadfast, knows exactly how to make our firm a success, and her drive to succeed in the business world surpasses any other person I know.

Add to that, the woman is a fucking goddess. She can walk down the street, and you can see men walk past her with their dicks practically saluting her.

Charlie Mason is the whole package.

The only area she can't get right is her love life. We're talking failure of epic proportions. She dated randomly throughout college, but something or someone always held her back. I didn't push, I wasn't the type of person to make her open up if she didn't want to. Yet, I did work hard to organize blind dates with the hottest guys in college. I mean, the ones that if Rocky weren't my husband, I'd have ridden them faster than a rollercoaster at Disneyland. The point is no one piqued her interest until Julian Baker came along.

There is no question he's Mr. Perfect, kind of scary because really there's no such thing. Everyone has a flaw, but with Julian, it's impossible to find one. When Charlie announced they were engaged, I was in shock because they had only been together a few months. It's like one of those cheesy rom-com movies—love at first sight then a happily ever after.

Something just didn't feel right, and as one of her best friends and business partner, I didn't hold back my opinion on the matter. She knows I'm a straight shooter, and this situation warranted a warning.

That was just the tip of the iceberg until that beautiful jerk walked back into Charlie's life.

Lex Edwards—billionaire extraordinaire.

I knew who Lex Edwards was. Rocky rambled on about him every time he was on page six. The guy had an abnormal obsession with Lex's life, and I'm surprised Charlie never stumbled across the same articles. But then again, her priority had always been on work.

In my lifetime, I never would have figured out it was the same man—*the* Alex who Charlie would scream out for in her sleep. Her waking up drenched in a cold sweat with tears streaming down her face was exhausting the first six months we lived together. When I pieced the puzzle together, I realized there was more to this story than Charlie let on.

Lex irked me. He completely rubbed me the wrong way. Not in the way I normally would like to be rubbed, but hey, the man's obscenely gorgeous. I hated admitting that vital piece of information.

He had some hold over Charlie, and without a shadow of a doubt, every time he was near her, her vagina celebrated like it won the Super Bowl.

Bottom line here—I loathed him.

My best friend was fucked up royally over what he did to her, and you always got to have your girl's back when the going gets tough. The thing is, I saw a change in him over the weekend in the Hamptons. He wasn't the man I thought he was. Okay, yeah, I was becoming a soft bitch, but he revealed himself this weekend, and I no longer saw him as the man who was splashed all over the tabloids. I saw a man who fell in love with a girl and did what he thought was right by everyone. Just because I saw this other side of him didn't mean I lightened up. No, I was still a bitch—a hot bitch who gave the best head to her husband.

I roll over to my side, checking my phone quickly before hopping into the shower. There are only a few emails, nothing important needing attention today. After showering, dressing in a pair of jeans and a loose shirt, my next stop is picking up Will next door. This is going to be hard. Will hated leaving his friends, so I decide to grab a quick cup of coffee from the kitchen to muster the energy to deal with his impending tantrum.

Rocky is pacing up and down the kitchen visibly upset about something.

"What's wrong?" I ask, pouring the freshly brewed coffee into a mug.

He throws the paper at me. It falls to the floor, my reflexes not reactive at this time of the morning. Bending down, I pick it up, my eyes darting to the article he points to.

My eyes scan over the words, each sentence burrowing inside my heart making it sink deeper and deeper. The nerve of these reporters to publish such bullshit, but Charlie won't believe that. I know her well—she's too emotionally invested in Lex returning to see how misconstrued the media can be, especially when it comes to billionaire tycoons and their love lives. The more money you have, the bigger target you are.

The house is eerily quiet. "Where is she?"

"She drove back to the city, asked me to take her car back." Rocky twists his hair, still pacing the area of the kitchen.

He's always had a soft spot for Charlie, treats her like a sister, and I love him even more for it.

"Where's Lex?"

"Still sleeping, I guess."

"Shit, Rocky. What did she say? Was she upset?" Clenching my jaw, I mirror Rocky's pacing, desperately trying to think of how to fix this. "Of course, she'd be upset."

Rocky stops me, latching onto both my arms to still my movements. "Babe, calm down."

I grab my phone and try to dial her number—voicemail.

Leaving a brief message, I text her as well. Lex needs to wake up. As the thought leaves my mind, he walks into the kitchen looking very content. He looks different, jubilant, like a man who got laid by the woman he's in love with.

"Morning. Have you guys seen Charlotte?"

If this were two weeks ago, I'd have gladly thrown the paper at his face and told him he was nothing more than a selfish manwhore, but like I said, something changed. He's different. I see this side of him that Charlie was once, and still is, in love with this happy, carefree, fun-loving guy who adores her. I wasn't surprised they were fucking all over The Hamptons. I wondered if they did it in the hot tub after we did. I told Rocky it was gross to jizz in the water, but he said with my tits bouncing in front of him all wet, he couldn't help himself.

Rocky and I glance at each other as Lex asks about Charlie again. With my arms folded, preparing for the worst, Rocky passes him the paper. Lex stares at it with confusion before his eyes dart back and forth. I brace myself as his skin flushes, the paper crunching into his fist as he throws it onto the floor. Grabbing his phone, he mutters the words 'you stupid bitch,' then he dials the number.

"Kate. Get me Victoria on the phone right now." He hangs up abruptly, leaning on the table for support. "Where is she?"

"She went back to the city."

"How long ago?"

"About half an hour."

"Fuck!" He slams his fist against the counter, startling the both of us. "This is the fucking press. Victoria is a business colleague and nothing more. These pictures are completely out of context. I've never touched the stupid bitch, nor would I ever."

I don't know why I believe him. The thing is that even though I disliked him, he proved me wrong, which is something quite unheard of. He loves Charlie. And yeah, I know the past was fucked up, but that was years ago, and they have both grown since then.

I just didn't understand why Charlie had this massive trust issue, and why she couldn't see how much he loved her. I also know tabloids can spin shit out of their asses and manipulate photographs. I learned that the hard way when there was a picture of Rocky a few years back at a sporting event, and it looked like a chick was blowing him.

This isn't about taking sides, but Charlie is stubborn, and right now, I can't help but feel sorry for the guy. Not that I'm going to tell him that.

We need to get back to the city as soon as possible and fix the damage that's been done. Charlie will shut everyone out, including me, because it's her defense mechanism. I try her number again—still voicemail. I ask Rocky to get Will from next door. It isn't long before Adriana and Elijah walk into the kitchen.

"Hey, guys, what's happening?" Adriana takes a seat at the table, grabbing a banana and peeling it. She glances from me to Lex, confused by our silence.

"Charlie's gone," I tell her.

"Gone? Where?"

I hand her the paper from the floor, watching as Lex is standing at the window gazing outside. His eyes are glazed over, his expression heartbroken. Maybe he knew, just like me, how Charlie would take this.

"Lex, is this true?"

"Are you fucking kidding me, Adriana?" he shot back.

"But the photos look, well—"

"What, Adriana?"

"Well, they look like what the article says."

"Fuck, Adriana!"

"Lex, calm down," Elijah warns him.

"Don't you get it? She finally fucking told me she trusts me and wants a future with me, and then this happens. This is so fucked up!" He slams his fist on the counter again, startling us. "Last night..."

Adriana puts her arm around her brother's shoulder, attempting to comfort him. "Last night, what?"

"Lex, we need to head back," I tell him, noticing the time. "Let me deal with her in the meantime. She needs to calm down. You need to make sure whoever posted this article retracts their damn words. Look, Will is going to be here any minute. Can you please not mention why she left?"

A few minutes later, Will walks in. He's elated to see Lex, who tries his best not to show any anger in front of the child. I have to hand it to him, taking a kid's feelings into account is hard to do when you are feeling like complete shit. Will asks where Charlie is, so Adriana quickly explains that something urgent came up in the city. He doesn't seem to notice anything else, but he begs Lex to ride in the car with us. Of course, Lex agrees, and that's the end of the conversation.

We pack our things and drive out of The Hamptons.

Adriana and Elijah take Charlie's car, and the rest of us take the RV Rocky borrowed from a friend. I sit in the back with Will as he quietly plays on his iPad. Every so often, he looks up and asks if we are home yet. I scour my emails for anything from Charlie. Nothing. Frustrated, I place the phone back in my bag and stare out the window.

Lex is texting furiously on his phone—the constant pinging sound keeps coming through. Thankfully, he at least has the decency not to answer calls because his words would be enough to make Will scared of him for life. A few moments later, my phone vibrates. I grab it out of my purse, Eric's name flashing on the screen.

"What do you want?" I answer, careful not to mention his name.

"Nikki." His voice is all high-pitched, typical Eric in panic mode. "What the hell is going on?"

"With what?"

"With Charlie. She texted me, and I found her crying in the basement of her building. She didn't want to tell me what happened, but Emma said there was some article about Lex being caught with his pants down this morning."

"Correct."

"Nikki, why are you talking like that? Oh wait, shit, is he with you?"

"Sure, okay, yes, get the papers drawn up."

"Okay, sorry, didn't realize. Listen, she's in the office, but... but... she's acting weird." His voice quietens, trying to explain it all. "She took a shower, got changed, and it was like a different person emerged from the bathroom. She told me not to forward any personal calls to her, make sure security doesn't allow Lex in the building, and she said no one was to enter her office, including me. I don't understand what I suddenly did wrong?"

Eric is hurt and betrayed, and I don't blame him for feeling that way. He doesn't know the Charlie I knew, the one who, when in that dark place, doesn't care for anyone.

"Let's meet at midday. We'll discuss any concerns, then."

I hang up the phone without saying goodbye.

Lex and Rocky glare through the rearview mirror. With Will in the car, we are unable to talk. A second later, my phone lights up.

LEX

Was that her??? Tell me what the fuck is going on.

I didn't appreciate him taking his frustration out on me considering it isn't my dick that landed him in this hot mess, but I sympathize with him. I cringe, not liking myself softening toward him.

ME

No, it wasn't her. I don't know what's going on apart from the fact that she has told our security you are not to enter our building so don't even try to see her at work, Edwards.

With his anger suppressed under his cold exterior, it's the last of the conversation as we cross the bridge into the city. The sky is gray as we drive in, a far stretch from the perfect blue we had experienced the past few days. The weather alerts predict severe storms for the next few days.

Rocky drives to the Waldorf where Lex is staying. As he pulls into the valet parking, I ask Rocky to park the car for a moment, so I can have a word with Lex alone.

We both exit the car, but I'm quick to stop him walking away without getting my thoughts out.

"Do not fuck this up any further, you understand? Let her cool down. She's stubborn, and if you push her, she'll run to Julian, and then you might as well say bon voyage."

The mention of Julian's name is enough to burst the vein popping on his forehead. Fury tears through his face as he bows his head with his fists clenched at his sides.

"What the fuck do you want me to do, Nikki? Stand here and do nothing? I need to see her and explain. You think I don't know full well that she'll run to him? That she's probably already with him."

"Explain what, Lex? She won't listen to you. I'm warning you, do not attempt to approach her. Let me speak to her, or I swear to God I'll chop off your balls and wear them around the city as earrings."

"I'm sorry, Nikki, I can't. I need to see her."

"Don't be a stubborn asshole. Once again, you broke her, and once again, I'm left picking up the pieces. When I met that girl, she was broken beyond repair. I don't know exactly what else you did besides leave her. You might think this is fixable, and maybe it is, but you need to back off right now."

Lex stares at me, defeated. His eyes no longer shine that green that he is known for. Instead, they look dark, the ramifications of this situation weighing him down. With his shoulders fallen, he walks away to the entrance of the hotel before disappearing through the glass doors.

Heading back to the car, I ask Rocky to take Will home as I head into the office.

After a quick drive, I enter the reception area and catch sight of Eric sitting in his office. I walk in, closing the door behind me.

"What the hell happened, Nikki?"

"Look, Eric, I don't want to get into the semantics. How is she?"

"A total mess when I found her."

"When you found her?"

"Yeah, on the floor of the basement. She was crying. She texted me to meet her."

"And now?"

"She's in her office. She asked that no calls be transferred to her because she's working on the Mackenzie case. She seems to be okay now. I can't believe Lex screwed her over again. I mean, those photos. *Wow!* Can't the guy keep his beautiful dick in his pants?"

"Are you fucking kidding me, Eric?"

"Excuse me?"

"I can't believe you actually bought that bullshit," I bark, infuriated by his thirst for gossip.

Stunned, he lets out a laugh. "What, you're defending him now?"

"It was a piece of poorly written trash with a pathetic attempt at Photoshop. Do you think that a man who flew back to Manhattan and almost blew a multi-million-dollar business deal would do that if he didn't love her? Do you honestly think that a man who makes billions of dollars a year would be stupid enough to fuck another business associate when he's trying to win back the only girl who holds his heart? It's people like you who keep these fucking tabloids running. Honestly, Eric, I expected more from you."

"Nikki, I'm sorry, but—"

"No buts, Eric. Stay out of this. Do not poison her mind, you understand? That girl is hurting right now even though she won't admit it. All your he's-a-jerk-and-you've-got-Julian talk isn't what she needs right now."

I storm out of his office, furious at his narrow-minded attitude. Taking in a deep breath, I head toward her office. I don't knock. There's no point, so I barge in unannounced.

Charlie is silently typing on her computer. What concerns me is how normal she looks. Her hair is pinned up in a perfect bun, her clothes are neatly pressed, she's flawlessly made up, and if you didn't know Charlie like I know her, you would think nothing is wrong at all.

She looks up for a brief moment, stunned to see me but is quick to bow her head and continue typing. The moment she looks into my eyes, it's there staring me in my face, the sparkle in her eyes has vanished without a trace.

"So what, you're not even going to talk to me now?"

"What would you like me to say, *Nicole*?"

Wow, she must be angry to be calling me Nicole.

"Well, for starters, Charlotte, a smart woman like yourself can't possibly believe the trash printed in that tabloid."

"Drop it. It's over."

"Over? It just fucking began, Charlie!"

She stops typing and adjusts her glasses. The silence is irritating me as I stand there tapping my foot waiting for her response. She lifts her head to meet my gaze as if on autopilot, unable to show any emotion.

"Why do you even care, Nikki? If you take his side, then you might as well go fuck him and to hell with you both. That's probably what you really want. I saw the way you were looking at him, asking him a thousand questions. He's yours for the taking."

The words hurt, there's no doubting that. At this moment, my rage takes over. I have to leave before I say something I'll regret. I turn to face her one more time before heading out the door, gritting my teeth as I'm barely able to hold myself together. I'm a lawyer and a damn good one. I fight for a living. I argue with judges until I'm blue in the face, but this is nothing compared to that.

This is my best friend, the one person who I never fight with.

"That man loves you. He'll do anything for you. Stop being a selfish little bitch and grow up."

Those are my final words before I storm out of the office.

No matter how hard I tried, I couldn't get her words out of my head. We have never really fought before, and the act itself was enough to bring me down.

Rocky's hand presses on my shoulders as he gently massages me. "Babe, it'll work out for them. They both need to get some perspective, and Charlie won't be thinking clearly right now. Just give her space."

"Do you think I'm wrong for understanding his side? Does that make me a bad friend?"

"You know as well as I do how that stuff is rubbish. Yeah, I read it for laughs, but I didn't actually take it seriously. They will work it out, babe. Please stop stressing. I don't like seeing you like this."

Charlie avoids me the next few days at work. According to Becky, our intern, she's busy seeing clients and attending courtroom hearings. The tension in the office is palpable. Eric also avoids me after our blow-out, running scared every time I enter the building, which I'm thankful for because I still want to slap his face with a double-ended dildo and tell him to harden the fuck up.

By Friday afternoon, I can't wait for the week to officially be over. Emma is inside my office as I pass on notes for an upcoming brief when a commotion stops us. Shrugging her shoulders, Emma informs me she'll check to see what's going on. Moments later, she returns, pleading for me to step outside my office before disappearing again.

"Oh, for God's sake, Emma, I'm not interested in office gossip," I lecture, head down as I continue reading.

"Nikki, seriously, you need to come out here. *Now!*"

I don't care for her disrespectful attitude, making a mental note to reprimand her after I sort out whatever it is that's disrupting my urgent deadline. I walk outside only to be met with an angry Lex banging on Charlie's office door. The security guards, the sad, pathetic, overweight donut-eating bunch of fuckers can do nothing to hold him back. I motion for them to leave, telling them I'll sort it out.

"Lex, what the hell do you think you're doing?" I berate him, trying to keep my voice controlled. "You can't come in here and disrupt our office with your personal problems."

"Where is she? I've given her four days, and she hasn't responded to any texts or emails, nor has she been home. Tell me where the fuck she's staying, Nikki."

"In my office, now," I demand.

Lex follows me into my office, pacing up and down, not pausing for a second. His appearance catches my attention —the messy hair, crooked tie, and an overgrown beard—a telltale sign of a man's sorrows.

I pull Emma aside for a moment as she hovers by the door.

"You make sure the office gets back to normal. I don't want anyone mentioning this to Charlie. Warn everyone out there that anyone caught discussing this will have to answer to me. You find out where she is, and if you need Eric's help, make sure she does not come into the office. You understand?"

Emma nods, scurrying out of the room, closing the door behind her.

With a restless week almost behind me and many sleepless nights, I'm officially over this bullshit. Charlie has chosen to ignore the problem rather than face it head-on, leaving me with a very devastated man inside my office.

"I don't know where she is," I tell him, calmly. "She won't talk to me right now. I told you not to smother her."

"Do you honestly expect me to sit here and do nothing? Let her believe all the fucking lies? I flew back in because I need to see her. I'll not leave until I speak to Charlotte." He bows his head, trying to gain some sort of composure. "I never wanted to leave her, Nikki. I always loved her. She doesn't understand how much pressure I was under back then. We were both so young."

I sigh, resting on the edge of my desk trying to listen without voicing my opinion. They have history, a lot of it, and Charlie only gave me bits of information whenever she felt like it. I don't want to drag myself into their mess, but curiosity gets the best of me.

"What exactly happened, Lex?"

He walks over to the window, gazing out into the skyline. Clearing his throat, I sense his vulnerability, and no matter how I prepare myself for what he's about to say, nothing can be stronger than the truth.

"It was exactly two weeks after prom, the night I told her I'd find a way for us to finally be together, whatever it took."

He explains what happened when he found out Samantha was pregnant, the pressure his family, mainly his father, placed on him. If anything were to happen to this baby, it would be all Lex's fault.

"Lex, I'm so sorry."

I don't know what else to say. I knew bits of the story but only from Charlie's side. To think how Charlie must have felt, to place myself in her shoes for just a moment, I understand now why she struggles to trust him. The pain she endured was nothing that I'd wish on my greatest enemy, but I also understand the enormity of being a parent. If anything does go wrong, how easy you can blame yourself. The responsibility of parenthood far outweighs anything else I've ever experienced.

"I was trapped and weak. I tried several times to call her but would hang up like a coward. The damage was done. I knew I'd hurt her, I apologized and begged for forgiveness. But there's something more, something she's holding back. I don't know what it is... please tell me what it is?"

He glances at me like a lost little boy desperate to find the place he calls home. What can I say? I have my suspicions because there are parts of her story which don't add up, but this isn't the place and this is not the person to be talking to. It isn't even my story to tell.

"Charlie's a very private person. It's only now that you've come back that she has opened up about that time of her life. Look, go back to London and do what you need to do. I'll keep an eye on her here. In the meantime, leave her the fuck alone."

"Why are you helping me?"

"Because she deserves to be happy, Lex, and you're it for her. That soul mate bullshit doesn't just happen for everyone. Sometimes it does if you're lucky, but you have to work hard at getting it right. It doesn't always fall into your lap so perfectly. She's my girl, so don't do anything stupid to screw this up. You love her? Then make sure this doesn't happen again, you understand?"

He nods, and hopefully, my words mean something to him. Otherwise, one push, and he's lost Charlie forever.

Walking into my apartment an hour later, Will runs toward me, crashing his body into mine as he wraps his arms around my waist. I hold him tight in my arms, smothering his face with kisses. His smile, as usual, melts my heart. I thank my lucky stars this beautiful child was brought into this world. In a time full of chaos and uncertainty, I can always rely on Will to make everything seem insignificant.

Rocky follows, leaning in to kiss me. "Long day, babe?"

"Exhausting. I'll tell you about it later," I say, squeezing Will until he complains he can't breathe.

"Well, there's someone here to see you."

I walk into the kitchen, and low and behold, I find Charlie sitting at the counter.

She smiles awkwardly. I haven't seen her since our fight, and to be honest, she looks like shit. Her skin's pale, not the usual glowing bronze, sun-kissed tan she normally sports. The dark circles around her eyes aren't hidden behind any makeup. She appears tired, drained, and I sigh as I notice how thin her frame is. She obviously hasn't been eating. It's only now I realize the magnitude of how much this ordeal has affected her.

"What am I doing, Nikki?" She sobs, placing her head down on the counter.

I throw my bag on the floor, extending my arms around her.

"I'm so sorry I said those things to you, of all people." She cries, her words are barely audible.

"C'mon, let's talk." I grab her hand leading her to the living room.

Rocky comes in with a bottle of gin, two glasses, and tells me he's taking Will to his mom's where they'll both spend the night.

It doesn't matter what names she called me, or what she accused me of.

All that matters is that she needs me and is finally ready to talk.

It's also the moment I realize my best friend is in a very dark place. I no longer take sides. I no longer act in defense. I'm going to hold her hand, walk along this dark path, and remind her that no matter what happens in the end, I'll forever be by her side.

THREE

LEX

There is nothing left to do but email her the truth. It has come down to this, and nothing else matters beside getting Charlotte to at least talk to me again.

From: Lex Edwards
To: Charlotte Mason
Subject: I'm Sorry

Charlotte,

Please just hear me out. All the stuff was fabricated. Victoria Preston is a colleague, and while she has made advances on more than one occasion, I have very firmly put my foot down. There is no other woman for me but you. Please don't do this to us. We are trying to make this work, and both of us need to trust each other. I'd never do anything ever again to betray you. I lost you the first time and am not that stupid to make the same mistake twice.

Talk to me please, baby. Don't do this. I know you read

my texts. Just please email or call or text me. Tell me
what you are thinking.
Lex Edwards
P.S. I love you Charlotte, my wife. That still hasn't nor
will it ever change.

The screen flickers as I stare into space. If I stare long
enough, the images morph into different shapes. This
consumes me, and for the few minutes I'd spent lost in my
computer screen, I forget the pain which pierces every part
of my soul.

The pain is tugging on my heart, begging it to come out
and play, go for a jolly stroll together.

The pain that ate me alive the moment she disappeared
that morning in The Hamptons.

I beg her to speak to me. I send emails and texts relent-
lessly but nothing. I even put read receipts on my emails,
but all I get in return is an 'unread.' Nikki warned me to
stay away but, how can I? She's my fucking wife. She said 'I
do.' *Is this my fault?*

Confusion plagues me along with guilt and remorse.
Maybe I could've done more. Should I have been firmer
with Victoria? The team I had built around myself
should've prevented this from happening. Why the fuck
aren't they doing their jobs correctly?

Yet, surely, she has to know how ridiculous this all is.

Why would I even look at another woman when Charlotte is mine? Was I not sincere enough that she couldn't
believe me after I said the words 'I love you' when I vowed
to be her lawfully wedded husband?

Questions, more fucking questions with absolutely no
answers.

I take a long drink of the flask tucked into the pocket of

my jacket. It burns as it makes its way down my throat, but the numbness it brings me makes life more bearable until it wears off. I'm not one to drink at work, and this unprofessional behavior is out of character for me, but I have no other escape.

The trip back to London was the longest flight of my life, and even worse was having to deal with my sister who flew back with me to make sure I was okay. Yeah, I guess I'm okay for a man who lost the woman he has been waiting for his whole life.

The afternoon dragged until I hauled myself to Preston Enterprises. Inside the boardroom, people around me were chatting, others preparing for our board meeting. Victoria, of course, was avoiding me, and the *New York Times* refused to retract the article saying their sources were reliable.

What fucking sources was what I wanted to know.

The room falls silent as I sit on one end waiting for her arrival. The other sheep in the room continue to sit quietly, twiddling their thumbs pretending not to notice how my fists are clenched ready to pounce on Victoria the second she walks through that door. Five minutes later, the devil herself appears.

"Good afternoon, everyone, I apologize for my tardiness." She places a pile of papers down, adjusting the screen ready for the presentation. Avoidance only works for a certain amount of time, and her time is running out.

"Good afternoon, Mr. Edwards. Nice of you to attend our meeting here in London," she says, not looking my way for even a second.

The projection screen slides down, and the lights turn off. The sheep turn around in unison to watch the screen. As the presentation begins, I can't help but use this opportunity to castigate her for her childish behavior which fucked up my life more than she can ever imagine.

"You avoid all my calls and emails. Tell me, Victoria, did you achieve what you wanted by feeding bullshit to the press?" I whisper into her ear.

She remains still, her posture straight as she focuses on the presentation. "There's a time and a place for this, Mr. Edwards, and now is *not* that time nor place."

My anger spikes. T*he stupid whore*. Who the fuck does she think she is?

"Don't play games with me, Victoria. You and I both know nothing happened and nothing ever will. Find a way to fix this, or Daddy will see that lovely picture of his best friend with his cock in your loose pussy."

She abruptly turns to face me. Even though the room is dark, I can see the shade of red forming on her face, her fury enough to satisfy me in this moment. I turn my chair to focus on the presentation, leaning back with a satisfied grin. Suddenly, profit and losses seem like the most entertaining topic in the world.

Sleep has become obsolete in the past few days. I gave up trying and instead focus on my counterattack while in the ring. My trainer, Hank, has never seen me so dedicated, even suggesting I play up against the big guns. Okay, I may have been angry, but being beaten up by professional boxers isn't on my list of things to do.

After the initial anger wears off, I know I'll have to fly back to New York to win Charlotte back, no more drowning my sorrows and wishing the problem away. I have to take action and prove to her once and for all this is one big lie. Even if it means I have to sit outside her apartment for days on end waiting for her to return home. I'm determined, and nothing is going to stop me now, not even Nikki's warnings.

Thursday night, eleven o'clock. I sit in the car opposite her apartment block, the windows dark, not a hint of life. I've been here for three hours and nothing. As every minute passes by, my rage grows uglier, slowly spreading to every part of me. My mind conjures up every possible place she can be staying, and as the bitterness starts eating away at me, I know there will be nowhere else she'd be staying out this late on a Thursday night except for Julian's.

The thought alone is like acid, burning my soul bit by bit. It isn't just her trust in question, it's mine as well. As long as he is living and breathing, she will run to him.

When the sun rises, I give up.

With my head spinning and mental fatigue plaguing me, I drive back to my hotel for some much-needed rest.

My eyes wander across the several invitations to bid scattered across my desk. After dropping the ball on many things, I have no choice this past week but to work nonstop to make up for lost time. I've fallen back into the trap, trying to control my emotions by throwing myself into work. I can't control my personal life, but this business merger is something I have complete command over.

Everything is ready to go, and I'm confident we're making the right decision by purchasing this company. I glance over the contracts but notice a section is missing. Huh, this is odd. I go over the paperwork again but still can't locate it. *Fuck!* With frustration, and running on zero sleep and bourbon for a staple diet, I dial Kate immediately even though it's after seven on a Friday night.

"Good evening, sir."

"Kate, where are the margin tables report for the Berkshire contracts?"

"It should be with your copy."

"Well, it isn't, okay?"

"Then I have a copy with me. I can bring it to you tomorrow."

"No, I need it now. I'll be at your suite in ten minutes."

I hang up, grabbing my wallet, taking the next available cab. Usually, Kate and I will stay in the same hotel. However, due to my last-minute decision to fly to New York, The Waldorf had no available suites for Kate. Instead, I put her up in the Four Seasons.

When I knock on her door, she opens it quickly.

"Good evening, sir."

"What on earth are you wearing?"

She's dressed in what could only be described as a fluorescent pink strapless dress. It's very tight-fitting and short. *Very short.* I'm drawn to her legs, long and lean sitting in a pair of strappy silver heels. Her makeup is bright, and her hair is left loose in soft curls. The oddest thing is, she's wearing a whistle around her neck.

"Oh, this?" she says while waving a hand over herself. "I'm going out with some friends tonight to some gay club. Apparently, there are certain dress codes one must wear to these clubs. I know, I know, I look daft, right?"

My attention focuses on a pair of black pumps sitting by the bed. My stomach weakens slightly as they look exactly like the ones Charlotte wore when I was fucking her on her desk.

No, this definitely isn't the time to stir things up.

"Here are the papers you requested."

Her eyes move to where mine are focused.

"Oh, sorry about the mess. I have a friend staying here for a few nights while she sorts some stuff out."

"She's here now?"

Kate laughs softly. "Yeah, showering in case she meets someone to hook up with at the gay club... like that's even possible. She's arse over tit in love with this jerk, but apparently, he's cocked up big style. Hey, if you want to meet her, I can always lure her out."

"I better head out and call it an early night. Say hi to your friend for me." I chuckle lightly, amused by her visit to a gay club. I've never been, nor will I ever want to. Women often baffle me with their interests.

"Will do... and Mr. Edwards?"

"Yes?"

"I hope it works out for you... with her, I mean. I don't know her, but I can see you love her, and that's all anyone needs."

I pause, thinking about her words. "See you tomorrow night." With the small amount of fight I have left in me, it's all I can manage to say.

It's only eight, and I have already done everything possible. Everything is set for tomorrow's meeting. I've been to the gym and showered, and now what? I hear a knock on the door. I open it to be greeted by Rocky and Elijah.

"Dude, you look like shit," Rocky roars.

I caress my beard, wondering what these two fuckers are doing here.

"Get changed, we're heading out," Elijah tells me.

"Where to?"

"Porky's! It's all-you-can-eat night." Rocky laughs.

Porky's turns out to be a seedy strip joint in the meat-packing district. I don't know why I honestly thought we were going to an actual all-you-can-eat restaurant. Rocky's sitting front row center, wearing *an I Eat Meat* truckers' cap. His eyes light up any time one of the girls does their show in front of him. I'm surprised he does this kind of thing. I'd have thought Nikki would've microchipped him or something.

The girls are nothing special, your typical fake tits, spray-on tan, fake eyelashes type of women, and all bleached blondes. They do nothing to ease my pain, not even when one tries to sit in my lap and rub her tits on my face. I can smell the alcohol on her breath, and her eyes are glassy. No doubt she did a line before she came on stage.

"Do you love this place or what?" Rocky cheers, waving a dollar bill in the air.

"Have you lost oxygen to your brain? Most likely from those extremely tight jeans you're wearing," Elijah points out.

I almost spit out my bourbon. They are fucking tight jeans.

"Hey! It's like the newest trend or something. Nikki picked them out for me."

"Did she make you wear them tonight so your dick couldn't get hard?"

"*No...* it can get hard. It's just really tight in there." He squirms.

"And the color? What is that, iris-purple?" Elijah questions.

"The fact that you even know that's pretty gay, dude. Besides, it's violet-blue."

I roar in hysterics as he mentions the color. Only a married guy like Rocky would wear *violet-blue,* most likely to scare off any pussy that comes near him tonight. As Rocky continues to justify his choice of tight, feminine-colored jeans, the topless waitresses continue to serve us drinks. By the tenth round, I am losing focus.

"I'm surprised Adriana let you out tonight. Wait... this better not be your bachelor party because this is way too tame."

"Me, out? I'm surprised Nikki undid your chain from the street post."

"At least I'm guaranteed great pussy every night. Elijah, it will happen to you when you get hitched."

"Please stop talking about Elijah and pussy. He's marrying my sister. C'mon, Rocky, this was supposed to be a pain-free night," I complain, twisting my neck to call the waitress back over.

"Oh yeah, my bad. Anyway, so look, all I'm saying is that sometimes you need to spice things up a little, keep that fire going. For example, once Nikki actually did use the dog chain on me. Made me eat her out for like an hour." He lifts his glass with a wide shit-eating grin on his face.

"I'm not a bondage type of guy. We're more into *kama sutra,* exploring different positions."

"Stop... Elijah. Just shut the fuck up right now," I snap, annoyed.

Raising my glass, I accidentally tip some bourbon into the peanut bowl. No one ever eats that shit anyway, except for Rocky.

Elijah frowns. "Perhaps we should change subjects."

"Oh, yes," Rocky shouts, clapping his hands with delight as a new group of women dance on the stage.

The music starts, and Madonna's 'Like a Virgin' plays over the speakers. The strippers strut their stuff on the stage, all dressed in white virgin-looking bodices with their little white thongs. The older girl pulls Rocky up onto the stage due to his over-enthusiastic reaction to the song.

"Damn, those jeans look even tighter when the spot-light's on." Elijah winces.

I scowl. "Fuck, I think you can see the shape of his balls."

Rocky moves on the stage, mimicking the strippers as they slide up and down the pole. The sight is good and bad at the same time. Moments later, he's surrounded by the three girls, tits all bouncing in his face. He looks like he is in titty heaven, that's until his face turns bright red, and his goofy grin is replaced by an embarrassed, forced smile.

"What's up with him?"

"I don't know." Elijah shrugs his shoulders. "You reckon he blew in those pants?"

"Fuck, he couldn't have. I don't know how you could possibly get hard in those," I wonder out loud.

"I don't know, but he looks uncomfortable. Wait, he's coming our way."

"Dude, why the face? You blow in your pants?"

"N... No," he stammers.

Rocky turns around, unsure of what I'm looking for until it stares me right in the face—a giant split in the seam of his pants right down the middle of his ass.

"Dude!" Elijah and I roar in unison.

"Fuck you, guys. It was fine until Destiny told me to crouch down so I could smell her pussy," he complains.

"Why the hell would you crouch down to do that?" Elijah asks, appalled at the act.

"Because I wanted to smell it."

"Dude, I don't think that pussy smells any good. More like a sea bass that has been sitting out for days."

"Oh shit, man." I almost cry. "Sea bass is one of my mother's famous recipes."

"I know," Elijah chuckles.

"I need more drinks."

The rounds keep coming, and the three of us are way too intoxicated to understand each other's conversation. I watch the strippers gyrate throughout the night. By then, my vision has blurred, and I know it's coming to an end before I pass out.

The music changes once again, this time playing Usher's 'Make Love in the Club.' It's soothing compared to the rest of the shit they played. A young girl walks slowly onto the stage. She looks different—a *brunette*. My eyes fixate on her. She's wearing a pale pink bra with a matching thong and long brown hair sitting above her waist.

She looks new, maybe a rookie.

Taking to the pole, she closes her eyes ignoring the men in the front who yell vulgar words at her. As she opens her eyes, they meet mine—big chocolate brown eyes fixate on me.

I feel a slight stir in my pants.

It's time to leave.

FOUR

CHARLIE

Delete. Delete. Delete.

The emails are coming thick and fast, but I choose to ignore them—*him*.

What is he going to tell me? It's all manipulated by the media, and he is the victim?

I'm stronger than this, I don't need him. If I can handle eight years without him, then I can get through this. At least, that's what I keep telling myself.

Eric came to my rescue in the parking lot. He saw me at my most vulnerable moment and wanted to take me up to my apartment, but I refused. Instead, he grabbed some of my things and took me to his place. I sobbed the entire way, and he looked at me, helpless. He was unable to ask the questions that lingered, and I was unable to give him answers, but I picked myself up the only way I knew how— burying my head in the sand, ignoring the situation, and pretending it doesn't exist.

After my big blow-up with Nikki, I avoided the office for a few days by working from home. I soon realized Lex would eventually track me down, so I needed somewhere else to stay, somewhere he couldn't find me.

Unlike anything I have done before, I reached outside my comfort zone and contacted Kate. She answered immediately, and thankfully, was willing to help me out for a few nights.

I'm standing inside the hotel lobby with my pathetic suitcase beside me. As soon as she sees me, she rushes to where I stand, throwing me into an embrace. Kate is exactly what I need at this moment—a friend not involved in this so-called mess known as my life.

Inside her suite, I instantly notice how nice the room is —an upgrade, no doubt. Surely, she must have been giving her boss serious head for this.

"Wow, this is amazing." I glance around the living area separate from the bedroom. "I can't thank you enough. I really needed a place to stay, life has just gone..." I sigh. "I'm sorry, I didn't know who else to ask."

"Hey, don't worry." She motions for me to take a seat. "Life has thrown me a giant curveball, too. Arsehole was banging that beastly bird in that pic on Insta. I said goodbye to that tosser."

"Oh my God, Kate. I'm so sorry."

"Better now than later, right?" There's a sadness in her expression, but she's quick to replace it with a mischievous grin. "Don't worry, I met this gorgeous Navy guy last weekend, and can I just discuss how yummy that rebound was? I'm so done and dusted with that Aussie jerk. Found better and bigger fish in the sea... one with better gills if you know what I mean."

Of course, I know what she means. His cock was bigger and better, always a plus.

"*Arghh,* excuse me for just one second, it's the boss."

She answers the call with an annoyed look on her face. "Good morning, sir."

She remains on the line while I walk toward the window admiring the view of the park. It's early morning in the city that never sleeps and is busy as usual, even with a storm due to come in over the next forty-eight hours. I watch as people scurry along, zigzagging in and out of the crowds, obviously late for work. The tourists are walking around in awe, snapping photographs of everything in sight. I watch the few homeless people who roam the streets, lost in their own little world. How, in that moment, I envy their strength to carry on every day despite their shitty circumstances.

"Yes, she got the contracts. No, I don't know. Her assistant refused to give me that information. Okay... okay, thank you, sir."

Kate hangs up the phone.

"Sir?" I tease, grinning. "Sounds kinda kinky."

"Oh, trust me, it's *not.*" Throwing her phone onto the couch, she gazes at me intently. "Charlie, you look like a truck ran over you. Tell me what's been happening. So, your love life has gone tits up?"

Tits up? I'm confused but assume she means upside down.

"I don't really want to talk about it. Everyone is pushing me, and I just don't want to think about it for a while if that's okay."

"Fair enough. How about we grab a drink tonight? Let's have fun and forget about our man troubles."

"Deal."

Kate's phone starts buzzing again, and this time she lets out a frustrated groan before grabbing it. "I'm sorry, I have to take this *again.*"

"Hello, sir. Yes... yes. No, there's no way out. Why? Because the board requested you be there. Uh-huh... uh-huh, look, I'll be there in ten minutes, and we can speak then. Yes... okay." She hangs up the phone, muttering profanities beneath her breath. "Bugger me, it's been a sodding week from fucking hell. I'm ready to explode after the shit that's gone down with work. Look, I've just gotta meet my boss. He's gone crazy, and is making it difficult to work for him even though it's not all his fault."

"Sounds like fun. Remember, think of me if he gets over this chick and needs some great rebound sex," I call out.

She laughs, exiting the room as I crash on the couch and stare at the wall.

Later that night, Kate and I went out for drinks, and I mean plural. We had a blast and even got chatting with a few guys. I wasn't into the whole thing, of course, but she took to a hot bartender.

The next morning, we're suffering from massive hangovers, and I was awakened by Kate's phone repeatedly going off.

Fuck, the damn thing never shuts up.

I pull myself off the sofa to reject the call, but thankfully, it stops.

"My head hurts. Who the hell calls you so early in the morning?"

"Argh, was it ringing?" She stands up, unsteady on her feet. "Shit. It's my boss. Fuck."

"Oh my God, Kate, come work for me. Seriously, what is his problem?"

"Yeah, I know, but I kinda understand why he's so short-fused. I mean this woman who he is irrevocably in love with isn't talking to him, and to be honest, it's not even his fault, you know?"

It sounds all too familiar.

"Well, if it isn't his fault, then he needs to make her realize that, whatever it takes."

"I think the damage has already been done."

"No, I'm sure it can be sorted," I say, thinking his situation couldn't be as bad as mine. "He just needs to be honest.

"Seriously, Charlie, fluorescent pink?"

"Yes, Kate. If I have to wear fluorescent yellow, then you have to wear pink."

"And the whistle?"

"Eric said you have to wear these colors and a whistle around your neck. I don't know the protocol of the gay scene," I huff. "Okay, listen, I need to take a shower. Eric should be here any second now. In the meantime, make sure you put on the dress and whistle, or he'll feed you to the gay herd, and let me tell you it's not pretty."

I close the bathroom door, taking a nice long, hot shower. As I stand here, my mind wanders to how long it has been since Lex touched me last. Yeah, like five fucking days. I thought about Nikki's words. Okay, so part of me is coming around, but fuck, it's Friday night, and I refuse to spend it wallowing or masturbating in the shower over someone I can't have.

Quickly dressing in my outfit, I examine my face in the mirror. I've lost weight, and the bags under my eyes are more than evident. I apply makeup with dark eyeliner, more so than usual to hide the circles. Placing my hair in a high-side ponytail, I adjust my strapless dress, ready to hit the gay scene. *Oh, wait, my shoes and whistle.* I leave the bathroom in search of these two most important items.

"Oh, hey, so I'm glad you were in the shower. You would've just encountered the beast."

"Who? Your boss?" I ask, amused.

"Yep, work matters."

"It's Friday night!"

"Everything is urgent with him."

"Why didn't you invite him to come out with us? Or better yet, you should've sent his hot ass into the bathroom to visit me. I surely could have used it."

"Oh, Charlie, I'm sure he'd have gladly taken you on." She laughed.

The knock on the door breaks me from my shower fantasy—it's Eric loaded with whistles.

"You said we had to wear one whistle, *E*," I point out.

He blows the whistle. *Ouch, it hurts my ears.* "I brought spares in case you forgot."

"Oh, we didn't forget. Trust me."

"Oh, hello there, darling!" He leans in kissing Kate on both cheeks. "You biatches look amazing. Are you ready to watch a bunch of gay guys get it on? I want to be walking like John Wayne tomorrow."

"Oh, my days," I mutter, shaking my head.

Kate laughs, pulling me along and closing the door behind her.

After waiting in line for only a short time, we're allowed to enter the club. Okay, so I'd never been in a gay club before, but it's exactly what I imagined. The club is dark, crowded, and the heavy scent of sweat lingers in the air. Eric calls this 'man juice.' The neon lights flicker like a light show, the techno beats bounce off the walls while I'm almost trance-like, and the atmosphere is euphoric. The men are wearing fluro jocks. I feel extremely overdressed, not to mention conscious of the fact that we look like the only women here.

"E, aren't you a little overdressed?" I yell over the music.

He grins, removing his pants and shirt and handing them to the coat guy who wears nothing but a fluro pink thong with the words 'Hands Off Snakey' written on the front.

Everyone has a whistle, all being blown to the beat of the music. We make our way to the bar where, thankfully, girls are hanging out. We look at each other, and although they are strangers, we throw each other a big smile and say hello. Well, at least we don't have to worry about sleazes trying to pick us up at the bar.

"So, what are we ordering to drink?" Kate asks.

"A round of Daisy Chains, please," Eric yells to the bartender.

"What's a Daisy Chain?"

"The drink, I don't know. The act, don't ask."

The drink turns out to be Sambuca shots. The smell of the anise is strong, and I wince as I swallow it. *Holy fuck, that is surely going to kill me.* Urgh, the aftertaste is rancid. The next drink is called a Candy Maker which is actually tequila.

The night carries on with lewd, homosexually-named drinks being served to us. We loosen up and start dancing. It doesn't bother me that I'm surrounded by sweaty males with bodies to die for, or the fact they all have their tongues down each other's throats. We just get lost in the trance, enjoying the carefree buzz. Kate is beyond smashed, and I'm not far behind her. As I dance, I feel my tiny purse vibrate. I pull out my phone, squinting to read the message.

LEX

Charlotte please, I am so lost without you

1 Voicemail message

My heart skips a beat reading the message. Maybe it's the Daisy Chains and Candy Makers that loosened me up, but suddenly, I feel the urge to listen to the voicemail and not delete it like the other dozen I had this week. I motion to Kate I'm going to check my phone, but she's too preoccupied being sandwiched in between two guys who love dancing with a straight girl.

I make my way over to the corner and press into my voicemail, covering my other ear to drown out the music.

Please talk to me. I can't go on like this. We said we would start over, but you're not here with me, you're not even talking to me. Charlotte, listen to me when I say you can trust me. This is not what it seems. I need you... I need us to be okay. Please talk to me.

The line goes silent, and the pang in my heart deepens. This man is my husband, so what the hell am I doing? *But it wasn't like it was a real wedding.*

Walking back to the bar, I push my way through the crowd unaware of my trance-like state. *Was I wrong in all this?* But how could that possibly be? The pictures looked real, and someone out there wanted me to see them. Who sent me this link? *Someone in love with Lex,* I thought.

"You okay, Charlie?" Eric asks, out of breath.

"Yeah. I think I need another Daisy Chain."

He laughs, pulling me over to the bar. "Was that Lex you were texting?"

"No, I wasn't texting. I read the text he sent me and listened to his voicemail. The first time I've had the courage to all week."

"C'mon, Charlie, even I'm wrong for judging, hear him out at least. You know you wanna get back to tapping his hot ass again."

"If only it were that easy."

"What's going on, ladies?" Kate rests her head on Eric's shoulder, slurring her words.

"Charlie just got a text and message from Le—"

The whistle blows loudly in our ears. We all cringe.

Apparently, it's conga time, but the gay version. And that's our cue to leave. Eric joins the gay train and waves goodbye.

Kate and I stumble our way home to pass out as soon as we walk through the door of the hotel suite.

I move my tongue around my mouth, it tastes bitter and cotton-like. As I swallow, I feel the nausea wash over me. Running for the bathroom, tripping over Kate lying on the floor, I barely make it to the bowl before the ramifications of last night's shots take place. I sit there minutes on end unable to peel myself off the cold tiles. I'm dying, there's no other explanation.

"Charlie, are you oka..." Kate pushes me aside taking my spot.

Oh, fuck no, I can't watch her puke as well. I run out of the bathroom pacing up and down the living area thankful that the trashcan stands by the small kitchenette and sink. That will be the last time I ever set foot in a gay club. *Ever*.

Hours later, we manage to shower and get dressed. I say goodbye to Kate, thanking her for making me forget and also letting me stay with her. We agree to meet up for coffee tomorrow before she is due to fly back home.

As I walk back into my apartment, the familiarity of it all overwhelms me. I'm exhausted, no doubt from the lack of sleep this week, the clubbing, and the extra work I took on to distract myself. On top of all that, I drank way too much, and my body is hating me for it.

I throw myself onto the couch, closing my eyes as Coco purrs beside me. A sudden ring startles me. Beside me, my phone is dancing on the coffee table—it's Julian.

"Hey you," I answer, my voice hoarse.

"You okay? You don't sound well."

My body aches all over as I straighten myself up. "Just coming down with something, I think."

"I was going to ask you if you were free for dinner, but never mind, rest up."

"No, it's okay, Julian. We need to talk anyway."

"Yes, we do need to talk. So, how about I pick you up around seven?"

"Um... how about I meet you there? Just text me the details."

I hang up the call, feeling guilty for avoiding having him here. I remember Lex's voicemail from last night. I remember how I felt when I read his words and heard his voice.

With a sudden curiosity, I scroll through my inbox. I find the deleted items folder and recover the emails he sent me.

He apologizes over and over again.

He promises nothing ever happened or ever would happen.

But it isn't those emails that make me look at him in a different light. It's the ones he sent me quoting one of my favorite songs. Songs he'd sing to me as I rested against his chest in our safe haven that was our cliff top back home.

A tear falls on my screen as the words linger. How does one stop what the heart wants? It's impossible not to see the pain I'm inflicting on him, and it makes my heart hurt, a part of it crying for the sorrow he is feeling. But this is about *my pain*. How am I to rise above it? How am I able to place my trust in him and let all the fears wash away? Can I hand my heart over to him? It thinks it belongs there, but once upon a time, it was asked to leave, and when it left, it took me along with it to a very dark place. Has he changed? Has his heart changed too? Will he see me and understand my fears, understand how fresh this all is? Or will he push me into the dark by questioning my insecurities, belittle me for my ability to run?

I can either hand my heart over or place it in a panic room.

I walk to my vanity and open the little wooden box. Inside sits the engagement ring Julian gave me and the wedding band that Lex placed on my finger.

Two rings, two different men.

I pick up the diamond ring and slide it on my finger.

I don't know what I'm doing, all I know is that tonight, I need to smile.

And if there's one person who can make that happen, it's Julian.

FIVE

CHARLIE

Nine Years Ago

I tried Alex's cell again, damn voicemail.

It was the morning after I saw him at 'our' place, and during the night, I had tried several times to call him. Maybe he was tied up with work. I hoped because the alternative was unbearable, and my paranoia grew deeper as more time had passed.

Something was off yesterday, and I sensed it despite Alex reassuring me everything was going to be just fine. He was demanding, physically, and while he had shown that side several times, yesterday was different. *As long as we love each other, that's all that matters* he kept repeating over and over again.

I walked into the kitchen, grabbed my wallet, and headed to the store. It was Saturday morning, and the streets were quiet, just the regulars eating their breakfast at the local diner. I walked into the grocery store and grabbed a box of Cheerios. Oh hell, and a Butterfinger while I was at it. Taking my items, I walked toward the counter.

Kaley.

She had been the death of me since junior high. I honestly believed she was some sort of human robot put on this earth to annoy the living daylights out of me. After prom, her vendetta against me tripled. She never explained why she hated me so much, and frankly, she wasn't worth my energy.

"Hi, Kaley," I reluctantly greeted her while placing my items on the counter.

"Shopping alone today?" She smirked, swiping each item as it pinged on the register. "No, um... boyfriend to help you out?"

"Excuse me? Seriously, you need to keep your lips shut, and by lips, I don't just mean the ones on your face."

So much for not exhausting my energy. I was tired, and my sleepless nights were catching up with me. Pulling my bills out of my pocket, I threw them on the counter willing this conversation to end.

"Oh, please, Charlie. You're a fool for thinking Alex would leave his wife for you."

I played dumb once again. This wasn't the first time she had insinuated that Alex and I were a couple. It had occurred several times now since prom. She had this obsession with us, and no matter how much she tried to rile me up, I always had to hold my head high and pretend she was full of lies.

"I mean seriously, Charlie, he has a family to worry about now. You wouldn't want to tear that baby's life apart, would you?"

What?

My heart started pounding in my chest, my skin suddenly felt on fire, the pit of my stomach threatening to cave in right there on the floor tiles. I must have heard wrong or she was making up lies again. Yes, remember, Kaley has a degree in serial bullshitting, but she stood grinning like she had won the lottery. *No. No. No.*

"What the fuck did you just say?"

Her eyes widen with a satisfied smile fixated on her ugly face. The cruel joke she was playing brought her joy, a foolish lie to see my world fall apart.

"I said that Alex and Samantha were sitting in a tree. First comes love, then comes marriage, then comes a little baby sitting in a carriage."

"You're telling l... lies," I stammered.

"Nope, I was there in the doctor's office when Samantha walked out and told me." Kaley leaned in, motioning for me to join her. "Apparently, they had some wild night a month ago, and Alex couldn't keep his hands off her. Totally explains why she's pregnant."

Everything started spinning, my world caving as I took in the information. I ran outside the store, vomiting all over the pavement. My chest felt tight, my breath uneven. Clutching my stomach, my mouth fell open as my legs began to shake, threatening to crumple to the ground.

Resting on the street post for support, I glanced across the street and saw Adriana. *She'd tell me it was all one big fat lie!*

I ran across the street to my best friend. Stopping dead in my tracks, she stood there without a hello or a greeting of any kind. Her face bursting with rage, nostrils flaring as her lips pulled back baring her teeth. *What the fuck was going on?*

"How dare you, Charlie? *He's my brother,*" she screamed.

"Adriana, please, just listen to me," I begged, no longer caring that she knew.

"Tell me it's not true. Please, I'm begging you, tell me it's not true."

Mrs. Edwards was sitting in the car, her head down refusing to meet my eyes. I ran over and banged on the window, but she remained still. I pleaded with her to look at me, to give me the answer that would either allow me to continue breathing or would end my life right here, right now. But she sat silently still, immune to my pleas.

"Charlie, you have ruined our friendship, broken my brother, and embarrassed yourself in front of the whole town. Leave us alone. Leave my brother alone. *Whore*," she yelled before opening the door to her mother's car. "Oh, and another thing, if Alex really loved you, how come it's Samantha carrying his baby? Think about that for the rest of your life."

The engine roared on the car, and within seconds, they had sped off down the street leaving me standing there by myself.

She answered my question, and so my life slowly started to disappear, the light was fading, the air was too heavy to breathe. I felt my body weaken. This was too much. I needed him. Where was he?

He promised never to leave.

He promised that his heart belonged to me.

He promised that he'd never touch her again.

My hands were shaking uncontrollably, and so I dialed his number again.

Disconnected.

My body shuddered, the walls spun again. *Tell me this isn't happening.* Not my Alex, he was mine. My heart and soul belonged to him. My life was nothing without him. *I can't go on,* I sobbed to myself. *I can't live in this world without him.*

"Miss, are you okay?" asked a lady walking by me.

I looked into her eyes, my vision blurring as I tried to focus.

That was the last thing I remembered before I passed out on the pavement and was embraced by darkness.

SIX

ALEX

Nine Years Ago

The voices filtered through the apartment.

It was now or never.

Avoiding my family since the day it happened would only get me so far. How did they expect me to react? All 'no worries, Mom and Dad, you did me a favor by dragging my butt here to San Francisco to stay with my wife and raise a baby I didn't even want.'

At first, I heard my mother. She sounded happy, and the words I could make out were those of anticipation, waiting for this baby to arrive. I dragged myself out of bed making my way to the mirror. The beard that had grown on my face annoyed Samantha, and that's exactly why I kept it there. The dark circles around my eyes had formed as a reminder of the nightmare I was living. I washed my face briefly before heading out to the living room.

"Alex, sweetie." My mother held out her arms as her face changed from delighted to worried. She knew not to mention anything about my appearance in front of everyone, something my father had no problem with.

"Well, Alex, it's nice to see you're taking care of yourself. I hope you plan to clean yourself up before returning to work on Monday?"

My father had arranged for me to be transferred to Saint Francis Memorial Hospital. What he didn't know was that I was just about to pull the plug on my medical career. How could I help people when I couldn't even help myself? His overbearing ways would stop if I could just muster up the courage. I needed to stand up to him. I needed to be a man.

"Emily, Andrew, please come out to the balcony. I have prepared some lunch. I know it was a long drive for you." Samantha ushered my parents to the balcony, leaving me alone with my sister.

Adriana stood by the window, avoiding me at all costs. She didn't look any better than I did, except no beard, of course.

"Adriana, please... talk to me," I begged.

Moments passed, and not a word was said. Would it always be like this between us? I missed my annoying sister. I fucked it up royally for her. And despite her not-so-warm behavior toward me, all I wanted to ask about was Charlotte.

"What would you like me to say, Alex?" she huffed in return, folding her arms, staring me down until I felt nothing but intimidated even though I towered over her small frame.

"I don't know, Adriana, that you understand." I hesitated, knowing I was pushing my luck with her.

"Understand?" she shrieked and let out a you-are-fucking-joking laugh.

"Okay, sorry, whatever."

It was at this moment I realized how alone I was in this, how there was no one I could confide in who would remotely understand what we had. I stood from the couch to make my way to the kitchen, abandoning this conversation.

"She left," Adriana mumbled.

I turned swiftly, almost causing myself whiplash. "What?"

"About a week ago. I don't know where to."

"What do you mean she left?"

"She left town, to go God knows where. But I'm not surprised after the humiliation she must have felt."

I raised my voice in desperation. "How could you not know where?"

"Because, Alex, she and I no longer talk."

"When was the last time you spoke to her?"

"I ran into her the morning all hell broke loose in town. She confronted me, and well, Alex, I was hurt. I said things I shouldn't have. I had no idea this was going on, and now I look back, it was so obvious. It was there right in front of my face, and the only reason I didn't notice was because I was too absorbed in my own love life."

"What did you say to her?"

Adriana bowed her head. "It doesn't matter. She's gone now."

"Tell me what you said to her!"

"I just told her to stay away... and that..." Her hesitation made me anxious. I knew she said something that would have pushed Charlotte to the point of no return.

"You mustn't have really loved her if you got Samantha pregnant," she whispered.

"Fucking hell, Adriana!" Placing my head in my hands,

I tried to ignore the pain spreading throughout me again. My poor Charlotte. How could I have been so fucking stupid?

"Alex, I'm sorry. I was so upset."

Taking deep breaths, the blame shouldn't be placed on Adriana. This wasn't her doing. I created this mess, and I would forever pay the price.

"No, I understand. It was never our intention to hurt you. She worried about you all the time, but we were so deep in this. I loved her... more than you can ever imagine."

"And now, Alex?"

"Love like that doesn't just disappear—" My voice faded.

Samantha walked into the room, interrupting our conversation. She must have known we were having a moment, and she looked annoyed that Adriana wasn't screaming at me. As I made my way onto the balcony, Adriana walked beside me, holding onto my body. Before we stepped outside, she hugged me tight, much to the bemusement of my father.

"Have faith, big brother. The right place and the right time, she'll be yours again," she whispered.

I wasn't sure I believed that fate would play a part in us being together again one day, but I did know this—my obligation to be a father to this unborn child had to be my number one priority.

And for now—I had to let Charlotte go.

SEVEN

LEX

Present

It is Saturday morning, and I wake up with the hangover from hell.

It's been a long time since I last drank myself into a stupor with a bunch of men, though Rocky's masculinity was questioned several times in those ridiculously tight jeans of his.

Thankfully, I wake up alone and not with a stripper from last night's shenanigans. Our meeting with the Berkshire Group is organized for seven o'clock tonight. It's the only time Gerald Huffman and his team can swing a time to meet. It doesn't bother me working on a Saturday night since I'm not twenty-one anymore, and my life doesn't revolve around club-hopping.

No, just strip clubs, apparently.

Kate agrees to meet me at the restaurant at six forty-five on the dot. This will give us fifteen minutes to work over our strategy, and I'm confident Gerald will sign the contracts tonight.

In a fleeting moment, the business savvy side of me kicks in. To say I've been distracted and off my game of late is an understatement, but with my confidence pieced back together, I'm certain tonight will work in my favor.

Unfortunately, in my pathetic state, I forgot to shave my beard. Thank my lucky stars the hotel has managed to have my suit dry cleaned and pressed at the last minute since I'd completely forgotten about it.

"Good evening, Mr. Edwards," Kate greets.

Kate is standing in the restaurant lobby, armed with manila folders and her usual corporate attire. After much consideration, I decided to give her a raise. Once tonight is over, I plan to sit down and have a discussion regarding her performance. The obvious blaring point is I have screwed up multiple times over the past few weeks, and Kate has always picked up where I fell short.

"I'm glad you could make it. No wild parties to attend tonight?"

"No, sir." She chuckles as if remembering something funny. "I believe we partied to our full capacity last night."

The restaurant is busy with waiters scurrying about carrying exotic dishes, the aromas enticing me. It makes me realize how much I have missed food. Yeah, I have barely eaten the past week. *What's fucking new,* I think. Johnny Walker and Jack Daniels have become my companions of late. I make my way to the concierge as Kate follows.

"Reservation under Edwards."

We follow the head waiter to our table. The noise is a little overbearing, just your typical Saturday clientele. I pull my phone out, checking my messages as I follow him through the crowd, lifting my head for a moment as the image catches my eye and halts me on the spot.

Kate is also checking her phone, running straight into

the back of me. "I'm so sorry, sir. I was checking my mess..." her voice trails off.

Charlotte sits there, her body leaning into *him*. Unable to move, my eyes are drawn to her like magnets.

Her face looks slightly different, perhaps tired. There's no smile, no spark in her eyes, no glow to her skin, and she appears gaunt. The light inside her has gone out.

Frozen on the spot, I stare, my name being called but sounding so distant. The bastard leans in further, gently reaching for her hand and entwining his fingers with hers. He cups her chin, and she smiles slightly prompting him to lean in further to steal what is *mine*.

I don't know how I move, but suddenly, I'm standing in front of them. Charlotte glances up, her mouth falling open in shock until her expression swiftly turns to anger. The dark circles around her eyes and the prominence of her cheekbones worry me. If this has been hell for her, then why is she here with him?

"Charlie?" Kate gasps before I can get a word in.

"Kate?"

What the fuck is going on, and how on earth do they know each other?

The Louboutins flashed before me. *It was her.* It was her last night in Kate's suite. It was her who Kate always talks about, her friend in New York with the fucked-up love life. All of it makes sense, and how utterly stupid I am not to even piece that equation together.

"So, I don't even deserve an explanation?" I grit, willing the shake of my fists to stop. "You run to *him* the second things get a little tough with us?"

"Are you kidding me, Lex? A little *tough* is that what you think this has been?" She laughs while gesticulating with her hands.

"Well, I wouldn't know, you won't fucking talk to me."

I clench my fists as her laughter slaps me in my ears. Does she honestly think this is one big fucking joke? My body stiffens, unable to compose myself, I'm barely holding on, the fury and rage consuming and controlling any rationality lurking within me. I'm a time bomb ready to go off at any moment.

"I'm busy here, Lex, as you can see." Her voice is calm as she speaks the words, her eyes directly on mine, not flinching for one moment. "Perhaps we'll discuss this another time."

Julian stands, creating a barrier between Charlotte and me.

"Okay, Edwards, she told you to leave."

Oh, so he finally found his balls, I think. *Yeah, soon you'll be fucking choking on them for trying to steal my woman.*

My temper gets the better of me. The room is stifling hot, my blood pumping like a volcano ready to rupture. There's nothing left to do but the obvious. I swing my arm punching him right in the face as he stands there before me trying to take my world away from me. If he didn't exist, she'd have come back to me, that murderous thought flashes before me.

The rage is overpowering as I try to swing at him again, the blood bouncing off his face as he screams my name, yelling at me, the voices around me in a panic. The image of Charlotte as she pulls Julian back caressing his face only adds to the violent behavior consuming me.

Kate is calling my name, pulling my arm back begging me to stop. "Mr. Edwards, please don't do this. You will regret it and lose her forever," Kate begs, holding me back.

If there's anyone who knows how Charlotte really feels, it's Kate, her new confidant. With the adrenaline still running through me, I turn to face Charlotte, ready to apologize for my behavior. Beg her to talk to me, at least to give me that. I really have no other option, I can't lose her again.

"Lose me forever? Too fucking late, Lex. You lost me a long time ago. I was just stupid enough to think it was fixable."

The apology is devoured now by rage again rearing its ugly head, the hurt and pain of her words stabbing me in the heart with a freshly sharpened knife. I need to let it out, how I really fucking feel. But people are watching, waiting for my reaction. This isn't some soap opera. This is our life, and I don't want them to hear the words I'm about to speak.

"*¿Quieres lastimarme por lo que te hice, Charlotte? Bueno, has ganado. Para citarlo, he terminado*. You want to hurt me for what I did to you, Charlotte? Well, you've won. To quote you, I'm done".

It's the only way I can say how I really feel, what is deep inside eating away at me. It isn't my fault. Call me arrogant, call me whatever the fuck you want. I know when I've fucked up, but this isn't one of those times. I lost my trust in her. I no longer want to play this sick, twisted game. Lex Edwards never gives up, but he also doesn't settle for second place. If only she didn't run to him, if only he didn't touch her, and if only I didn't see a slight spark in her eyes as he leaned in to kiss her.

Charlotte continues to stand there, smothering Julian until he angrily walks away. She starts to follow, but stops, turning back to face me one more time. "I was actually here to tell him it was over."

Her sullen expression gives away the words I needed to hear only minutes earlier.

As she walks away from me, the restaurant patrons busy themselves pretending to ignore the scene I caused. Mr.

Berkshire stands in front of me, a look of confusion on his face. *Fuck! Now I have to deal with this.* Thankfully, Kate takes over most of the dinner meeting because I can barely think straight. She knows what she's talking about, and every so often Mr. Berkshire asks me a question which fortunately I'm able to answer. By the end of the night, Kate has him signing the contracts, which for Lexed is a huge deal.

It's a little after nine when we're done, and Mr. Berkshire shakes my hand congratulating me on hiring such an intelligent assistant.

Outside the restaurant, I know Kate will finally ask me what I'd said.

"What did you say to her?"

"Kate, drop it. It doesn't matter anymore."

"Are you fucking serious, Lex?" Her tone throws me off, her abusive language and her calling me Lex all in one sentence. Since when did we cross the line from boss to friend? "For the past month, I have watched both of you in agony. She loves you so much. All along it was you that she'd go on and on about. Had I known, maybe things would have turned out differently. You actually love one another, yet neither of your stubborn fucking heads can seem to comprehend that. I don't know what you said back there, but believe me, if you want her then go after her. You need to shit or get off the pot and fight until you're blue in the face. Show her you can't live without her."

"What the fuck do you think I've been trying to do these past weeks? Sitting around, watching TV, scratching my ass? It's over now, Kate... I'm done. I have no more fight left in me."

I walk into the liquor store next door and purchase the strongest whiskey they have in stock. The clerk looks at my blood-stained hands until I pull out my black Amex. Without a single word, he scans my card and passes me the receipt to sign before placing the bottle in a brown paper bag.

As I exit the store, Kate stands there watching me take a swig from the bottle. The whiskey is smooth with an almighty kick.

"Why are you doing this to yourself?"

"Because I fucking love her, and it hurts like hell."

"And that bottle is going to fix it?"

I don't answer her, raising my hand in the air to say goodbye and make my way to my hotel a block away.

As I enter the lobby, I run into Victoria who's checking in.

"What do you want, Lex? Don't worry, the *New York Times* is retracting that statement, so you can keep your pornographic shots of me to yourself," she hisses.

I take another swig of the whiskey. This time the burning has stopped, and the liquid feels smooth as it makes its way down my throat. Victoria is decent-looking, I mean when she isn't so conniving, I can see that she's a head-turner. The slutty black number she's wearing is enough to get me hard if I try to concentrate. Who knows what I'm thinking anymore? My mind's spinning, and I just want to forget everything that happened tonight.

"I don't care about the pictures anymore. Come with me."

I pull her arm as she looks at me confused by my sudden change of heart. I press the elevator button, and as the doors open, I drag her inside, pressing the button to the penthouse suite.

"What the hell's wrong with you, Edwards?"

When we reach the penthouse level, the doors open,

and I pull her hand to my door. As I swipe the card, she asks me one more time what the hell is wrong.

"You want to fuck me? Well, get inside before I change my mind."

With a grin widening across her face, she runs her fingers along my cheek before following me inside and closing the door behind us.

This time, I'll make sure Charlotte and I are completely *done*.

You want to hurt me for what I did to you, Charlotte? Well, you've won.

To quote you, *"I'm done."*

EIGHT

CHARLIE

I sit opposite Julian at a restaurant downtown. The tension is palpable, and no matter how I angle the situation inside my mind, it always comes back to the same thing.

Lex.

The restaurant is busy for a Saturday night, and it only dawns on me as I look around and notice almost all the tables taken, we should've chosen something more intimate to have an important discussion regarding our future.

Clasping my knees together beneath the table, I'm unable to make eye contact with Julian. I have no clue how to begin ending things with him. My mind is a train wreck of emotions from a terrible week of no sleep and too much alcohol.

As my hand lays flat against the pristine white tablecloth, he places his own on top, a glimmer of hope sparkling in his eyes as our gaze finally meets.

"Julian, we need to talk about us."

He leans in, cupping my cheek. A familiar touch of

warmth but no longer the touch I *crave*. The guilt of my indiscretions allows his hand to linger longer than necessary, knowing this will be the last time he touches me, and most likely the last time he'll look at me lovingly.

It is now or never.

I have to tell him it's over.

I know where my heart belongs despite the hurt and humiliation plaguing me each time I remember the last time Lex and I were together.

I study his face, almost as if we will never cross paths again, admiring his hazel eyes, the way they comfort me and make me feel secure. Everything about us was so easy before Lex walked back into my life. We have no past to haunt us, and until that day in the restaurant, there was no one else between us or meddling with our relationship. It was just all us, and if the universe worked differently, it probably still would have been only us.

As he tilts his head and leans forward to kiss me, a faint smile plays on my lips as I allow myself a moment of closure. Julian will always be the beautiful man who swept me off my feet, and no matter what happens from this moment onward, we'll always have those memories.

He deserves better, and even though I'm going to hurt him by ending what we have, one day he'll look back and thank me. Maybe not now, but one day, one person will love him and only him.

My train of thought is interrupted by a loud commotion. As I turn my head toward the sound, my mouth drops at the sight in front of me.

Lex.

He's standing beside our table with an attractive blonde.

Wait, is that Kate?

What the hell?

It all falls into place.

The flying back and forth coincidentally with Lex's time here.

The controlling hot boss with a fucked-up love life, pining for this one woman.

My posture stiffens, frozen and unable to move from the enormity of this discovery. A heavy feeling erupts inside my stomach, making me queasy and breathless while I sit here completely silent with no words. I can't believe this is happening. Why didn't I see the signs? Her voice rings in my head. *It's not his fault he lost the woman he loves.*

"Kate?"

"Charlie?" she gasps.

"How do you know Kate?" Lex barks, interrupting us.

My eyes dart between Kate and Lex. Undoubtedly, he looks like beautiful hell. No matter the pain he bestows upon me, I can't deny my heart begging for him. His normally bright eyes are dull, almost lifeless. My eyes are drawn to his unkempt beard—unruly and very unlike him. Despite my reluctance to paint this picture of him inside my head that what happened didn't affect him whatsoever, I'd be stupid to deny that the man standing beside me is suffering much like me.

Kate clasps her hand over her mouth as the realization of the situation sets in.

Lex asks why I haven't returned any of his calls, raising his voice at me without a care in the world that everyone is watching us, including Julian. His overpowering alpha trait is rearing its ugly head like I've seen a dozen times before. The need to control this situation is the only thing on Lex's mind, and jealousy is fueling his anger right now.

With a slow and disbelieving head shake, the color

drains from Julian's face. The pain etched all over him only cements my guilt, and as I go to apologize to Julian, his head jolts up, the momentary pained expression turns maddening. With his eyes burning like wildfire and nostrils flaring like a bull ready to attack, he stands, warning Lex to back off.

My hands begin to tremble, dreading the two men standing face to face in a stand-off in front of everyone.

It all happens so fast.

Lex punches Julian square in the face, Julian stumbles as he is knocked back, the blood pouring from his face splattering all over my pale blue dress.

Rage consumes Lex like burning hot lava as Kate places her hands on him, holding him back while trying to calm him down. Without even thinking, I touch Julian's face, his nose dripping blood and the corner of his lip cut up. *This is all my fault.* Julian doesn't deserve this—he's done nothing wrong.

I grab a napkin holding it gently to his face and caressing his cheek, overcome by guilt at the pain I'm causing him. Why can't Lex see Julian isn't to blame? The big illuminated arrow is pointing right above *my* head. I'm the instigator of the tangled web here, not Julian.

"Fuck you, Edwards," Julian spits, catching me off guard, almost pushing me over. "She doesn't want you. If she did, she wouldn't be sitting here with me right now. Game over! Fucking leave her alone."

"Mr. Edwards, please don't do this. You will regret it and lose her forever," Kate begs.

"Lose me forever? Too fucking late, Lex," I croak, mouthing words with no stamina left in me. "You lost me a long time ago. I was just stupid enough to think it was fixable."

I laugh at the irony. I'm beyond defeated, physically exhausted, my head throbbing, my stomach weak. I desperately need to sit down and catch my breath or more so, I need to be alone—indefinitely. My thoughts are jumbled, this situation is too much. I'm tired, suddenly so very tired.

His demeanor changes, and his posture straightens. I wait for him to reveal his true self—he already did by violently blaming Julian, but I don't expect him to communicate to me the way he used to, our most intimate form. Instead, he speaks in Spanish. As he says the words, my brain interprets them quickly and much to my horror, I understand what he says.

You want to hurt me for what I did to you, Charlotte? Well, you've won. To quote you, I'm done.

I stand there shocked to the soles of my feet by his words. Paralyzed by the words I never expected to hear from the man who promised me he'd move heaven and earth to make me his. In this sick mindfuck of a game we play with our own lives, I never stopped to realize the damage I could cause because it was always about *me—my* feelings, *my* hurt, and *my* pain.

And now, it's finally over.

I follow Julian's lead like a lost little girl, but there's one thing I still want to say if only he didn't react the way he did, if only he didn't beat Julian to a pulp.

With Julian well ahead of me, I turn around to be met by Lex's wounded expression. I can go over to him, beg of him not to give up on us, but we are beyond broken. The hurdles between us just keep coming, and despite my love for him, there's no Band-Aid to repair the damage already caused.

Taking a few steps back, I draw in the distance between

us to stare him directly in the eye, with a finality in my weighted gaze. "I was actually here to tell him it was over."

Refusing to see his reaction, I turn around swiftly as Kate calls my name. She catches up with me, grabbing my arm forcing me to stop.

"I'm sorry, I had no idea it was Mr. Edwards. Please, you have to know it was all fake. I was there, Charlie. I was there when Victoria threatened him, and he told her to fuck off. You need to trust me."

"Kate, I'm sorry. I just need to let him go."

I walk out of the restaurant to Julian who's in the middle of the sidewalk. We both stand, the cold night upon us, yet I'm numb, unable to feel anything but guilt. Julian's eyes are blazing, ready to air everything out in the open. *No more lies, Charlie.* This is my chance to do the right thing.

"Is it true what he said?"

"Let's go back to my place and clean you up first," I offer, saddened by his bruising face.

"Charlie, I asked you a fucking question!"

I bow my head, my eyes clouding as tears drop like an endless waterfall. "Yes, Julian. What he said is true. The truth is, I love him despite all his flaws. More than you can ever imagine."

"I'm not going to stand here and beg you to choose me," he croaks, the pain lingering in his words.

The hurt is much more than I imagined. I love Julian, just not in the same way I love Lex. They may have been different types of love, but it still hurts like fucking hell. I'd spent the last eight years battling the pain caused by my foolish actions as a teenager only to experience a heightened version of it once again.

There's only one thing I need to do. This is it, no

turning back. *Let go of him, Charlie. You don't need him as a safety net. Set him free.*

And that's what Julian has become, a safety net.

My heart belongs to one man, always did and always will. That man may have told me we were done, but I can't give my whole heart to Julian, and that's what he deserves—a woman who will make him her world.

I slide the ring off my finger, having only placed it back on before I came here, and hold it before him.

"Charlie..." he barely whispers, his voice hoarse, almost cracking. "We're so good together. I need you... you don't understand how much I need you."

"I'm sorry, Julian." I choke back the sob stuck in my chest. "You don't know how much I wish this turned out differently, I really do, but I can't live this lie. I can't help how I feel."

I extend my hand out further, this beautiful ring in all its glory represents what our life could've become. No matter what happens from this moment onward, no one can ever take away Julian being the first man to propose marriage to me. It will forever be a beautiful memory to cherish.

Shaking his head with a grimace, he stares at the ring and finally takes it from me, clutching it in his hand. With a look of sorrow, he leans in, placing a final kiss on my lips.

My tears cascade between us, falling onto our kiss as our final goodbye.

Pulling away, he turns around without saying goodbye, without a single word and steps off not looking back.

Bringing my shaking hand to my forehead, I glance toward the restaurant, contemplating if I should talk to Lex, but the thought alone overwhelms me. More so than ever, I need to be alone.

With my head hanging in shame from my careless behavior and pain I've caused everyone, I raise my hand and hail a cab to head home.

No good will come from my company tonight.

And once again, the darkness has found me.

But this time, it's all my own fault.

NINE

CHARLIE

Nine Years Ago

"Charlie, look, I've had enough of this moping around and wasting your life away."

I was sitting on the chair, facing the window, watching the rain fall against the windowpane. It was unusual for it to rain in the summer, but then again, nothing surprised me anymore.

The gentle tapping against the glass was almost soothing, a noise I welcomed to drown out the incessant voices in my head telling me he chose *her*.

I continued to stare, crippled by the pain which had taken away my reason for living, my reason for breathing. Time was passing by. I didn't know what day or month it was. All I knew was I needed to escape. The memories were everywhere I turned.

"I've spoken to Grandma Mason." Dad cleared his throat, unable to look at me. "She wants you to go stay with her, and frankly, I agree with her."

My body shuffled on the chair and I turned to face him.

The memories of my grandmother were fond from the handful of times I had spent with her. I recalled my sister telling me Grandma and Mom had some sort of beef. She didn't know what it was, but she thought Grandma didn't want Dad to marry her. I was young when she told me, and perhaps, unknowingly, it tarnished my image of my grandmother as I always took my mom's side.

"Grandma Mason? I haven't seen her in years. Do you mean in Connecticut?" I asked, alarmed.

Connecticut was on the opposite side of the country. I wasn't ready to completely let go, my home is here, and Dad was here.

"Yes, Connecticut," he says, lowering his gaze. "I love you, Charlie, but you need to get your life back together. This town is no good for you, and I'm no help. I need to be on the road to pay for this house. You should be in college come fall and experiencing life. I don't want you to regret things because you're waiting for him to return."

"I'm not waiting for h-him to return," I stammered, trying to defend myself. "Even if he returned, he has a family now."

The words cut like a knife, slicing and tearing me apart at the thought. I'd spent too many nights wide awake, wondering what they were doing. Torturing myself as I visualized him rubbing her stomach while he sang lullabies to their baby. How happy he must be to have a family, completing the package of their so-called marriage. I'd even gone as far as to picture what their baby would look like —*beautiful*. And then it would hit me in a new wave of pain, everything I had imagined we could've had one day was all being experienced in real time with her.

But Dad was right. The whole town hated me. I was the mistress whore. I had nothing left. I had been stripped bare, and all my dirty laundry had been aired for all to see. People judged me, calling me names.

I'd avoided going into town now so as not to run into Dr. and Mrs. Edwards. I'd heard from Finn that Adriana and Elijah left for the summer, but he didn't know where. Most of the kids in school were busy traveling or getting ready to settle into their college dorms.

Finn, of course, was busy with Jen. They were as steady as you could get and had enrolled in community college to stay with each other. I'd thought about it, but not wanting to be a third wheel, there was also no reason for me to stay here anymore.

I'd gotten into the University of California where Adriana and I had planned to attend together. Aside from that, I applied to Yale but was waitlisted. Studying law was something I'd toyed with but moving across the country at the time terrified me. As a result, I hadn't gotten in anyway and still hadn't heard from them.

"But I haven't been accepted into college on the East Coast?" I said out loud, suddenly feeling the weight of my decisions. "I guess I could take a gap year or apply to community college, maybe even work?"

"There are options, Charlie," he reassured me. "I just need you to be happy, okay?"

I ran to my dad and hugged him tightly. His overpowering smell of Old Spice comforted me. I buried my head into his shirt clutching onto him for dear life, scared to say goodbye, but knowing I wouldn't be okay if I stayed here.

"I'll miss you, Dad," I sobbed into his shirt. "This falling in love business is hard."

"Me, too. More than you can imagine, kiddo." He held onto me, kissing the top of my head before letting me go. "And one day, you'll fall in love with someone you'll love and will love you back just the same. I know he'll treat my princess the way she deserves to be treated."

"Oh, Daddy!" I buried my face deeper into his chest, allowing my tears to fall as he clung to me tightly. I never considered myself a daddy's girl, but he had been here for me more than my mother, and I would never forget that.

I walked up to my room, pulling a suitcase from the spare room closet. I opened my dresser, pushing aside my clothes, looking for it. Underneath my shirts, I pulled out the jersey, *his jersey*. I still hadn't washed it, and I allowed myself to do the one thing I said I wouldn't do—I lifted it to my face and inhaled the scent of the fabric.

It was him.

I sunk to the floor and held onto the shirt, the tears falling and soaking the fabric. It was finally time to say goodbye. Alex was never coming back. He chose to leave me and walk away never to return, and so I mustered up what little strength I had and finished packing my bags.

The next day, after another sleepless night, I stood at the doorway, looking at my room one more time.

My bedroom no longer looked inviting, the walls were stripped of any memory reminding me of my best friend. This room, cold and empty, had no more life left in it, so as I closed the door, I was saying goodbye to this life.

I sat perfectly still, this feeling of being so insignificant overwhelmed me. Around me was chaos with people rushing to board their planes, others brimming with happiness as they welcomed family and friends. Then there were those waiting to say goodbye with tears and hugs, some trying to remain brave, but like most people, it only got you so far. Even amongst all that commotion, there were others who sat like me, headphones in place, drowning in their fate, their destination.

"Charlie, you don't have to do this. Who cares what people think? If they got a problem, then tell them to become good friends with my fist."

The battle had been fought. I'd lost and had no fight left in me.

"I deserve it, Finn. What on earth was I thinking?"

"You weren't thinking. You were infatuated with him. Okay, so what, he's a college major in medicine. C'mon, Charlie, you could have anyone you want. He's married—"

"You don't think I know that? Finn, I didn't choose this... I mean it was my choice in the end, but it was impossible to push aside how I felt about him, and I thought he felt that way, too."

"Charlie, he's a guy, he thinks only with his dick."

"No... that's not true. What about you?"

"Well, I was thinking about my dick when we had sex. Yes, I know, even though my dick couldn't follow directions for shit."

I laughed for the first time in a month, and it intensified to the point that people with their headphones on turned around to look at me, but I couldn't stop. It was the relief I needed, and Finn just sat there looking at me, slightly amused and equally offended by my ability to laugh so much at his pathetic dick.

"Gee, Charlie... I know it wasn't great but... *ouch*," he complained.

"I'm sorry..." I laughed harder. "I was remembering when you were looking for the hole—"

"Oh, c'mon, Charlie, it happens to the best of us."

"And you were like, are you sure this is your vagina?" I roared.

His grin widened, and uncontrollably his shoulders moved, his laugh barreling out as he remembered the moment.

"Well, I didn't think our first time should be doing it back door. Jesus, Charlie, I was hopeless. If it's any consolation, I have gotten better, much better," he claimed with a wiggle of his eyebrows.

Catching my breath, the laughter slowed down, and I smiled at Finn. He was a massive part of my life that would no longer be a five-minute walk down the road, and so the tears fell, and without fail, he pulled me into him as I clutched his chest.

"Hey, listen to me. I know where the hole is now. Jen can attest to that."

"Finn..." I scolded softly.

"I know, Charlie, we're not gonna have these moments, but you're only a five-hour plane ride away. We can still call each other every day, and you're gonna kick ass in college and make me proud. I know you can do this. You need to move on. I know you loved him, but you need to face the fact that he chose his life, and it was without you. You're eighteen, Charlie, plenty more guys out there, and now it's your turn to break their hearts."

"I can do this," I chanted to myself. "You're right, I'm eighteen. It was simply my first love, and I have so much to experience in college. I'll forget about him... won't I?"

"Maybe... maybe not. But I'm certain that even though you may not forget about him, there will be someone else who'll knock your socks off and know where your hole is." He laughed.

"I love you, Finn. I couldn't have asked for a better best friend."

"I love you, too, Charlie. Always will."

He hugged me tight until the announcement came for the final boarding call. As I said my goodbye, I realized that it wouldn't be forever, and Finn would always be a part of my life as much as Alex was. With my headspace slightly clearer, it occurred to me Alex really was my first love, the kind you read about in romance novels. Everything I felt was textbook—the grieving for the loss of what we had—and while I wouldn't have wished for an ending like this, I was able to, for a moment, believe that I could put this behind me.

All I had were memories. He was gone in the flesh—where to, I had no idea—and so I boarded the plane with a glimmer of hope that across the other side of the country, I'd find Charlie Mason again because I missed her.

I missed the girl I used to be.

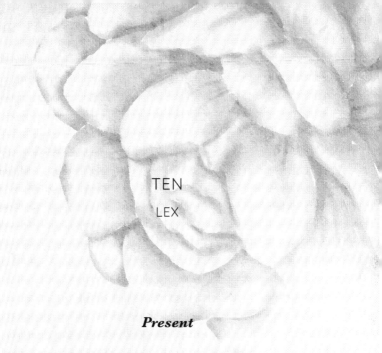

TEN

LEX

Present

I roughly cough like I've swallowed a bunch of razor blades.

My eyes are shut tight, and I'm unable to ignore the fire clawing up my throat. Water, I need water. Struggling to open my eyes, they sting as the light hits my retinas. What the fuck is wrong with me? I give up trying, burying my head under the pillow to fall asleep again.

Attempt number two—this time I take it slow.

As my eyes open, the bright light burns once again. It's the fucking sun. I pull the sheet above my head to block out the light. Something feels off against my skin.

I pull the sheet tighter against me. What the hell is it? It's wet and sticky. My eyes are still closed, but I can feel it against my torso. I place my hand down searching for this odd thing annoying me, scraping my palm against my body until I find it toward my ribcage. Clutching it in my hands, I bring it to my eyes.

It's a condom.

Fuck!

Startled by the discovery, I sit up unwillingly staring at this piece of rubber, a result of my pain. I fucked up big time! What the fuck have I done?

"Nice of you to wake up."

The sound of a voice makes me jump. I'm not alone.

"What are you doing here?"

"I'm guessing you don't remember any of last night?"

I strain my brain trying to remember what happened. I drank so much—I mean a lot. The entire bottle of whiskey and even raided the hotel room mini-fridge.

Inside the hotel lobby, I saw Victoria and dragged her to my suite. I remember the shrill in her voice as she unbuttoned my shirt and ran her hands along my chest. She mumbled words like 'finally I get a piece of you' and other dirty shit, but then it became a blur and I think, well, hope, I blacked out.

I rub my face, wishing this away. "What did I do?"

"What do you think you did?"

"Please tell me I didn't?"

This could affect my business. Victoria will have something to hold over my head for the rest of my life. How could I have been so unbelievably stupid?

"And why would you want me to tell you that you didn't?"

"Because... because..." I can't say her name. It's still too raw. I told her I was done, but was I really done, or is this some mini-break? I don't know the right answer, but I know enough that I don't want to jeopardize anything in the future because I was drunk and fucked up, and I mean big fucking time.

"Just tell me, okay?"

"No, you didn't," Kate assures me. "I stopped it."

"You stopped it?" I ask, shocked and confused by her comment.

"Yes. I knew you would regret this, so drastic times called for drastic measures."

"What did you do?"

The worry creeps in, but I'm also relieved nothing happened. It was my fucking lucky day all right, whatever it was that saved me.

"I called Eric."

"You did what?"

"I called Eric. He met me, and we got access to your suite. Victoria was all over you, and, well, she told us to piss off, but we said no. If it meant we had to sit here and watch, then so be it."

"And then?"

"She said fine and to watch, I s'pose trying to call our bluff, so we did. You even said to me I was free to join in if I wanted, but Eric wasn't allowed."

I bury my face into my hands. "I'm so sorry, Kate."

"Apology accepted," she states, awkwardly. "Well, she got annoyed and realized we weren't going anywhere, so she yelled at us, then finally got her stuff and left."

"And the condom with the..." Slightly uncomfortable, I don't want to say the word in front of her, but I think all sense of professionalism flew out the door kicking and screaming last night. "The... um, you know what's inside?"

"Oh, that's just coconut juice. Eric thought you needed a lesson. Go ahead, smell it."

"I'll take your word for it."

As I sit there, I let out a big sigh that Kate saved the day once again. I couldn't help but feel self-conscious of the fact I was shirtless as she sat across from me. She must have sensed it as well, throwing my Yankees T-shirt over, which I gladly put on.

"Kate, I could've fucked up big time," I say, barely above a whisper.

"Yes, you could have. I knew you would regret this, and Charlie would never in this lifetime forgive you for it despite you two not being together."

"But who's to say she didn't fuck Julian in the past week or even last night?" The words leaving my mouth are enough to allow the rage inside me to boil over once again.

"Because she wouldn't. Both of you need to learn the meaning of trust because without it, how can you give yourself completely to another person?"

"There's nothing left to give. I'm heading back to London tonight and staying put. Any New York work can be handled by you or even Peters. Yeah, send him over to handle the press of the new office."

"Is this how you're going to leave it?"

"There's no other option, she made that clear."

"There always is, you just don't want to open your eyes," she tells me, rather rudely.

Maybe that's the case, but I'm sick of being in this love triangle. All I ever wanted is her. Alone. No one else. When it comes to us, there's always someone else involved.

"I don't want to talk about this anymore. Thank you for stopping me last night, but this topic is off-limits, you understand?"

"Yes, sir." She stands and walks away, defeated.

I was harsh and I know she has good intentions. But I need solitude.

Fuck, I'll do anything to erase all this mess right now.

"Hold still, Lex!"

I stand on this podium-looking thing in the middle of Adriana's guest bedroom. She places pins along the hemline, circling both legs. This is the last thing I want to do after battling a hangover all day.

"Okay, done. Not bad, big bro."

"I feel like a penguin. Why do the suits have these tail things?"

"Because it's a classic tuxedo, you doofus."

As I glance around the room, the three matching dresses catch my attention. The wedding is just over a month away, and there's no way of avoiding it no matter how much I kick and scream. I thought of several excuses to back out of attending, but I owe this to Adriana plus, I'd never hear the end of it from my mother.

Yet the cold, harsh reality is that I'll have to see *her*, and I will have to walk down the aisle with *her*. Staying true to wedding traditions, I'll probably have to dance with *her*. A whole lot of touching with someone I can't have.

"I know what you're thinking. You'll have to see her in a little over a month, have to walk down the aisle with her, dance with her."

Lifting my head, I gaze at my sister with an incredulous stare. "Seriously, Adriana, what the hell?"

"I know, right?" She nods her head, resting her hands on her lap. "It appears as I'm getting older, I am becoming more psychic. Either that or you're easy to read."

Adriana packs up her pins and places them in her sewing kit. Sitting on the floor cross-legged, she looks me in the face. I know the look, so I decide to avoid it by walking behind the screen and changing back into my jeans.

"Look, Lex, if I have to rearrange partners and stuff, I can."

"No, Adriana, this is your wedding. Don't change anything," I almost demand, the masochistic side of me wanting to smell Charlotte's scent as she walks beside me. "We are adults and can behave for a few hours."

"Like *six* hours, Lex."

"What! Your wedding goes for six hours?"

"Well, eight if you include the ceremony."

This is why I don't do weddings. I hate all this shit, and it's just for show, anyway. You don't need to spend ridiculous amounts of money and invite hundreds of people to show how much you love each other. Fuck, eight hours of pretending to smile. I recall my own wedding to Samantha years ago, it was the same old bullshit and for what? America has the highest divorce-rate statistics. I've got one under my belt and am about to go for round two.

"Listen, I've got a flight to catch. I better go."

"To London?"

"Yeah." Slipping my hands into my pockets, my gaze shifts toward the floor. "So, look, I won't see you until the wedding."

"You're not coming back to New York?"

"No, Adriana. Please don't ask. Not now," I beg, not allowing her to get another word in. I wave goodbye and head out of the guest room only to be greeted by a nervous Elijah in the hallway.

Blinking rapidly, he scratches the back of his neck unable to look my way. I don't know what his problem is, but I have no time to ask questions, or I'll miss my flight back home.

"I was just leaving, Elijah."

"Listen, Lex... I, um... well, there's um—"

"What?" Frustrated, I push him aside until I stop dead in my tracks.

She's here in the living room.

"Sorry," he mumbles. "I tried to warn you."

I shoot him back an annoyed look. He could've warned me if he wasn't babbling like a schoolgirl.

Charlotte is standing by the door, avoiding my heavy stare. With my heart racing a million miles per second, I can't ignore how different she looks.

She's wearing low cut jeans, a gray hoodie with 'Girls Do It Better' printed on the front, and her Converse. Her hair is tied back in a rough ponytail, but it isn't her clothes or even her hair that catches my attention—it's her face. The color of her skin is pale, almost dull without her usual rosy cheeks. Compared to when I saw her yesterday, she looks extremely tired with dark circles around her eyes, and they also appear swollen. She's been crying, and I ache just to reach out and touch her, caress her face and take away the pain she's living, but I'm the one who said it was over.

I can't go back on my words, can I?

But she's my wife. To have and to hold till death us do part.

I swallow hard, riddled by hurt as the memory of her sitting across from Julian and caressing his face last night at the restaurant comes swinging back like a giant wrecking ball.

"Oh, hey, Charlie. I thought you were coming after eight?" Adriana asks, nervously.

"Sorry, Adriana, I have something on tonight. I hope you don't mind... I need to do this fitting now."

With her gaze fixating on Adriana, ignoring my presence in the room, my anger begins to boil beneath the surface. She has something on tonight after eight.

What? Like a date?

Or an all-night fucking session with Julian?

My mind is going crazy. The guilt I feel when I see her eyes has turned into rage.

I have to leave before the rage and hurt turn into something not even I can control, and I do something else I'll regret for the rest of my life.

Turning around, I kiss my sister on the cheek and silently wave to Elijah standing on the other side. With heavy steps, I walk toward the door, placing my hand on the doorknob as Charlotte stands only inches away.

Unwillingly, my lips part, the scent of her perfume is lingering in the air between us making it impossible for me to breathe. I can't fall for this again and get tangled up in this mess of what we have become. So, with desperation, I quickly turn to the door and exit the apartment, shutting it behind me.

I half-expected her to follow.

Beg me to talk to her.

But I also know how deep her pain goes. Much like me, but we're both hurting for different reasons. And with my heart chained down unable to fight any longer, I quickly leave the building and hail a cab straight to the airport.

Back home and as far away from *her* as possible.

ELEVEN

ALEX

Nine Years Ago

I was lying in bed reading *Time* magazine—the only thing keeping me sane these days.

Samantha walked into the room not saying a word. Unlike her usually talkative self, she remained awfully quiet removing her earrings, sorry, one earring. *Why would she wear just one earring?* Shaking my head, I ignored the unusual fashion choice and watched her slide out of her dress. Despite our strained marriage, she looked sexy in this newly purchased red dress she had worn to some dinner tonight with her sister and friends.

As she stood near the dresser, her naked body reflected off the mirror. The growing stomach was evident. My lips pressed together in a slight grimace as my eyes caught sight of it. Slipping her nightgown on, she climbed into bed.

I was just about to ask her how her night out with the girls was when I smelled it—*Brut*.

Pulling at my ear, my gaze fixates on the wall straight ahead. I had my suspicions, having spent months sneaking around behind her back having an affair, I knew the signs. But what the fuck could I do? It wasn't like I was innocent in all this. I had been the one who broke our marriage vows first, but what kind of marriage were we trying to fix when both of us had succumbed to our desires to be with someone else.

She looked down at her hands where I noticed the missing wedding ring.

"Alex, we need to talk."

"About the fact that you smell like Brut, or that you aren't wearing your wedding ring?"

Samantha snapped her head sideways, her face turning from sad to bitter. "I don't need a lecture. I fucked up, just like you did."

I put the magazine down knowing all too well we would have this conversation again. No matter what I did, she held my affair with Charlotte over my head. How the fuck were we supposed to raise a baby in this? Our relationship had turned all shades of fucked-up, and both of us together were toxic.

"Alex, the baby, it's..." Her eyes began to water, and suddenly, very unlike Samantha, tears fell down her cheek. They came hard and fast, quiet sobs as her chest heaved from the outburst of emotion. Seeing her in this state was a rarity, and unable to hide my own guilt, I patted her hand willing her to calm down.

"The baby... it's not yours," she cried out.

My eyes widened as my gaze became unfocused. With words trapped beneath my running thoughts, I tried to ignore the hardening of my stomach while continuing to grasp her words.

"What did you just say?"

As silence fell upon the room, time only fueled my

anger. Baring my teeth, my eye began to twitch as the adrenaline kickstarted into attack mode.

"It's not your baby. I lied. I'm sorry! We didn't make love that night. You were out drunk, and I saw you... I saw you holding her. I saw the way you looked at her. I couldn't handle it, and, well... Christopher was there." She continued crying before reaching over to touch me.

"Don't you dare touch me, Samantha." I pushed her hand away, jumping out of bed in a fit of rage. "You fucking spiteful bitch! Do you know what I gave up for this baby? And now it isn't even mine."

I could feel my body shaking, my fists clenched, and without thinking, I smashed my fist through the bathroom door, my hand throbbing in pain, but the physical pain so much more bearable than the pain inside my chest. Pacing the space in front of me, I was struggling to come to terms with the fact that I had lost Charlotte all because of this vindictive bitch.

"I thought I was doing the right thing for our marriage, but no matter what, it always comes back to *her*. I'm so sick of living in her shadow. Do you know you talk in your sleep at night asking her to come back to you? Do you know how it feels to be second-best?" she screamed. "Chris is different, he wants me and our baby."

Her voice calmed down, yet too bad for her, all I could see is red.

"Fucking hell, Samantha, I've lost Charlotte because of you!" I stormed into our closet, changing into my jeans and sweater. I grabbed my overnight bag putting in some spare clothes. Leaning into the back of my closet, I rummaged around in my old football helmet. There, in a loose cavity in the lining, was the one thing I kept—a picture taken of her on prom night. I allowed myself after three months to finally look at the picture, my heart sinking as I didn't expect the tsunami of emotions that came with seeing her face again, even if it was only a picture. Placing the final things in my bag, I walked out of the closet. Samantha was still sitting on the bed sobbing.

"I'm so sorry, Alex," she wailed.

I walked over to her, my anger intensifying. Sliding my wedding ring off my finger, I placed it on the bedside table. This should've been done months ago, and if I had been strong enough to have done it then, I'd still have the girl I love in my life.

Leaving the house in a rush, I threw my items into my car knowing exactly what I had to do.

I grabbed my phone, dialing my sister's number praying she'd pick up. The second I heard her voice, relief washed over me.

"Adriana, can you meet me at the airport in two hours? Bring your passport."

"Yes, Alex."

She didn't ask why nor attack me with questions.

If anyone knew me better than I knew myself, it was my sister.

And with her by my side, I knew I'd find Charlotte... again.

TWELVE

CHARLIE

Present

They say if you love someone, you're supposed to set them free. What if it's the other way around? They set you free. Am I supposed to fly back? Or am I supposed to leave it up to fate? There's a high chance fate isn't on my side, my wings having been clipped, and without them I can't soar.

This was me after Lex told me he was done.

The storm set in that night at the restaurant where I broke the heart of the one guy who actually loved me enough to want to be with me despite what I'd put him through. But it wasn't fair, life wasn't fair. Why didn't I love Julian the same way I loved Lex? Life would have been easy then. Okay, so it wasn't the love that set me on fire, but he was safe and solid. No past, no memories.

Yet he deserves better than me, better than this roller-coaster I put him through. I did to him just what Lex had done to me all those years ago. How can I cause so much pain when I know firsthand how much it hurts to be treated like that?

It starts to rain, but I walk at a normal pace, the people around me scurrying for cover and looking at me like I belong on another planet, but I don't care. It all feels so insignificant now. The cold rain is drenching my barely-covered body as the fabric of my dress clings to my skin, and I shiver uncontrollably.

As I enter my apartment, I make my way to the bathroom ignoring Coco purring by the door. Turning the bath on, I let the hot water steam up the room. I wipe the mirror with my hand to look at my face. My mascara is smeared under my eyes, my lipstick is long gone, and my hair is a wild, tangled mess. I strip out of my clothes and climb into the hot bath, a small slice of heaven in a fucked- up situation.

Sinking further, I let it spread over my body. The warmth provides me with security for a short time, but then the water slowly becomes cold, and the reality hits me just as hard. After a solid hour, I climb out and make my way to the bedroom. Putting my pajamas on, I tuck myself in, willing myself to close my eyes.

It's the first night I have cried myself to sleep since the morning I left The Hamptons.

The next day, I do everything possible to keep myself busy. I go for a run, but without Kate, it isn't the same. I do my laundry and grocery shopping even though I have zero appetite. I clean my entire apartment and then watch three movies back to back hoping for some comic relief. It's only six in the evening, but I decide to go to Adriana's early for the final fitting for my dress she keeps nagging me about. It isn't until about an hour ago when I realize I promised Will we'd watch the meteor shower together on his rooftop at eight.

I welcome the drive to Brooklyn, deciding to take my bike out. As I drive onto her street, I park the bike, pulling my helmet off. Okay, Brooklyn isn't my favorite place to leave the bike, but I made friends with the guys down the road last time I was here, and they told me they had my back. Well, so far, they did anyway.

I make my way up to her apartment and knock on the door. Elijah answers, but when he sees me, his face appears panicked. I can't blame him, I know I look like fucking shit. There are just some things that makeup can't cover.

"What are you doing here?" he asks, looking back into the living room.

"Fitting. Apparently, I've lost weight, and Bridezilla says I need to fatten up to fit back in the dress."

"Oh, right, the fitting. Wasn't that supposed to be after eight?" Again, he turns around, the sweat beads forming on his forehead.

"Uh, yeah, but I have to see Will tonight, so I was hoping to get this done early. Elijah, are you okay? Did I catch you in the middle of something?"

Oh My God! Was Elijah having an affair, hence the panic? I seriously need to stop watching *The Bold and the Beautiful.*

"Just hang on a sec, Charlie..." He scurries out of the room leaving me to wait confused by his odd behavior. It isn't long before I hear the familiar voice. Panicking, my body freezes. I'm unable to move, unable to run away like I so desperately want to.

Fuck! It's him.

I don't want to be here, but it's too late. His voice gets closer and closer. Turning the corner, our eyes meet for the briefest of seconds. His stare freezes over like winter's ice, robbing me of the warmth which spreads throughout me each time our gaze meets.

Adriana panics as well, asking me why I'm early. I explain my plans for tonight, and in a flash, he says goodbye to them, ignoring me, and walks out the door.

He looks amazingly beautiful.

And I miss him so much.

My stomach is in knots when I realize how easy it is for him to ignore me. He's truly done, and that inkling, the little ray of hope, walks out the door with him. I'm left standing here, mustering any bit of dignity I have left.

"Char... c'mon, let's have coffee before the fitting," Adriana offers.

"When you say coffee, you meant vodka, right?"

She laughs as we walk into the kitchen. I sit at the small round table, flipping aimlessly through a wedding magazine that sits in front of me while she starts the Keurig. The pictures are all one big blur. I need a distraction, anything to stop me from remembering the way he looks, the way he gave up on me, again.

"We won't talk about him."

"Thank you." It's all I can manage to say.

Handing me a cup of steaming coffee, she leads me to her guest room where I change into my dress. I can't help but look over at the suits that are hanging on the rack, especially the one with the Post-it note scribbled with Lex.

"Adriana, when did you really know Elijah was the one?"

She removes the pins out of her mouth, placing them back into her sewing box. "I think it was my first year of college. I mean, yeah, I always fantasized about marrying him. I'm sure you remember how much I talked about that in our senior year.

I nod with a smile. "Yes, you did."

"I sure did love him, but you know it was high school, and I was only eighteen. Then the first year of college was rough. We were apart, and I had lost you. Lex had gone AWOL, and I really felt alone. I made some friends on campus, and there was this one guy, Matthew. He was great, your typical college jock, sweet and a great friend." She smiles at the memory before continuing, "One day he made a move, and I froze. I didn't see him that way, and I apologized that I gave him the wrong impression. Naturally, being a great guy, he understood, but then I asked myself what made me stop. And then I realized Elijah was the only one who'd ever kissed me, the only one who had ever touched me, and I didn't want that to change. I knew I wanted him for the rest of my life but trying to propose to a guy takes balls."

"You proposed to Elijah?"

"No, although I was close to doing it. He proposed to me. It was our second year of college, and he was studying art. I never really saw much of his work because it was very private to him. One day, he invited me to have dinner in his dorm room. Not the most romantic of settings but, of course, he'd decked it out with a million candles. Anyway, he said he wanted to show me what his assignment was, it was supposed to be something that captured you. He pulled the curtain away, and there was this black and white painting. It was me.

"But the thing was it looked so familiar, the scene, and then he told me it was when we used to sit by the lake and watch the sunrise. We never took photographs of that time, but he told me he knew he loved me even back then, and that image will be forever engrained in his memory. I was touched, of course, but what caught my eye was that the portrait of me sitting by the lake had something different. There was a wedding band in the painting. It stood out because everything was black and white, but the band... it was gold. I started to cry, and then he got down on one knee and asked me to marry him."

"Oh my God, Adriana. That's so sweet." I choke back the tears threatening to fall. "You guys are soul mates, you know that, right?"

"I wouldn't marry him if I didn't think so myself." She grins.

"You deserve only the best... I really mean that."

With a sigh, she gazes at me sympathetically. "In the end, Char, it will all work out. I promise you."

It's well after midnight when I crawled into bed that night. The fitting went well, and according to Adriana, I'd lost a few pounds. It's not like I needed a reminder of why my jeans feel loose around my waist.

As I lay alone in bed, the thoughts keep plaguing me, especially the way Lex ignored me. His face, tonight, the way he avoided looking at me, the way he couldn't even say a word to me made my stomach queasy. The images, the memories of us standing in that gazebo saying 'I do,' he was my husband, and it hurt like fucking hell that he had forgotten that. Now what? Do we get a divorce? Annulment? Was it actually valid?

It's the second night I have cried myself to sleep.

I'd spend the majority of the week with Will, taking him to school, picking him up from school, taking him to the park, museum, and library, practically visiting every part of Manhattan. Nikki encourages me to take the week off since my cases are quiet, and I gladly welcome the break looking for any distraction to get me through this tough time.

Despite a tiresome week seeing every sight possible, I can't shake how ill I feel. I barely sleep and wake up in hot and cold sweats. I blame my binge drinking for my immune system taking a massive hit.

The vomiting hasn't stopped, so I narrow it down to Will's stomach bug. He caught it early last week, and I've been around him when he was contagious. Even in my sickly state, I try to get in some time at the office until Nikki sends me home, refusing for the rest of our staff to become infected. When I try to argue, she pulls out the health and safety policy of our team, which I can't argue with.

By Tuesday, I'm told not to even step foot in the office. I hate being home alone. It gives me too much time to think. By Wednesday, I'm going insane, and I don't feel any better.

Sitting on the couch certain I have some deadly disease, I decide to drag my sorry ass to the drug store. I'm out of Pepto-Bismol and Advil and need something stronger to battle whatever is wrong with me.

Dressed in my sweats with my purse in hand, I wait for the pharmacist who is busy talking to a lady who looks like she's about to pop out an elephant. I half-smile at her as she rubs her belly, complaining to the pharmacist about the terrible heartburn she's having.

I'm not really listening to the entire conversation, but something about her piques my interest. Despite her complaint, her face glows, her long red hair has that shine, the one they always say pregnant ladies have. Her loose dress hangs comfortably over her stomach, and her ankles are as swollen as tree trunks. I wince at the thought of being in so much pain.

However, she still looks beautiful, and then it hits me like a ton of bricks laced with acid.

My period.

In a panic, I scroll through my phone unable to locate my calendar. My hands shake as I fumble through the apps, finally locating it. I go back through the months. I get my period like I normally do but my shot. *Shit.* Unable to calm down, I search in panic, and there it is, the reminder to get my shot over a month ago.

"Miss, can I help you?"

Staring blankly into her face, I'd be lying if I smiled and said everything's okay. I don't need help, not when the weight of my mistake comes crashing down like a vicious storm.

Without warning, I fall to the cold floor, my chest heaving as vomit sprays out of my mouth hitting the area surrounding me. A scurry of assistants come to my assistance with a bucket and cold towel. The voices surround me, but my body continues to shake, the heaving persistent. Gasping for air, I struggle to breathe, another person handing me a paper bag. I take it from her, placing it on my mouth and sucking in the air.

In the midst of this breakdown, I motion for my phone. With trembling hands scrolling through the screen, my vision begins to blur, but I manage to find Nikki's number. I dial it, passing the phone to the lady beside me. She talks, panicked, but I rest my head against the hard concrete desperate to shut my eyes.

I don't know how long I lay on the floor, not until I hear a familiar voice yelling for everyone to back the fuck up.

"Charlie, Charlie... look at me?"

Nikki is kneeling beside me, her brows wrinkling as she stares at me waiting for a response.

"Nikki," I croak, barely able to say her name. "I want to go home..."

"Charlie, I really think we should call the paramedics."

I shake my head, still struggling with my words. "No... please don't."

"But Charlie—"

"Nikki, stop! Just help me stand. Please."

She grabs my arm, and I manage to stand though unsteady on my feet. I beg again to go home, but before we do, I ask Nikki for a favor as I wait on the chair with a brown paper bag.

I sit on my bathroom floor beside Nikki in a catatonic state staring at the three pregnancy tests, each a different brand, all lying side by side marked with the two blue lines which have decided my fate.

"Charlie. Three tests can't be wrong. They're all positive."

I continue to sit in silence, not even blinking as I watch, hoping for a miracle that the lines all become one. Just one line. My vision clouds, why is this happening? The lines are staring me in the face—nothing can make them change. Closing my eyes, I pray that this is an awful dream, and at any moment I'll wake up, and everything will be back to normal, but minutes later, I open them, the reality a huge slap in the face is still staring at me.

Nikki shifts closer to me, placing her arm around me, pulling me into her. "Look, girl, I'm sorry, but I gotta ask... whose?"

Turning to face her, I search her eyes for any sort of judgment. She's my best friend, and if anyone understands, it will be Nikki. I close my eyes again, remembering the past few months. Who I fucked, where I fucked, when I fucked, and what the fuck did I use?

I ramble through my thoughts which are causing my head to ache, a migraine now imminent. I used condoms, I gave head, and he fucked me in the ass. My body sinks and the weight of my actions causes me to shake again. Any self-respect I had for myself disappears along with my dignity.

I'm a whore, a slut, whatever you want to call it. I say the names to myself, my head screaming on repeat. My behavior is beyond disgusting, and now I have to pay the ultimate price.

"Nikki... I don't know."

"Oh, Charlie, it'll be okay. Look at Will. Rocky and I couldn't have been in a worse situation, but we made it work and look at him. My life doesn't exist without him."

"But you had Rocky."

"Yes, I know," she admits. "But why on earth would the father not want to be part of his baby's life? Either way, you've got two great men, and both will make great fathers."

"Because it's all too complicated. Nikki, I can't do this... I can't be a single mom and have to look at this child every day and see the face of its father. I don't understand how this happened."

It isn't a question because no matter how it's answered, it won't erase anything.

"Well, sweetie, it's quite simple... you got caught up in the hot sex and forgot about Mr. Semen and his million buddies."

"Nikki, I married him."

"What?" She raises her voice, her eyes wide in shock.

"That last night in The Hamptons, we got married. Don't ask me how he pulled it off. I still don't know, but it happened. He kept asking me to marry him, and he took me to this house. Outside in the gazebo, the man, he performed the ceremony."

"Are you fucking with me? You married Lex? You're Mrs. Edwards?"

"Please don't tell anyone. I don't want to talk about this anymore."

"So, you are married to Lex, and this may be Julian's baby? My God, Charlie, it's like *The Young and the Restless*." She shakes her head while muttering something to herself.

I don't know how long I sit there, numb, unable to process how fucking foolish I feel for being caught up in all this. I don't cry, not one single tear has been shed since my breakdown in the drug store. Maybe I should have, I wanted to, but I couldn't. I'm unable to feel the pain now like I have some sort of shield. Staring blankly at the tests, it feels like hours later when I speak again. "Nikki, you need to get back to Will."

It's all I can think of. She has a family who needs her— her son needs her, her husband needs her. Family. Why does that word frighten me to the core?

"Charlie," she says softly, moving a loose strand of hair away from my face and tucking it behind my ear. "They're fine. Do you want me to make you something to eat?"

I laugh out loud, very loud, unable to stop, hysteria finally taking over—the tears of laughter roll down my face. Nikki can't cook to save her life—the irony isn't lost on me even in the state I'm in. She laughs along with me, and minutes later, we both sit there trying to catch our breath.

"Okay, so can I order you something to eat? Charlie, you

need to eat, whether you like it or not, it's not just you that you need to take care of now."

Sure, I know that.

The memories come flooding back to me, the pain now overwhelming as the tears leaving my eyes are tears of sadness. I can't stop sobbing uncontrollably as the fear sets in. I can't be a mother. I'm not able to carry this baby inside me nor do this all alone. Nikki holds onto me, and sometime during the night, I fall asleep curled up in a ball on the bathroom floor.

I wake the next morning on the floor, a pillow under my head, and my grandmother's knitted blanket covering me. I sit up, quickly searching the room, but it's empty. *Wait, did I dream all this?* My body aches as I take in my surroundings. I had slept on the bathroom floor which only means one thing, I'm really pregnant. I hear the click of Nikki's heels on my floorboards. She's dressed, ready for work, and must have gone home sometime during the night.

She hands me a mug. Thank God, I need coffee. Taking a sip, I scowl as the taste of tea lingers in my mouth.

"Don't look at me that way. No more coffee for you."

"Nikki, one cup won't hurt."

"No, it won't, but you don't know how to drink only one cup a day. Listen, I have the Henderson court meeting in an hour. Will you be okay? You know I wouldn't leave, but I've been working on this case for months."

"Of course, I understand. I'll just get changed and see you in the office later."

"Look, I'd rather you rest, but I get it. You need the distraction. Just promise me if you feel ill, you'll go home right away? I'll have my people watching you, so don't try to be a hero today."

I nod, silently. Nikki grabs her briefcase and makes her way to the door and turns around to face me.

"Charlie, you'll always have us. Rocky, myself, and Will. We're your family. Even when you have lost hope and think you're walking through this pain alone, remember, we are here for you no matter what you decide."

I smile, though it's painfully forced. As she closes the door, I sink back onto the floor, my tears falling without my permission. The walls feel like they are closing in, the roof caving on top of me ready to bury me under its weight.

I have to find the strength just to get through this one day, and maybe tomorrow, I can start answering the questions I have been desperately pushing aside.

In a zombie-like-state, I shower and change into a simple pair of black dress pants, a white collared shirt, and my black boots. Unable to even think about hair or makeup, I place my hair into a bun and apply a small amount of foundation and mascara. I don't want to raise any alarms with Eric, or anyone else for that matter, so I grab my lipstick to touch up the rest of my face. At least I look somewhat decent.

As I step into the office, I feel different. The confidence I usually carry with me is shattered. Instead, I carry this burden, this thing, this... I can't even bring myself to say the word.

I take a deep breath and close my eyes. I have to do this. Do what? Carry on with work or raise this... again that word. I can feel everyone's eyes on me like they all know. In a self-conscious move, I scan my stomach. Impossible, I'm only, what, a few weeks along? Fuck, I don't even know. I will have to get ultrasounds, hear the heartbeat.

No, not now, not here at work.

"Charlie, you're back! Do I have stuff to tell you..." Eric

glances around the room, then grabs onto my arm, ushering me into my office. I place my purse down and sit in my chair.

This chair feels like home, the comfy plush leather gives me a sense of power, and I love it. Well, I used to love it. Now flashes of Lex sitting on this chair plague me. The way he takes over, the way he demands me. I close my eyes for a brief moment while memories torture me every second I continue to breathe.

"Charlie, hey, girlfriend," he calls, snapping his fingers in front of me.

"Sorry, E... okay, so what have you got for me?" I focus on Eric because if anyone can make me feel normal for a split second, it's him.

"Are you okay? I mean despite, you know... and having this bug which, by the way, don't pass it on to me. I have a hot date with that Latino guy who works out at my gym."

"Wait. What happened to that other guy?"

"Long story, but the short version is I caught him getting blown by the busboy at La Rouges last week."

"I'm so sorry." I frown, letting out a sigh. "Why didn't you tell me?"

"Girl, you got your own worries."

"Sorry, I've been a really shitty friend."

"Yes, but it's justifiable, sweet cheeks. Anyway, so guess what?" He claps excitedly, again.

"What?"

"Emma fucked Tate last night in the parking garage downstairs."

"No way!" The pitch of my voice is so high, it even startles me.

That's the last thing I expected to come out of Eric's mouth. I know Tate sleeps around, but as long as it was outside the office, I never asked him about his personal life. Despite Eric's gossip mouth, I pray this union of theirs won't affect our office and ability to work together as a team.

"Yep, I swear. She didn't tell me, but you know how I get my brows waxed with Lyle down on six? Well, he saw them and texted me last night."

"Let's call her in."

I smirk, dialing her number. She picks up immediately, and I ask her to join us in my office to discuss a brief.

Moments later, she walks in, and I'm not surprised when I see she is dressed differently from her usual attire. Without a doubt, she's gone the extra effort to spice up her usually tame wardrobe. She's wearing this thin, black pencil skirt which hugs her body in all the right places. Her blouse is a chiffon cream color and slightly unbuttoned, and her pumps are new, in fact slightly higher than she normally wears. *Oh, she is so trying to impress.* This will be fun— interrogation is my specialty. I am a lawyer, after all.

"Morning, Emma. You look awfully nice today. Special occasion?"

"I, uh... um... thanks, Charlie. How are you feeling?"

"Better. Thank you for asking. So, the Jensen case. I hear you and Tate have been making good progress. Ahead of schedule, I see?"

"Yeah, we've put in a lot of hours as we're close to closing this one."

"So, I see. And Tate hasn't been working you too hard? You know, pushing you beyond your limits?"

She coughs as I say it, her face turning bright red while she stares down at the floor shuffling her feet awkwardly. "No, um... not at all. He's been quite attentive to my, um... needs."

The silence falls across the room as we wait for which

one of us will cave. I know Eric won't last long, and that's why I love him. He has no filter, and during times like this, his normally annoying trait is a godsend.

"So, when you say attentive to your needs, do you mean the way he shot his cannonball into your love purse on that red Mercedes downstairs in the parking lot?" Eric asks in a serious tone.

"Eric." I laugh uncontrollably.

"OMG, Eric, how do you know that?" Emma panics.

"Lyle saw you, and don't worry, he won't say anything because I offered to pay for his next five brow appointments. You owe me big time, girl. Now spill the juice."

And so, she tells us the story of how last night unfolded, how for months there has been this awkward tension between them, but nothing came of it. Last night they were working late, and he offered her a ride home. Before she knew it, they were getting it on in the parking garage.

"And how was it?" I had to ask, desperate for any distraction, including Emma's forbidden love affair.

She closes her eyes for a second. "It was... I don't know what to say... like, amazing doesn't cover it."

"Emma, are you in love with him?"

"Oh no, nothing like that. It's just that I've never been with a real man, you know? I mean he's thirty-one, and I'm twenty-two. The guys my age can't find a G-spot if you handed them a GPS and a tour guide."

We burst out laughing. I can't argue with her. Eric, of course, is in a league of his own and had to throw the question out there that was burning a hole in his pants.

"And... you know... did his goods match up to his feisty personality?"

"Let's just say it matched and then some."

Eric and I look at each other and happy-clap like old

times. It's this that I miss, this carefree chit- chat. For a moment, I feel safe, but it soon disappears as I look down and stare at my flat stomach, soon to be a daily reminder of the mess I've gotten myself into.

I spend my lunch hour working through the mountain of emails that have piled up. My stomach hurts, but it's an unusual pain, something I'm not accustomed to. I ask Eric to grab me a sandwich, maybe I'm just hungry. As I wait for him to return, I continue to drink water to pass the time while my queasy stomach churns.

Rocking back and forth in my chair, the room begins to feel stifling hot. Placing my hand against my forehead, my skin is on fire. Removing my blazer, I fan myself to cool my body temperature down.

I must be dehydrated. That's it. With a desperate need for cold water, I walk out of my office to be greeted by Eric. He looks hazy, but I realize it's not him, it's me.

The room starts to move, and I clasp at my chest while struggling to breathe. Eric's voice echoes in the background, his panicked words making no sense.

Around me, I see shadows, but the spinning only blurs my vision until all I see is darkness.

THIRTEEN

LEX

I have every email answered and every meeting scheduled and prepared. The stationery holder on my desk is perfectly organized—I have exactly eighty-two paperclips in that holder—and I even cleaned my keyboard, removing each key and wiping it down.

This is what happens when you work seventy-two hours straight with no sleep.

By Thursday, I'm losing my mind, bored and demotivated. I need a distraction, anything to wake me from this miserable life I'm currently living. My phone buzzes, and I check the caller ID. I let out a small laugh at the name gracing the screen.

"Dude, it's me."

There's only one person in my life who calls me 'dude.'

"Wait, did Nikki give you permission to call me?"

"Funny, Edwards. Listen, we haven't organized a bachelor party for Elijah."

"Rocky, Elijah isn't one of those pussy-watching types of guys," I tell him, bursting his pornographic bubble. "You saw him squirming at the strip club."

"Of course, you'd say that, he's marrying your sister. Listen, Adriana told me Saturday night is his only free night. Vegas... are you up for it?"

Normally, I'd have hung up on him ages ago. Actually, I probably wouldn't have answered his call to begin with. But I have grown accustomed to somewhat enjoying his company and being around other men for non-business purposes. I hadn't done this since college, and that feels like a lifetime ago.

"I'm in."

"Great! All right, so Adriana suggests Elijah's cousin and two college buddies plus your dad."

"My dad?"

My dad is the last person I want to see right now. I can't even recall the last time we spoke.

"Yeah, why not? Adriana tells me he's young at heart."

"Look, whatever." I ignore it, knowing that arguing with him is futile. "Okay, so what have you organized?"

"Nothing. Was hoping you could pull some strings?"

"Leave it to me."

We end the call minutes later after the conversation went stale because Rocky starts talking about some European movie. I pull out my contacts list and call George, the owner of a few hotels in Vegas. Calling in a favor, I book the penthouse suite mentioning the occasion. He says he'll take care of the rest. Done in one conversation, just the way I like it.

I fly over to Vegas but not without Adriana giving me a lecture on appropriate bachelor party behavior. She went on and on, and luckily, I was forced to board the plane giving me an excuse to end the call.

We arrive at the Palms early Saturday afternoon. George outdid himself again, pimping out the suite with everything you could possibly imagine. Topless waitresses stand at the door taking our jackets, offering us drinks, and basically anything else we want. As Elijah walks in behind me, his face cringes as he avoids looking at the tits on parade.

"Okay, so why the Elvis costume?"

Scratching my head, his sequins shine back at me like I'm watching a burlesque show.

"He's the King, and we are in Vegas."

"Okay, so again, why the Elvis costume?"

"Because I've always wanted to dress up as him, and seriously, I can't do this in Brooklyn." He shakes his head in disbelief as another waitress attempts to serve us a shot. "When I caught wind that you were planning it, I didn't expect this."

The response does not satisfy me, but hey, his prerogative, I guess. We make our way to the bar and sit on the stools waiting for the rest of the party to turn up. Over the next hour, four of Elijah's college friends arrive as well as two of his cousins. He does the introductions, and they are a laid-back bunch, not as geeky as I expected, except for the one dressed up in some sci-fi costume. When the hell did this become a costume party? It isn't long after that my father arrives.

"Andrew, I'm glad you could make it."

Elijah shakes his hand as my dad eyes him up and down, amused by his attire.

"How could I miss my favorite son-in-law's bachelor party?"

"I'm your only son-in-law." Elijah chuckles.

My dad pats him on the back. The mutual admiration they have for each other is always evident, and in ways, I'm envious of the relationship they have because all I ever seem to do with my father is butt heads. I turn away, not wanting to be caught looking.

It's been months since I have seen Dad. In true Andrew style, he hasn't aged one bit. He looks to be in his forties, at best, even though he's in his mid-fifties. His brown hair is still slicked back in the same style it has been for years, his emerald-colored eyes an exact match to mine. He turns my way with a slow and steady gait.

"Son, nice to see you." He extends his hand, and I shake it like it's a fucking business meeting.

"Dad, always a pleasure."

"So, I hear the merger at Lexed was quite a success. Well done."

"We are where we projected we'd be. Even better, actually."

"Your dedication has paid off. Your sister tells me you've been spending quite a lot of time in New York."

I'm certain he knows. Adriana tells my parents everything. She can't keep a secret to save her life. Hence, why she's their favorite. There's no avoiding this. Watching him furtively, I can't believe we are back to talking about this subject again. We never saw eye to eye about Charlotte, and as far as my father is concerned, I broke marriage vows, and that's the crux of it.

"Just spit it out, Dad. What do you want to know?" I throw back whatever liquor is inside the glass in front of me, wiping my mouth as I finish. Turning to face him, I stare into his judgmental eyes. "That I saw Charlotte again? That she looks utterly amazing? That she's successful and moved on?"

"I'm glad she's doing well," he mentions, calmly. "She always was a smart one."

"Seriously, Dad, that's all you're going to say?"

"Lex, what would you like me to say?"

"I don't know. That I should leave her alone? That I shouldn't have started all this shit again?"

"You're a grown man. What you do with your life is your decision."

Laughter erupts inside my head. The hypocrisy, years later, from a man who controlled my life when I needed to make it out on my own. Now it's my decision? How very parental of him.

"Funny, because that advice is nine years too late. Maybe if you let me make my own decisions back then, I wouldn't be living this fucking nightmare right now."

"Son, listen to me—"

His sentence is cut off as Rocky enters the room. "I'm here, motherfuckers!"

Rocky cowers as soon as he catches wind of my dad standing next to me.

"Oh, sorry, Mr. E."

"Rocky, please, your language doesn't offend me. Besides, it's a bachelor party. I wouldn't expect anything less."

"Shit," he mouths with a grin. "Then let's get this motherfucking party started."

Rocky walks over to the sound system and cranks up some music, Sir Mix-A-Lot's 'Baby Got Back' begins to play loudly. As the beats plays, Rocky makes himself designated bartender for the night.

We are in trouble.

"A toast to Elijah, Mr. Kama Sutra himself. Oh, shit, sorry, Mr. E!" Rocky blurts out realizing his Kama Sutra comment may not have gone down well with my dad.

"Please, call me Andrew." He taps on his chest as the

aftermath of the shot settles. "Damn, it's been years since I've had one of these. Not since the night Emily and I—"

"Oh, hell no, Dad," I'm quick to interrupt him, scowling at the thought. "That's some fucked-up shit. Please don't bring up stories about Mom."

"C'mon, Lex, Elijah said your mom's a MILF." Rocky chuckles.

"I did not!"

Elijah's face turns completely red. I didn't know whether to feel sorry for him or punch his goddamn face.

"Well, I don't blame you. She still knows how to..." My dad trails off as my eyes widen in disgust. "Sorry, son, no more talk about Mom.

"We can talk about Charlie, then." Rocky elbows Dad with a smirk. "Will that be more suitable?"

All eyes fall on me, aside from Elijah's friends and cousins who are on the balcony talking to the waitresses. It's the last thing I want to talk about. I grab the bottle of Patron in front of me and pour a double shot. It burns but eases the hurt lingering inside of me. I bang the glass on the counter-top, pouring another. Rocky looks at my father who just sits there, amused.

"What exactly do you want to talk about, Rocky? The way I fucked her on her desk or the way she fucked me on mine? Tell me, I'm sure you'll have a good old laugh." My tone is bitter. No matter what, I can't escape her, but I have to try because I can't go on like this, trapped in a nightmare. I've done this too many times to count, and the result is never good.

"Dude, look, I'm sorry."

"I didn't think so."

This party has hit a low point. I grab the bottle and pour the remaining shots. Placing my arm around Elijah's shoulder, I make a toast. "To Elijah. Thank fuck, I can officially hand over my sister to you. Cheers!"

We raise our glasses, then swallow the drink.

The night kicks off with the guys playing poker and the topless waitresses serving us buffalo wings and other deep-fried wonders. After losing a thousand bucks to the nerdy sci-fi dude, I grab a beer this time and walk onto the balcony.

The view is impressive. The swimming pool is illuminated in bright blue as the LED lights surround it, and not so far in the distance, the rest of Vegas twinkles in the night.

As I lean against the glass railing, the dry Vegas heat does nothing to cure my wandering thoughts. The heat, compared to London's chilly air, is extremely uncomfortable.

"So, it's a touchy subject, then." Dad is leaning his elbows on the railing beside me, scotch in hand as he stares into the night just like me.

"Look, Dad, there's nothing left to say. It's over between us."

"Never figured you for a quitter."

His words sting. I'm not a quitter, but I'm also not going to stand by and be second best. Where the hell is this coming from? From him, of all people?

"Can't always have what you want."

"So, you want her, then?"

"Dad, just drop the charade. You never liked her... you were never shy to admit that. It's over between us. Nothing more left to be said. We tried again, and it didn't work. It's just not meant to happen."

He takes a swig of his scotch, the stench lingering in the air between us.

"Did I ever tell you the story about how your mother and I met?"

"No," I mumble.

"I was quite a womanizer back in the day. I spent most of my late teens screwing everything in sight. When I went to college, I used the whole doctor thing to my advantage. Worked like a charm with the ladies." He smiles as if remembering the time so fondly. "So, one day I met this girl, Cassandra. She tamed me. I studied hard, and she was everything the other girls weren't, so I proposed, and she said yes. On the night of our engagement party, I finally met her family. I was freaking out over meeting her parents, so it never occurred to me that it was her sister I should be worried about."

Taking a step back, I tilt my head to the side. "Holy shit, are you talking about Aunt Cassie?"

"Yes. Her sister, your mother, was the most beautiful woman I had ever met in my life. The moment I saw her, I was in awe. Drove me crazy. She was shy but so unbelievably kind-hearted. I fell in love. We started seeing each other behind Cassie's back, but one day we were caught, and all hell broke loose. Emily was disowned by her family and the whole town. It was hell."

Unable to string a sentence together, I try to absorb this new information. My parents always seemed drama-free, and to think all along, they started a sordid affair just like me.

"But worth going to hell and back?" I question, raising my brows.

"Worth every second, but son, I didn't want that for you or Charlie." Letting out a heavy sigh, his stare falls to his feet. "I thought I was doing you a favor. I thought you'd get over it."

"But I didn't."

"No..." He lowers his voice. "You didn't."

The revelation of his intentions left us with an awkward silence. I never truly understood why my parents meddled in my life and made decisions, which in hindsight, were mistakes. I understand now why my dad wants to protect me having been in a similar situation, but no one else can ever understand how much I loved Charlotte back then. And that, alone, should've been the very reason I fought everyone to keep her in my life.

But I didn't. I was a coward, and nothing will ever change that.

Our momentary silence is short-lived as Rocky runs onto the balcony squealing like a woman. "She's here, she's here!"

With Rocky, it only means one thing—stripper.

We sit at the bar when suddenly we hear the crack of a whip. *Holy fuck, what the hell?* Elijah is waiting, holding his breath, worry plastered on his face. The crack of the whip the second time echoes throughout the room.

"My name is Madame Kiska," she growls in a dominant tone.

Her thick Russian accent is somewhat sexy. Kiska sounds familiar, then I laugh to myself. Kiska means pussy in Russian. She's Madame Pussy. Rocky sits wide-eyed and ready for whatever she will dish out, Elijah the complete opposite. She runs her finger along Elijah's jaw, the latex making a slight sound. Cupping his chin, she squeezes it tight and whispers something in his face before slapping him.

I struggle to hold in my laughter, but her icy stare puts me in my place. Rocky sits there like he has ants in his pants. The music plays, and she does her act on each one of us. The alcohol keeps coming, and much to my amusement, even my dad participates. He laughs as she cracks her whip, and I can swear on my life she breaks out of character a few times and smiles at him. Elijah's friends enjoy themselves—these guys probably never got laid. One of them keeps rubbing his crotch, no shit, his hard-on pointed out like an eyesore. I swear, a fucking bunch of geeks.

Me, well, I just miss her.

Nothing in this world, no other woman can compare to my girl.

Her lips, her scent, just her.

I close my eyes knowing I can't go there, so I grab the closest bottle to me which happens to be vodka and take a swig. Motherfucking fuck. I let out a loose cough as it makes its way down.

With that feeling of being watched, I scan the room, and standing by the large glass doors is my father watching me intently. He shows no sign of emotion on his face. Taking a drink, he looks at his phone and grins as he types something. I walk over with my bottle of vodka, discarding the glass and calling it mine.

"What's got you so happy?" I ask miserably.

"Just a text I got."

I know that look. It's the kind of look I get when Charlotte texts me. *Fuck! What the fuck!*

"What the hell, Dad?"

"Relax, it's your mother. I can show you the text if you want."

"No, I'm good, thanks. Fuck, you two are a couple of freaks."

He grins foolishly. After thirty fucking something years together, he's still in love. I should be praising him, but knowing Mom is on the other end probably sending him dirty texts is enough to make me shudder.

"Anyway, I'm heading off. Got me a date with my freak."

"Date? Mom's in Vegas?"

"No, son. It's called Skype. Maybe you should use it sometime." He pats me on the back and says goodbye.

Even my dad is getting laid more than me. I need a mind erasure as quickly as possible. The vodka bottle is nearly empty and what better opportunity to see what Madame Kiska is up to. Not surprised one bit, I walk out to the main living area to find Rocky in his boxers, hands cuffed, and feet chained. She runs her whip along his torso as he mouths off vulgar words at her.

"You keep your mouth shut, you understand? Only Madame Kiska can speak!" Her accent is strong as her whip cracks along the floor.

"Hey, Rocky, how about a selfie for Nikki?"

"Yeah, yeah! C'mon, Rocky!" Elijah slurs his words. His Elvis suit is still on, but for some reason, he's wearing aviator shades even though it's almost midnight. Fuck, Adriana is gonna kill me. He's beyond wasted.

"Nah, fuck, guys, don't! She'll fucking have my balls."

"Thought she already did." I chuckle.

Elijah grabs the keys that hang on the back of Madame Kiska's belt, much to her disapproval. He dangles them in front of her, Rocky begging someone to un-cuff him. I hold my phone up ready to take a picture.

"C'mon, Elijah," I roar. "This pussy needs a selfie."

"I'm serious, you guys. Don't you fucking dare. She'll have your balls, too."

Elijah continues to dangle the keys, but Rocky being double his size, attempts to reach out for them, knocking them out of Elijah's hands. I scramble for them as they fall to the floor. Now, this is fucking fun. I throw them to Elijah as he catches them with two hands. Rocky continues to beg, but this is way more entertaining. Elijah tells me to go long, and before I know it, I'm standing near the doorway.

"Leexxx, this one is to win the Super Bowl." He throws the keys with force. In my intoxicated state, I pretend to leap like a football player but miss as we watch the keys fall into the pool.

"What the fuck!" Rocky's girly scream echoes in the room.

Elijah and I run over to the pool, scratching our heads in unison.

Elijah stares blankly into the pool. "I guess they're gone."

"You guess they are gone?" Rocky repeats.

"Dude... you're screwed." I break out into hysterics, Elijah following me.

"Get the fucking keys!"

"All right, keep your panties on."

It's a warm night, and without even realizing I'm fully dressed, I dive into the pool. I search the bottom as much as I can, given my state of intoxication I am barely able to see straight.

I come up for air. "Sorry, it's gone. I'm sure she has another set."

We run inside to find Madame Kiska. She's rubbing her tits in that geek's face. We interrupt the floor show to ask about the keys. She cracks her whip at the interruption until she realizes what we said. "No, I don't have another set. Why the hell did you guys do that?" Her accent disappears and is more notably replaced with a southern twang.

We explain the story again hoping it makes sense, forcing her to pull out the spares.

"These are real cops' handcuffs," she panics, shuffling off the geek.

Lifting Rocky's wrist, she points to the handcuffs where LAPD is engraved on the side.

"Shit, dude." I whistle at the predicament. "I heard only cops have the master key."

"We can't go to the cops," she almost cries. "They'll ask me where I got them from."

"Where did you get them from?" the three of us ask.

"Long story. My ex, pimp, or whatever you want to call him, was in the LAPD."

"So, you stole them?" Elijah confirms, keeping a straight face.

"Stole, borrowed, same difference."

"I don't give a goddamn fuck about you, woman. I need these cuffs off, and you're coming with us to the police station."

An hour later, the four of us enter the police station—the handcuffee, the Madame, Elvis, and me dressed in normal attire but still soaking wet from my dive in the pool.

"So, how can I help you gentlemen and madame tonight?" the cop behind the desk asks.

Elijah clears his throat. "We kinda handcuffed my friend."

"Uh-huh, so why not get a pair of bolt cutters?" the cop questions.

We look at each other, neither one of us wanting to talk.

Rocky breaks the silence. "Um... they kinda belong to the LAPD..."

The cop walks around the desk and lifts Rocky's wrist.

"Do you realize it's a federal offense to steal property from the police?"

"Yes, sir," we answer with our heads bowed.

"Who do they belong to?"

The three of us swing our heads to face whatever her name is. She remains silent until she caves under our glare.

"Mine, but I can explain," she wails.

"Go ahead."

She explains the story, the cop barely buying it. The longer she drags the story, the deeper in shit we all become.

"You know that you should be all doing a night behind bars for this offense?" His tone is deadly serious.

Oh fuck. The slammer? Fucking Rocky and Elijah. This isn't on my bucket list. I can see the sweat dripping off Rocky and Elijah's foreheads. If it weren't for the alcohol, I probably would be panicking the same.

"Do you think this is the first time I have seen this?" asks the cop.

"Uh, no, sir, I mean yes, sir..." Rocky answers nervously.

"Well, which one is it?"

"I don't know, sir."

The cop laughs, shaking his head. "You out-of-towners are no different from the rest of them."

As soon as I realize he isn't serious, I break out in a small smile. The cop takes out his key to undo the handcuffs, and I get an idea.

"Sir, can I ask you for a small favor first?"

The cop stares at me strangely.

Moments later, Elijah holds up the mug shot board with some random number next to Rocky as I take the picture.

I hit send.

"You're dead meat."

It takes not even a minute for my phone to ring, so I press the speaker button when I answer the call.

"What the fuck is my husband doing in jail, Edwards!"

I fall to the floor in hysterics along with Elijah. Unable to breathe from Nikki's continuous cussing, she finally threatens Elijah that she will tell Adriana everything. It's contagious. Soon the whole room is laughing, including Rocky.

It will definitely be a night to remember.

The next week is mainly spent in meetings and fighting every battle under the sun. Suddenly, work has become insane, and I'm putting in eighteen-hour days if not more. In the past week alone, I flew to Chicago, Boston, and Vancouver. I'm due next week to speak at a conference in Paris. I am reluctant to leave London again, just that nagging feeling that something isn't right.

On a dreary Friday afternoon, the rain is pouring, covering the skyline. Employees start filing out of the boardroom after a presentation on current market trends. Kate sits across from me, fidgeting with her phone and bouncing her feet under the table. Her eyebrows draw together, and every few seconds, she lifts her eyes to look at me only to drop them again moments later. I sit still, tapping my pen on the desk as I watch her with a tight expression.

"I'm waiting..."

She glances up at me. "I'm sorry, sir, it's just... nothing."

"Great, well, nothing means you can get back to your desk and finalize the travel arrangements for Paris."

Hesitating, I wait as she looks ready to open her mouth, but instead, she walks away, closing the door behind her.

It happens again, twice, then I call her back into my office. Seriously, what the fuck is wrong with her? By the fourth time, I've had enough.

"Kate, tell me what the hell is wrong that's making you so unproductive today?"

"Excuse me, sir?"

"Whatever it is, you've tried to tell me four times in the past hour. Let me guess, you're handing in your resignation?"

"Oh no! I enjoy my job... somewhat."

"Okay, then what? I'm not a mind reader, and you're wasting my time."

She shuffles her feet, wringing her palms. With her head bowed, she mumbles something.

"I can't hear you. Speak up."

"Charlie's in the hospital."

"What?"

"She was admitted a few hours ago. She's been very ill lately, but then she collapsed and had trouble breathing. Eric called me."

"And no one thought to call me?"

"Sir, the history, you know—"

"I'm her fucking husband!"

"Excuse me, husband? I don't even know where to begin with—"

"Book the next flight for me."

Overwhelmed with panic, I grab my phone and dial Nikki's number.

Voicemail.

I dial Adriana.

Voicemail.

I try every fucking person in New York.

Voicemail.

My grip tightens on my phone as I press it against my forehead, willing my eyes to close. My chest begins to tighten, terrified of what state she's in, my imagination running wild with possibilities.

Kate returns fifteen minutes later with my flight details. The plane is leaving in two hours from a different wing as she's booked a private plane. I don't care about the cost, I need to get back to the States now.

The hours pass by in a blur. Occasionally, I nod off, but my mind refuses to shut down. Still haven't heard from anyone, and this cold-shoulder nonsense will be the death of me.

It's just after midnight when I run through the doors of the hospital. The nurses quietly sit behind the desk. They see me and immediately tell me, "No visitors."

I throw some money at them to which they demand even further that I leave. One goes as far to call security, not that I care. A doctor walks past, and I grab him by the coat, begging him for answers, for anything.

"So, you must be the boyfriend?" he questions, looking at the chart.

"Husband," I correct.

"She was admitted this afternoon with breathing difficulties. Chest X-rays found she has a collapsed lung caused by pneumonia. She's severely dehydrated, so we have her on an IV and a mild sedative to help her sleep. I think your biggest concern must be the baby. We ran the tests, and all is well."

The medical jargon isn't lost on me, but my body stiffens, paralyzed with the one word he said. Did I hear correctly? You can't have heard that. You haven't slept properly, and your mind is completely fucked.

I rub my ear, making sure it's clear. "Excuse me... repeat the last part?"

"We ran the tests, and all is—"

"No," I berate him. "The bit before that."

"Your concern for the baby?" He quirks his brow. "Sir, are you okay?"

My eyes widen, the blood draining from my face. I grab the chart and find the room number—eight.

I almost gravitate to her room until I'm standing inside watching her lay on the bed with her head facing the other way. I fall on my knees beside her, hold onto her hand, placing it against my mouth. The smell of her skin is enough for me to break down inside. I miss her like fucking crazy, and now she's carrying my baby.

Charlotte is carrying *my* baby.

"Why didn't you tell me about the baby?"

I remain by her side, clutching onto her hand like my life depends on it. Only the persistent sounds of the monitors beeping, the glorious sounds of life, echo in the room. In the dark of the night, the stark white walls and linen can't be seen, only the warmth that radiates off her skin, but that's all I need—her and now our baby.

A baby.

The word replays over and over in my head. A human being is growing inside her that's half Charlotte and half me.

My emotions are scattered. I'm not ready to be a dad, but then part of me knows I'll have Charlotte for the rest of my life, and we will raise our own family and grow old together.

That part of me outweighs all the anxiety I feel.

Unable to hold back a smile, I mouth the words to myself.

A baby.

I need her to wake up, so I can tell her I was wrong for saying I was done. I love her so much, and now that she's carrying my baby, I want nothing more than to take her home and spend the rest of my life with her and our child.

On the bed, she continues to lay perfectly still, almost in a catatonic state until a slight whimper escapes her lips. My eyes search her face for something, but all I see is a blank stare until she turns her head further in the opposite direction.

I wait with bated breath for her to speak, for any words to ease my worry.

"I didn't tell you, Lex, because... because it's not yours."

FOURTEEN
CHARLIE

F ar in the distance I start to hear noises, the beeping of machines and the clicking of feet bouncing off the walls around me. There's a faint whisper, maybe the sounds of voices, but I'm not sure. I remain still, the heaviness weighing me down. I attempt to lift my arm, but the weight is so heavy it tires me quickly. I try again. No, it's too heavy. What's happening? Where am I? I try to open my eyes, but all I see is darkness, so I fall back asleep.

I wake up, this time feeling some light shining on my closed eyes, almost like a pink glow. Struggling to open them, slowly more comes into fuzzy focus. I see stark-white walls, everything bright. It hurts my eyes forcing me to close them to ease the pain. The smell, it lingers in the air like the smell of sterilization. It's familiar, and I know where I am, but I can't say it. I attempt to scream, but my throat is dry and aching so I'm unable to make any sound, and all that comes out is a tiny whisper. "What happened?"

"Charlie?"

I turn to face where the sound is coming from. Nikki and Eric are by my bedside. Eric is repeatedly rubbing his face, stopping momentarily to bite his nails. Beside him, Nikki is more composed, watching me with a worried expression. They both reach out to touch my hand.

Nikki leans over and taps the red button which hangs on the wall. Between them, they say something, but my eyes close again, heavy and weighed down with exhaustion.

There's more noise now and standing at the foot of my bed is a doctor. Removing the chart from the bed railing, his eyes scan across the notes before he retrieves his pen from his coat, scribbling on the piece of paper. I want to ask him why I'm here, and more importantly, what is wrong with me, but all that comes out is a rasp.

"I'm Dr. Schultz. How are you feeling, Miss Mason?"

Nikki passes me a cup of water which I gladly take. With the cool liquid easing my throat, I clear it with more effort, willing to speak. "Tired. Sore. What happened to me?"

"You have a collapsed lung caused by pneumonia," he states, watching me with a gentle gaze. "We have you on an IV because you are severely dehydrated. Don't worry, the baby is fine. We ran all the necessary tests, and the baby is doing very well."

There's that word again.

I close my eyes, desperate to shut out reality. Taking a deep breath, I open them to see Eric's eyes wide in shock.

"Baby?"

Nikki shakes her head, warning Eric to shut the fuck up.

"In the meantime, Miss Mason, we need you to get plenty of rest, and if you feel uncomfortable, the nurses can give you a mild sedative. I expect you'll be here for another few days."

Dr. Schultz places the chart back at the foot of my bed

before leaving the room. I want nothing more than to ignore everything right now, including the questions Eric is itching to ask.

"Okay, Charlie, I won't ask until you're ready." Eric's voice is calmer, and I can see he's more worried than he is itching for gossip. "Do you need anything? Food? Anything from your apartment?"

I want to be alone, and to get that, I send Eric on a mission to grab me some things from home.

"Okay, so I've got everything written down. I'll also make sure Coco is fed."

"All done, Eric," Nikki tells him. "Mrs. Landry, Charlie's neighbor, has taken Coco in the meantime."

"Great," Eric says with relief. "The last time I was there, she tried to claw my new suit."

Eric says goodbye leaving me alone with Nikki.

Dragging the chair closer to me, she takes a seat, resting her hand on top of mine. "You scared us, you know," her voice softens. "Charlie, I know you don't want to hear this, but you have a baby to take care of. It's not just about you now."

Staring at the ceiling, my heart is hollow. There's a truth to Nikki's words, but speaking them and being in this situation, are two different things. Although I can trust her with my hopes and fears, the cold, harsh reality is that I don't trust myself right now. Desperate to be alone, I nod my head softly before turning to face her. "I know," I murmur. "I just need rest."

Nikki stands then leans forward to kiss me on my forehead. "We're your family, Charlie. Always here for you, no matter what." Promising to be back later tonight, she leaves the room, and I welcome the isolation.

Many thoughts climb into my head, all vying for top

place. The more they circulate, the more my emotions tangle themselves in an intricate web. Various forms of pain, humiliation, and remorse threaten to drive my mind into a dark place of no return. Taking deep breaths, I force myself to be rational, counting my lucky stars I'm still breathing, but in the end, darkness perseveres.

Exhausted, I close my eyes willing all the noise to stop.

Inside a restless sleep, other sounds filter around me. The hospital ward is busy, the voices carrying up and down the corridor, the faint sound of the radio in the nurses' station playing. I focus on the sound—I know what it is, and I close my eyes trying my hardest not to focus on the lyrics of this one particular song. I want to scream at them to turn it off. I don't want any reminders that *he* exists, no sad love song to reiterate how pathetic my life has become.

Silence—all I need is complete and utter silence.

I repeatedly press on the red button, begging them to turn it off. After my outburst, the nurses give me a mild sedative to help me relax. It isn't long before I fall asleep, my body and mind finally resting.

Sometime during the night, I feel him. His warmth washes over me. I have to be dreaming. His fingers entwine with mine, that jolt of electricity awakening me, but I remain still, closing my eyes.

He speaks like the voice of an angel, but I'm not prepared for what he says. I am not prepared for him to know about this baby. And as I attempt to lay perfectly still, I begin the internal battle of what to do, what to say. I can't do this again. Nothing has changed. It's the same cycle of emotions consuming me and chaining me down.

There's no strength or will left in me, no fight. I'm defeated, beaten down, a shadow of my former self.

This journey is no longer one I want to take.

I love him more than I even love myself.

But I need to protect him, even if it means he will never know how much I truly love him, and how I'm willing to sacrifice everything so he doesn't experience the greatest loss possible to mankind. And the only way to protect him will be to destroy him at the same time.

He deserves better than me.

If I hurt him, then he'll never return.

Hurt him, Charlie.

Hurt him so bad that he'll no longer love you.

Hurt him so he will no longer come after you.

Hurt him so bad that he will wish you don't exist.

The voice inside is telling me what I need to do.

"I didn't tell you, Lex, because... because it's not yours." As the words leave my mouth, I bite my lip until it bleeds to stop myself from screaming his name, to stop myself from reaching out and begging him to hold me and make all this pain go away.

But it's the loss of his touch, the footsteps that disappear into the night that forces me to realize what I've just done.

Once again, I'm all alone.

The tears roll down my face, and it's déjà-fucking-vu again, lying in a cold hospital bed for the second time in my life, crying out for someone to save me.

FIFTEEN

LEX

I drop her hand.

With my head bowed, the words she whispers shatter every part of my existence. Is this another chapter in the nightmare replaying in my head? No, this is real, and I'm fucking living it.

Barely able to stand, I walk out of the room with no sense of direction. I don't know where I'm going. I have no idea how to get out of this hospital, how to get out of this nightmare, and how to pretend *she* never existed.

I have nothing.

The realization that the control of my life is taken away is the biggest burden I now carry. Outside in the cool night, the rain starts to pour as I stand there unable to move, unable to decide the simplest thing—where do I go now? Maybe it's hours later, maybe it is minutes, but somehow, I find the strength to lift my arm enough to hail a cab. The yellow cab with its bright lights pulls up, and I climb in.

"Where to, buddy?"

The question is simple, but I stare blankly at him. He asks again, this time with a lot less patience.

"JFK."

The driver remains quiet, listening to his music as the city passes by in a clouded haze. My mind has turned numb, not even processing our approach nor his first warning to pay the fare, then get the hell out of the cab.

Inside the terminal, the huge black television screen with all the flight information listed is spread out before me. I stand there reading every line, memorizing the destinations, flight numbers, and times. I don't know how long it's been after I arrived that a large gentleman in a security uniform walks toward me.

"Sir, is there a reason why you've been standing here for over an hour?"

An hour, time was lost on me.

The baby isn't mine.

"I'm sorry. I'll leave now." I walk toward the counter to be greeted by an over-friendly woman.

"Can I help you, sir?"

The baby isn't mine.

"Where is your next plane going?" I ask.

"Excuse me?"

"I want a ticket on your next flight to wherever it's going," I answer, defeated.

"Um, sir... that's an unusual request."

I see her make eyes at the security guard. "Maybe, but the woman I have loved for nine years told me tonight she's pregnant with someone else's baby, so perhaps you can understand my need to get the hell out of this city?"

Pursing her lips, her expression turns into one of compassion. I don't need a pity party, I simply need to get out of here.

"We have a flight leaving in an hour to Alaska, sir."

"That's fine, I'll take that."

"The last-minute fare on this ticket is twenty-one hundred dollars." She searches my face, waiting for me to tell her it's a ridiculous price like I give a shit about money. I pull my Amex out of my wallet and pass it to her. She takes it, surprised by my lack of consideration for money wasted.

The baby isn't mine.

How can it be *his*?

"Here's your boarding pass, sir. Flight 793 boards from Gate 11 in approximately thirty minutes."

She hands me my boarding pass, and I walk away in search of the gate. Finding it, I sit in an isolated section of the lounge.

The baby isn't mine.

How can it be *his*?

Was she fucking him the whole time?

My Charlotte, my wife, is carrying another man's baby.

There's nothing but white noise in my head, but I sit here silently, still numb, staring into space waiting desperately to board the plane to take me anywhere but here.

The flight is bumpy, but what did I expect from a last-minute flight sitting in economy. It didn't even occur to me to ask for business class, but I assume on a run-down plane like this, business class will be no different. I close my eyes trying to drift off to sleep. The constant wail of an infant a few rows back leaves me no choice but to place the free headphones over my ears. With a little more peace, I try again, but of course, it's impossible to clear my mind.

The baby isn't mine.

I spend the following week remote fishing somewhere in the middle of Alaska. The town is small yet very accommodating. It's amazing how sitting for hours on end with professional fishermen waiting for a bite can ease your troubles, that is until I know I have to finally leave.

The convention in Paris is four days away plus back-to-back meetings.

My phone has been turned off the entire time I have been here. I only messaged Kate before I boarded the plane to Alaska to tell her I would not be contactable for the week.

She replied at the time with a simple, "Okay."

I don't allow myself to think about *her*, it's like pouring salt on a wound. The questions go around and around in circles.

On my last night before heading to Paris, I do the inevitable and turn on my phone knowing I have to face the world again. The beeping doesn't stop for two hours straight, even though the signal I'm receiving is weak.

969 work emails.

Seventeen texts from Adriana.

Ten texts from my mother.

Seven texts from Rocky.

One text from Elijah.

One text from my father.

Zero from Charlotte.

The baby isn't mine.

I quickly scan through the texts first. Adriana is in panic mode. My mother is worried. Rocky's worried at first, but then starts sending me videos of girls getting fingered by other girls. I have to admit I'm slightly amused, but unfortunately, they do nothing for me. Elijah sends me some Paulo Coelho quote about survival. My father's words are simple —he tells me to do whatever it is I need to do. That's odd, I expected a lecture about how much of a disappointment I am to him and our family.

Back on European soil, something changes. The old Lex roars back to life like venom seeping through my veins, and my confidence comes back ten-fold. I learned to rebuild myself, control my life, and demand this world revolves around me, and today, for the first time in what feels like weeks, Lex Edwards is back and on his usual warpath.

Dressed in business attire, a far cry from the awful-looking fishermen gear I sported only a few days ago, I make my way into the conference room and deliver my speech. Every single pair of eyes are on me, some laced with curiosity and many with fear. A part of me desperately needs this old me back, not realizing how my work is engrained in me despite allowing my personal life to dictate my emotions.

I conclude my speech with a round of applause, my concentration shifting to Victoria seated a few rows back. Of course, she'd be here, but I still managed not to speak to her since that infamous night in my suite. I walk down the steps and make my way to where she's seated, ignoring the eyes watching my every move.

"Come with me," I whisper in her ear.

She follows my lead toward the exit and a vacated boardroom next door, away from prying eyes. I want to apologize for what happened, but I also need to forget. I place my hands on her blouse toying with her buttons.

She pushes my hand away, gently. "Lex..." her voice lingers. "You don't want to do this."

I gaze into her eyes.

She's wrong.

I have to do this.

I need to do this.

Make me forget, Victoria. Make me forget that Charlotte is carrying another man's baby, that I mean nothing to her, and she fucked him then she fucked me. Make me forget she's tainted, that another man's touch is ingrained and growing inside her. Make me forget we can never be together, that I'll forever have to look at their baby and realize I was second best.

Make me forget Charlotte ever existed.

"Honey, while I'd like nothing more than to have your cock in my mouth, this isn't what you want. I've never been what you want."

I'm surprised by her words. Is this reverse psychology? This isn't the Victoria I know. With an incredulous stare, I shuffle back.

"We play this cat and mouse game, but the reality is you love Charlotte. Lex Edwards actually loves another human being." She laughs, holding onto my chest. "Lex, go and make this right. This isn't you. This isn't the strong, confident ballsy Lex who pushes my buttons and who is also a genius in the business world."

"She doesn't want me," I mumble with my head bowed, my confidence dissolving in a heartbeat.

"That's impossible. No one can resist Lex Edwards. Look at me." I gaze into her eyes, not knowing what I'm supposed to be looking for. "You built this empire from nothing. You've fought in boardrooms with some of the most powerful men in the business world. My father is threatened by your power and *no one*, I mean *no one*, has ever challenged him like you do. You can't lose this battle because this battle will be your toughest, but it will come with the greatest reward at the end. You understand me?"

I nod, half-listening to her because the reality feels completely different.

"Now, let's go back in there and try to convince the Hanson Group to sell us their shares in the Wilson Division," she states with confidence. "Word is that John Hanson is desperate to offload because he has a failed merger in Hong Kong, and it has cost the group a lot of money.

"Victoria... I'm sorry for what happened back in New York."

She shrugs her shoulders. "Consider it forgotten. Besides, I have my eye on someone else if I can get his gold-digging wife to detach from his arm for two seconds."

Victoria, the shrew, will find a way.

"You're persistent, I'll give you that."

"Yes, and imagine me with the Prince of Luxembourg. What a powerful couple we would make."

"Going for royalty now?" I shake my head with a knowing grin. "You never cease to amaze me."

We walk back into the room, ignoring the curious stares from associates who have nothing better to do than specu-late. I don't really care what they think, or even the false news which will spread, I have nothing else to lose, and with that in mind, I do whatever the hell I want to.

Paris actually turns out to be a great accomplishment. We managed to sign on new business, and I'm in my element for the week I spend there. It turns out that back-to-back meetings with new investors as well as business expos provided me with the solitude that I was desperate for.

But all good things must come to an end, and once again, I find myself alone at a loss with what to do.

I'm still not ready to go home, so I flip through my phone and look for places I want to visit. For some reason, Brazil catches my eye. I was there years ago for a business trip, but something draws me back. I don't know what it is, but it feels like a pull almost.

I book my flights, and the next day, I touch down in Rio de Janeiro, still wondering why I chose to come here.

Wandering the streets of Brazil, I feel like a nomad, alone and with no purpose. A bottle of tequila becomes a permanent fixture in my hand. This city comes alive at night, the crowds freely dancing in the streets, the samba beats echoing through the night. It's easy to get lost in this diversity as I make my way through the streets not really knowing where I'm heading.

Women reach out for me, beautiful women, offering me their bodies for a night like that's what I need. It's hard to resist, but as I stare into their blank faces, it feels wrong. It's only *her* face I want to see, so I walk away until the noise lessens, finding myself in a quieter part of the city.

The buildings look more worn down, dilapidated even. The crowd appears different now—rougher. They are no longer friendly and are eyeing me with caution, almost on guard like I'm some sort of threat.

I see a neon light flashing and enter the bar—the tequila is running low in my bottle.

Inside, the music is more somber, the bar not too full, just a bunch of drunks drinking away their worries. I pull up a seat and ask for a shot. The man beside me pats me on the back like he's my long-lost friend. I motion to the bartender that all drinks are on me, throwing a wad of cash onto the bar surface. Fear is no longer apparent as the crowd cheers, saluting me, then going about their own business. The drinks keep coming, and my vision becomes more blurred. The man, my new best friend, speaks to me in Portuguese telling me about all the pussy he has fucked this week. His story is somewhat entertaining, and provides me with the welcome distraction I desperately need.

But then he goes quiet.

And my mind allows itself to think.

I want to beat the living shit out of *him* for touching *her*, for implanting his baby inside her.

I don't want him near *her*.

I wanted him *dead*.

I fumble for my phone, the screen jumbled. I think there's a text, I'm not sure. Where is Bryce's number? I need him to finish Julian off. Get rid of him once and for all.

My friend slides over another bottle of tequila. That worm, shit, I never thought I could drink a worm, but I fucking do.

What was I doing again?

The bottle is empty.

I realize I've run out of cash, or the cash no longer sits in my pocket. I fumble for more, only to notice it's all gone. I was robbed. Panicking, I place my hand over the secret pocket in my jacket, and relief washes over me as the plastic card still remains. Thank God for my Amex.

It's time to leave, so I stumble out of the bar with my friend in tow. As the door opens, I squint, the light is so bright. I check my watch, but it's missing from my wrist. Fuck!

It has to be the early hours of the morning or past midnight, I don't know. As my eyes adjust to the light, I immediately recognize the 'Christ the Redeemer' statue overlooking Rio de Janeiro, but the light that comes off it is so bright it hurts, almost stinging my eyes. I ask my friend why it's so bright, but he laughs and tells me it always lights up at night and rambles on about Jesus being his savior, but this isn't a little light—it's shining directly at me. I ask him again, he laughs once more telling me the tequila is making me see things, that the worm inside the bottle has a way of poisoning the mind. Yeah, so I am beyond intoxicated and has to be why my imagination is playing tricks on me.

The warm air greets us as I try to ignore the light until this little girl catches my attention. Her father is holding her hand. *Odd,* I think, *to be on the streets at three in the morning.* She looks small, her clothes are tattered, and her hair a wild mess of brown curls. She complains like a little brat to her father until I realize what she's saying. She's complaining about the light, the way it shines so brightly it hurts her eyes.

I turn around and run to her side. Kneeling to her level, I ask her if she sees it too, and she nods. Almost instantly, her father pulls her away, cursing at me and scolding her for talking to a stranger. She cries as he pulls her away, his voice speaking fast in their native language until I hear the name Carla. *Isn't that Charlotte in Spanish?*

She runs back to me, her father yelling her name. The little girl asks me one more time if I see that light too. I nod, giving her a small smile before she runs back to her father.

I stand there—this light, this girl named Carla, this sign.

Fuck, my head hurts.

That's the last thing I remember before I pass out, slumped in the alleyway against some old crates.

God knows how much later as I take in my surroundings, I know that someone is watching over me.

I'm alive.

The memories of last night flash before me—the light, the girl named Carla.

With my back resting against the dirty brick wall and the stale stench of trash surrounding me, I rub my face vigorously trying to come to terms with what happened.

I try to think about this more rationally.

Yes, she said the baby isn't mine, but I remember what

Bryce said about the psych ward. Is she reliving a memory, lying in a hospital bed, déjà vu and shit? I know Charlotte, and she wouldn't actually fuck Julian, not willingly anyway. Maybe it was a one-time thing like after the Victoria shit that went down. No, that would've been too soon. If she already knew she was pregnant, then it would have happened at least over a month ago.

Okay, so maybe I wasn't in the picture, that's possible, but she wouldn't do that to me, not after everything we've been through. So realistically, say she fucked up once, and it is his, do I let go of her for a lifetime?

There's only one question remaining.

Is she worth it?

I know the answer and fuck the fucking universe with all its fate and destiny bullshit. If I want something to happen, I'll make it happen—no matter what it takes.

She was mine all along, and once again, I, Alexander Edwards, vow not to stop, not until she's mine again.

SIXTEEN

CHARLIE

Time has become a blur since the night he left me. Well, should I say the night I foolishly pushed him away?

I no longer know what day it is, suspended in this 'no man's land' struggling to climb out, looking for any sense of hope, but it's impossible. I'm on a familiar downward spiral, and by the seventh day, I know it's near. I'm about to fall into pieces and forcefully be thrown back to a place I swore I'd never return.

This isn't how it's supposed to be.

I was supposed to hurt him, push him away for good.

And the greatest punishment I bestowed upon myself is remorse.

With Coco nestled on my lap purring as I stroke behind her ear, I'm certain she senses a life forming inside of me. Her head is nestled into my stomach, her body pressing gently as if to protect my unborn child.

We sit for what feels like hours until the repetition of the moment I pushed him away becomes too much for my mind to process alone. With a desperate need to drown out the voices and seek external help, I dial his number, each ring fueling my desperation.

Just as I'm about to give up, on the verge of tears I had tried my hardest to hold back, he answers my call. The familiarity of his voice calms me, and with only a few words spoken, enough to express my desolation, he gives me a time and place to meet him.

I don't sleep that night waiting for tomorrow. Tossing and turning, my dreams are plagued with nightmares, and after my third jolt of waking up in screams, I shower, dress, and sit on the couch willing the time to pass.

The coffee shop is a short cab ride away. In a more secluded part of the shop, I sit quietly wringing my hands until he arrives. Sitting down, he motions for the waiter to bring him an espresso as I order a decaf. *I hate decaf.*

Across from me, he watches with a pitiful gaze. I know by reaching out to him, I'm once again forever in his debt for what he has done for me. He smiles as he takes a sip of his espresso, his self-composure always confident, and a small part of me is intimidated by how much power this man has over me.

How decisions he chose affected my life—for the good or for the bad, the jury is still out on that one.

"Thank you for coming on such short notice."

"Charlie, I know enough to know why you called me."

With my hands shaking, I remain silent choking back the sob. He places his hand over mine, a gesture of comfort, of ease as I stare into his eyes.

Does he know what I've done?

Does he know the mistake I made?

"I don't want to go back there... I don't want to go back to that place."

My chest begins to heave, and my breathing becomes

difficult as the room becomes stifling hot. Knowing I'm on the verge of a panic attack, he rubs the top of my hand and demands I take deep breaths.

"You don't have to," he assures me, squeezing my hand tight. "You can make the decisions here. This isn't about fate, Charlie. This is about you understanding that life will deal you a card, and sometimes it's of the lowest kind, and it forces you to make the best of a situation. You're already better than you were by knowing you needed to call me. You've proven what you can accomplish, what you can get through if you believe in yourself and accept what is. Now you're faced with a crossroads, so what road do you take? Do you take the easy route and run and hide as fast as possible, or do you take the long winding road? In the end, the possibilities are endless."

Just like that, he places the ultimatum in front of me.

This is *my* decision, but I know I have already thrown fuel into the fire, and although I'm living this nightmare, Lex's nightmare is ten times worse. The pain I forced on him is of pure hatred, and why would I do that to the one person I love more than life itself?

"I've said things... things to hurt him."

"But you still love him?"

"I never stopped," I whisper, bowing my head.

"Charlie," he says softly. "Choose your destiny and never let go of that. One day this conversation will be history."

"How do you know that will happen?"

"Because if you really want something, I mean like *really* want it, you can have it. You just need to find the willpower and strength. Look at the end picture and stop focusing on the pain you're feeling right now."

I manage a small smile, knowing he's right. I've done

this before, resurrected myself when I thought it was the end. And I'd made promises to my grandmother, to him— the promise to live my life to the fullest.

"I can't thank you enough, Dr. Edwards, you know... for what you've done for me. I mean, my life... you know... I wouldn't be here if it weren't for you."

"It wasn't me, Charlie. I have my faults, too." He lowers his head, toying with the wedding band on his finger. "You reached out and needed my hand to lead the way, but the walk, the journey, you did that all by yourself. Thank yourself, Charlie, not me."

Leaning over, careful not to spill our beverages, I hug him tightly. Despite what he just said, my gratitude toward him can't be ignored. Everything I am today I owe to him. The only way I can repay him is to move forward, find a better place, be that better person. I've been given a second chance, and now a third.

"Remember what I said..." he reminds me as I pull away, "... this is your choice, your decision, your destiny. You want something... then *you* go for it."

I nod, understanding what I need to do to fix this catastrophe I created. It's going to be the biggest fight of my life, but if what he says is true, if I look at the end picture, I won't go down without a fight, without placing every morsel of hope, every bout of faith, every ounce of trust in us.

"Have you spoken to him?" I ask, hesitating.

Dr. Edwards purses his lips. "Yes."

"Oh..."

"He's not in a good place, Charlie."

Of course, he isn't in a good place. Neither would I be if I found out the woman I love is having a baby with someone else. And just like that, it clicks.

I'd walked a mile in his shoes, feel the pain of knowing

exactly that. When I found out he was having a baby with Samantha, it hurt beyond comprehension. But I wasn't even given a chance to do anything before he disappeared out of my life. No explanation. No goodbye.

"Dr. Edwards, there's one more thing... I need... a favor."

"Charlie, you know you can ask for anything."

"I need... I need you to do a DNA test..." I trail off, ashamed this is even an issue.

Some things are worth fighting for.

When your heart won't stop loving, then it's not ready to give up. He doesn't judge or pity me. Instead, he chooses to understand and once again guide me along the right path. We say our goodbyes, but I turn back one last time because I need to say it again. "Dr. Edwards?"

He turns around to face me, his strikingly handsome looks on par with his son.

"Thank you... again," I murmur before he walks out of the coffee shop with a smile on his face.

I take in a deep breath, gazing at my reflection in the mirror. The dress Adriana designed is absolutely stunning, the color blush matching my skin tone perfectly thanks to a last-minute spray tan Eric convinces me I needed.

The strapless gown sits snug around my breasts which have decided to grow in the last week, pumped full of hormones making them really pop out. Adriana made some minor adjustments since I have lost weight around my waist from my inability to hold down any food in the morning, but that appears to have eased in the last two days.

My hair is styled in soft curls parted to the side, and the

only piece of jewelry I am wearing is the phoenix pendant. Reaching for the necklace, I run my fingers over it, closing my eyes while I take in another deep breath. I'm unable to push aside the nerves, knowing I'll see him for the first time since that night in the hospital.

Sometimes in life you wonder how you ever got through something, a moment when life meant nothing. The past month has been nothing short of hell. Time is moving slowly, but I'm stuck in my own personal hell, waving my wand of pain over those I love and over the only man I've ever loved.

I have no one to blame but myself.

That's what makes this harder.

My talk with Andrew made me realize I can't give up, but I cannot push him either. There are several times when I nearly caved, dialing his number, sending him a text, and even as far as speaking to Air France on the phone ready to divulge my credit card details, but I chickened out at the last minute. Of course, I want to see him, but there's the uncertainty of his reaction, and I need to be in the right frame of mind to handle any hurt or rejection he might inflict upon me. He is a guy, after all, and his natural reaction would be to fuck everything in sight and forget about me, the super-bitch who's knocked up with another man's baby.

Oh, how I would do anything to take back what I said, to take back the hurt I caused him, but what's done is done. I'm officially all cried out, and now I'm here on Adriana's wedding day where I'll finally meet my destiny, the one I choose to follow.

"Charlie, I know you're scared," Eric murmurs while fixing the back of my dress.

"Scared would be an understatement. E, what if I've damaged him so bad that he can't even look me in the eye?"

Eric places the bottom of my dress down, standing behind me as he gazes at my reflection in the mirror. "My mom always said that you can tell how much someone loves you by looking them in the eyes. Look him straight in the eyes, Charlie. The answer will be there."

I nod, although the thought of not seeing any love for me weighs heavily on my mind. Can I look into his eyes? What if I fall harder, and he isn't there to catch me?

"And if all else fails, just look at his crotch and hope for a wave hello or the one-eyed salute."

"You're terrible." I laugh.

"Weddings bring it out of me."

There's a soft knock on the door followed by Kate poking her head in. Eric motions for her to enter. He knows we need to talk, so he leaves us alone to check on Adriana.

I have only managed to communicate with Kate by text. This is the first time I've seen her since the restaurant episode.

"Charlie, you look gorgeous. That color is amazing on you," she says, nervously.

Kate looks stunning wearing a navy off-the-shoulder chiffon dress. With her hair cut shorter into a bob, it's styled to the side with a French braid and colored in a lighter shade of blonde.

"Thanks, Kate." With my hand clutching my stomach, I try to calm my nerves again, willing to get out my apology. "Listen, I'm so sorry for allowing this to come between us."

Her shoulders instantly relax as if she has been holding in her breath just like me.

"Charlie, seriously, we are both at fault. How did we not

figure out we were talking about the same guy? I'm sorry for being distant the past month. It's been difficult handling everything on my own. I've been pushed beyond my limits, but I suppose what doesn't kill you makes you stronger, right?"

"I can imagine, and yes, it certainly does..." I pause, unsure if I should delve even further into this topic, but my heart desperately needs some sort of reassurance that I'm not about to walk out into a battle zone unprotected. "Kate... I love him so much it hurts to breathe without him. But you know it was me who pushed him away. This is all a mess. I'm hoping he'll give me another chance."

With a sigh, she shakes her head. "Charlie, he loves you. Mr. Edwa... I mean, Lex... has never looked at anyone the way he looks at you. Trust me, I've been around. Bollocks, I didn't mean for it to come out that way."

I laugh, placing my hand on her arm, reassuring her. "It's okay, I get it, he has a past. One day on a drunken rant you can spill all his dirty little secrets to me."

"Oh God, he'd fire me if he ever found out I spilled the beans."

"You really love your job, don't you?" Curiosity gets the better of me. She has voiced on several occasions that her boss was a pain in her ass. I wonder what it is about Lex that makes her enjoy her job. I personally can't imagine working for such an arrogant prick, but then again, I'm stubborn and want things my way, especially when it comes to work so I can't talk.

She hesitates before answering, "You know, I do love my job. I actually look forward to waking up every day and going to work. It's such a challenge, and I love the interaction with some of the most intelligent and powerful people in the business world. Mr. Edwards... Lex... is such a great mentor, if you ignore the fact that he has mood swings like a lady waiting for her Aunt Flow."

I laugh out loud, it's so him. Pulling her into an embrace, we squeeze each other tightly. "Thank you, Kate, for being a great friend. I've missed you."

"I've missed you, too, Charlie." She smiles, her blue eyes radiating. "You deserve to be happy. You both do. You know he's here already?"

"He is?"

"Yes, he arrived not long ago."

"How does he look?"

"Um... nice... in his suit," she says, shrugging her shoulders. "Clean... he looks happy to be here."

"Okay, I didn't ask you to describe his dad. How does *he* look?"

"Oh, Charlie, that's kinda awkward for me to answer..."

Pouting my lips, my eyes widen as my stare fixates on her.

"Don't give me that puppy-dog look. No fair," she complains, checking herself quickly in the mirror beside us. Turning around to face me again, she crosses her arms in defiance. "Okay, fine! He looks hot, the tux is top-notch against his body. His face is cleanly shaven after that ridiculous fisherman's beard he had been sporting the last few weeks. His hair has been cut kinda like that hot vampire dude from those movies. He looks pretty content. There... are you happy now?"

I'm happy, and although he could've grown the biggest beard known to man, I'll always think he's beautiful. There's no other man who can measure up to him in my eyes.

"That wasn't so hard now, was it?" I tease.

Adriana walks into the room with Eric. We gasp as she

stands in front of us, her face beaming. She looks like a princess. Her dress is ivory, not the traditional white, but it's a showstopper. The bodice is strapless and has lace embroidered all around it. The skirt is full like a ball gown, the middle section accentuated with a silk bow. She's everything I imagined she'd be on her wedding day. My eyes begin to water, and I blink, trying to avoid ruining my makeup.

"Adriana... you look..."

"I know, right?" Her smile is contagious. "But don't you cry and mess up that beautiful face of yours."

"Adriana, today is all about you."

"No, it isn't, Char." She squeezes my hand, staring into my eyes with a hopeful expression. "I need this to finally happen just as much as you two. You've always been special to me, and I know why... because you're a piece of Lex."

I don't want her to have to focus on anything but her and Elijah. With that in mind, and my nerves consuming me, I offer a soft smile and admire her standing in front of me for the last time as Adriana Edwards.

"Okay, bitches, it's showtime!" Eric claps.

Adriana takes in a deep breath. I reach out for her hand, noticing it's perfectly still. Not a single shake comes from her delicate hands. This is everything she's been waiting for as long as I've known her.

Elijah and Adriana chose to have the ceremony at a beautiful church not far from New Haven. The nostalgia of being back in Connecticut isn't lost on me, but instead of remembering a time in my life when things were out of control, I focus on the beautiful nature surrounding the tall white church.

Snow has fallen around us, and with our jackets still on, the air is cold, but none of us seem to care. Adriana has always wanted exactly this, and the universe granted her the perfect winter wedding.

We stand inside the foyer of the church with the doors closed to the main area. Everyone removes their jackets, handing them over to Adriana's aunty. There's a flurry of activity, everyone fussing over Adriana, the photographer trying to capture the perfect moment.

I stand back and watch my best friend, watch this moment that's all hers. I feel someone stand beside me—it's her mother, Emily. She watches alongside me, admiring her daughter. It's her moment as well, and what a moment for her. She has been waiting for this just as much as Adriana has.

"Charlie," she utters, reaching out for my hand, squeezing it tight as we both watch Adriana. "I'm glad you're here. It wouldn't have been the same without you."

Emily has been a mother to me when my mom decided to up and bail because life got too hard. Yet, she is another person caught in the tangled mess Lex and I created for ourselves. I sense, in her touch, the sorrow she feels for how we ended our own relationship—the callous stare she gave me when I just found out Samantha was pregnant and begged Adriana to talk to me while Emily waited in the car.

I had broken her family, disrespected her the same way she had done to me by abandoning me that day I begged for help. But none of us expected any of this to happen, and each one of us played a part heavily riddled with emotions.

The wedding coordinator shouts at everyone to get into place and begins the countdown.

Five... four... three... two... one.

The doors spring open, the orchestra playing 'Pachelbel's Canon' as the two little flower girls begin their walk down the aisle.

"This is it," I whisper, with a smile. "You ready?"

Adriana beams, nodding. "Waited a lifetime for this."

I turn back around, standing in place, and then I'm in front and about to start my march.

My eyes fall upon *him*.

With my heart pounding so loudly, I realize how easy it is to fall in love with Lex. The hardest part comes now, showing him how much I need him, how much we both need him—for the rest of our lives.

And as his head lifts and our eyes lock, the beat of my heart becomes completely still.

There's no tomorrow without him.

Alexander Edwards will forever be the only man to capture my heart.

And I refuse to live life any other way.

"You know, Elijah, the car's got a full tank of gas... it'll get you as far as D.C."

"Thanks, but I've been waiting for this day my entire life..." he pauses, waving to a few guests who have arrived. "Thank you, Lex, for helping me, you know, to be able to kick cancer's butt, but most importantly to be able to marry my girl. I know this isn't easy for you... but thank you."

I pat Elijah on the shoulder. "You're taking on the responsibility of Adriana, I should be thanking you."

"Soon, it'll be you, buddy."

I've always had a close relationship with Elijah even when things were strained between Adriana and me. Unlike everyone else, he never meddled or judged my behavior. He listened, offered advice if deemed necessary, and I could always trust him.

"I married her, Elijah, the last night at The Hamptons."

Elijah's mouth falls open as he tips his head to the side.

"Huh? How? For starters, you need to apply for a

marriage license, and then there's a twenty-four-hour waiting period. Is this some wedding prank you're pulling on me?"

"I bribed the city clerk, offered to pay for a new community hall he was currently trying to fund. It happened, Elijah, but after the way I treated her, I don't know if she still wants to be married to me."

"In the words of Rocky, dude, *far out*. For what it's worth, congratulations, man." He went in for a quick man-hug before the other groomsmen arrived.

We take our place at the altar, and suddenly, the nerves begin to eat away at me. I mean, Christ, I'm not the one getting married here, but after a month of not seeing her, well, *this is it*.

This is the decider.

Will I be able to look at her the same and still love her despite it all? Will I see my Charlotte or will I see this baby, *his baby*?

Taking deep breaths, my palms begin to sweat, and almost like he knows, Elijah places his hand on my shoulder, squeezing it tightly. The guy isn't breaking a single sweat, and that, folks, is love in its purest form. I swear, my sister is lucky to have found him.

I push aside the nerves to the best of my ability as the music begins, focusing on Adriana and Elijah's moment.

Adriana is anything but traditional, depending on her mood. I expected the wedding march to play on the piano but, instead, a string quartet plays as the two flower girls walk down the aisle. I have to admit, they are kind of cute in their little dresses, and I'm never one to think kids are cute.

Next comes the bridesmaids. I know there are two walking down the aisle, then Charlotte will follow. I watch in anticipation as Adriana's friend and Elijah's cousin walk down the aisle. The girls are pretty, but my focus isn't on them, and I don't even notice I'm holding my breath in anticipation until my chest tightens.

My heart stops when I see her standing at the entrance of the church wearing a pink-like strapless dress, the fabric and lace sitting perfectly against her skin.

I scan her face, searching for something, and instantly, her eyes meet mine.

The force of her presence is powerful, encompassing, and perfection is underrated when describing her beauty. In just one glance, one stare, every beautiful moment we have shared overshadows the pain we have managed to survive.

With my hands clasped over each other, respecting the ceremonial duties as I stand here as best man, I watch Charlotte walk down the aisle.

And once again, my heart starts beating.

How can we make this work?

Every step closer to me, the warmth rushes over my entire body. With a look of contentment and a gentle smile playing on her lips, she fixates on Elijah until she takes her position on the opposite side. Almost instantly, her eyes fall upon me again.

My mind dares to explore this moment, just us, one day her walking down the aisle to be my wife in front of everyone. A proper ceremony. Maybe that's why this all went wrong? Like fate saying 'hey, you rush me, so I'll fuck up everything for you guys.'

And just like that, our future is sealed. One moment, a simple act of the woman I love walking down the aisle is all I need to guide my heart and head in the same direction.

I want her and everything that comes with her, including this baby.

We have to make it work. I have to find a way to deal

with him in our lives, but it's that or nothing. If she loves me the way I love her, we can make this work. We can do therapy or co-parenting bullshit. Maybe the universe can work me some favors and have him give up all rights. Fuck, will you listen to yourself? She's already your wife, and so far, the universe has at least given me that.

I just need her to know that nothing will change her being Mrs. Edwards.

The music plays louder, and Adriana walks down the aisle with my father holding onto her. My mother is a basket case, sitting at the front dabbing her eyes with a tissue. It's all so overwhelming, and Adriana looks amazing.

The ceremony starts, but I can't help sneaking a look at Charlotte every chance I get. She still looks the same, definitely a lot healthier than when I saw her last. Her skin appears more sun-kissed, her eyes shine again, the light has been switched back on, and her smile—when I catch her smiling at me, I can't help but smile back.

I wouldn't be a man not to notice her tits. Pregnancy looks good on her, but this isn't the time nor place to imagine her naked. I almost need a dose of holy water to wash away the sinful thoughts lingering in my mind while standing here in the church.

And then, I notice the phoenix pendant sitting on her chest. That has to mean something.

My gaze is broken when the priest announces them as husband and wife. The crowd claps loudly, and the newlywed couple exchanges their first kiss.

Mr. and Mrs. Evans.

The two of them are overcome by joy while holding hands and proceeding their walk down the aisle as the happy newlywed couple, leaving us to go next.

Extending my arm out with my mouth curved upward into a smile, my body is hyper-aware as she gracefully links her arm in mine, and a jolt ricochets into every crevice within me lying dormant since the last time I saw her. Beside me, she jumps slightly, and I'm certain she feels the same thing.

As we walk down the aisle, all eyes are on us, and being so close to her is driving my senses wild. With the scent of her perfume and the essence of her skin, I so desperately want to pull her aside and talk to her, but not before kissing her beautiful lips and owning her in every possible way.

But cameras are shoved in our faces and surround us wherever we turn.

Outside, people throw rice at the happy couple.

Rocky, being a sports junkie, throws a hard shot at Elijah, smacking him in the face. I burst out laughing alongside Rocky, but Elijah shoots us an annoyed look while spitting out rice from his mouth.

Charlotte is pulled away to take photographs, the loss of contact unbearable, but I have to ignore the pang as I stand there watching her and the beauty she portrays, and I can't help feeling sick but a good sick. Like that butterfly feeling that makes you want to puke. Okay, that came out wrong, but all I know is that I can't take my eyes off her no matter how hard I try.

The photographer steps back for a moment, allowing me to talk to her. With every step I take, the words jumble in my mind unable to form a sentence. This feeling of no control is unsettling.

"Hi." It's all I manage as I stare into her eyes, completely at a loss for words.

"Hi, yourself."

The photographer grabs us once again, and before we know it, we are lost in the wedding chaos. The Rolls Royces pull up to the church, and we're separated yet again.

It shouldn't be a long drive to the reception, but, of course, in wedding tradition, a million pictures need to be taken from a pose by the pond, under the tree, against the cars, in the cars, you name it, and it is done—three times! It's fucking freezing out here, and Bridezilla demands we take our coats off for the pictures.

The photographer suggests a picture of the bridal party with their respective partners.

Again, I think it might be a chance to speak to her.

As we pose beside the frozen pond, the fussy photographer snaps pictures, directing us every which way. Beside me, Charlotte's skin is shivering, and I don't blame her since she wore only the dress with nothing covering her. Adriana has a death wish, I'm certain of that.

With disregard for the photographer's directions, I remove my suit jacket and place it around Charlotte's shoulders, worried she'll experience hypothermia and so will the baby.

"Thank you." She smiles, her teeth chattering.

"Um... Lex, what are you doing? We need one more photo?" Adriana barks.

"It's fucking freezing. Seriously, for the love of God, let's go."

"Fine." Adriana's teeth chatter as she crosses her arms to protect herself from the cold. "You win. Now, let's get this party started."

Once again, chaos disrupts as the wedding coordinator commands everyone to go back into their designated cars but not without warning us of our upcoming responsibilities upon entering the reception hall.

On the drive over, sitting with Elijah's cousin and friend, we crack open the bourbon and cheer to the groom sitting in the car in front of us. When we finally arrive, and with the alcohol settling nicely in my nervous system, we're asked to escort our partners once again for the grand entrance into the room.

"We meet again, and thanks for the jacket," Charlotte offers with a smile as she laces her arm in mine.

"Remind me never to get married in winter..." The second it leaves my mouth, I instantly regret it. *What the fuck is wrong with me?*

Charlotte's shoulders move up and down as she laughs. "I don't like winter either, so at least we agree."

"Sorry, I meant—"

We're interrupted as our names are called. Together, we walk through the double doors to a cheering crowd, then take our seats at the table.

I'm seated next to Elijah. It doesn't bother me until he keeps leaning over to his other side and kisses Adriana. It's fucking awkward, and the champagne they serve is for pussies. Just before the starters is to be served, I decide to make a quick dash to the men's room then grab something hard at the bar.

On my way there, I run into Rocky and Nikki in the hallway. I could swear she had her hair in a bun at the church, and now it's out, sitting messily on her shoulders.

"Babe, can you excuse us for a second?" Nikki asks Rocky.

He walks back into ballroom with a giant smirk on his face. That fucker just got blown. Nikki's lipstick appears fresh as if it was reapplied minutes ago. I wouldn't put it past them.

"First of all, that prank you pulled wasn't funny. However, it serves him right for begging for the floorshow."

"I can't argue with that one," I reply with a small chuckle.

"Look, you know me, I'm just going to say it how it is. I was there when Charlie found out. She's very fragile right now... I want you to take that into consideration."

"Nikki..."

"No, Lex, look... I'm butting out. This is your business. She's your wife now. All I ask is that you take good care of her, okay? She's family to me."

I nod in silence. Charlotte means a lot to many people, and in no way, moving forward, do I want to hurt her anymore. Then, I remember Nikki just said Charlotte is my wife now. So, Charlotte told her. *Does that mean what I think it means?*

Nikki walks away, leaving me standing alone thinking about what she said and forgetting my urgent need to take a piss.

I quickly duck in and out of the bathroom, then make my way back to the table. Entrée is served, and we all sit there chatting amongst ourselves. I know it's almost time for the speeches, but some moron in the crowd keeps tinkering with their glass. It's that stupid tradition where one person starts tapping their fork against the glass and the whole room follows which forces the couple to kiss. It's like the tenth time it has happened tonight, and after close examination, I realize it's Rocky who always starts it.

Looking over at Rocky, I shoot him a fuck-off-and-stop-doing-that look. With a wide grin, he raises his glass to me before drinking it all in one go.

A few moments later, the MC announces it's speech time. Thankfully, I'm second in line though I'm not worried about speaking in front of everyone. This is nothing compared to the large auditoriums where I have given speeches and presentations in front of the most powerful people in the world.

But I'll have to follow my dad.

And that's something else.

Dad is up first, and I know his speech will be emotional given Adriana is his only daughter. I recall my first wedding, his speech, and how everyone cried. This will be ten times worse.

"Thank you all for coming here today to celebrate the marriage of my beautiful and only daughter, Adriana, and my new and hopefully only son-in-law, Elijah."

The crowd lets out a small laugh. My father is always witty, engaging people when needed.

"Ever since Adriana could talk, she was obsessed with weddings. Her first failed marriage was at three. I walked into the living room and found all her dolls and bears dressed up sitting in rows. Adriana was wearing a Cinderella costume with a crown. I asked her what she was doing, and she said she was getting married and waiting at the altar for her groom. I couldn't help but be amused by this little girl's imagination, so I asked her who her groom was, and she simply replied, 'Alex.'"

Laughter fills the room as I recall the memory. At the time, I was nine and having a little sister around was rather annoying.

"Her second failed marriage attempt was at the age of eight. We were due to move to Carmel in about a week. Adriana came rushing through the house with a basket full of items. I asked her why the rush and what was she doing. She explained that she was eloping in the backyard, and that we all needed to be there because she was marrying the next-door neighbors' kid before we left. I explained to her again that marriage wasn't something you committed to with just anyone. I still remember her exact words to me. 'Daddy, if I don't lock him down now, then God knows who I could end up with.' I'm thinking little Jimmy next door must have been glad we decided to move three days early."

The crowd, again, let out a laugh, my mother beaming as my father continues, "As for her third marriage attempt, now this one *will* last. Elijah," he says, raising his glass toward him. "I have never seen a man so in love, so taken with a woman as much as I have seen you with my little girl. You're the light in her day, the contentment in her night. You have given her so much joy and happiness, and anyone who can make my little girl smile the way you do, well, that's the only thing a father can wish for his daughter. So, to a lifetime of happiness. Please raise a toast to the newly-wedded couple."

My mother, an absolute wreck, is sobbing into her pile of tissues. I have to admit, it was a pretty good speech. My father hugs my sister tightly before leaning over to give Elijah a quick man-hug.

Rising from my chair, I button up my jacket before walking toward the stage. I clear my throat, ignoring my sweaty palms. Why do I feel like I'm the giant elephant in the room, and the only person watching is Charlotte?

It is now or never.

I straighten my posture, it's showtime.

"They say love is a noble act of self-giving, offering trust, faith, and loyalty. The more you love, the more you lose a part of yourself, yet you don't become less of who you are, you end up being complete with your loved one. This couldn't ring any truer as I tell you the story of how I watched their love for one another unfold..."

From my left side, I see Charlotte staring intently at me, never turning away.

"The first time I met Elijah was when I came home from college. Adriana had this habit of waiting for me on the porch steps every time I came home, something she had done from the moment she could walk. On this particular day, she hadn't, something I thought she had outgrown, which saddened me somewhat. As I walked into the house, there was only one sound I could hear, the laughter of my sister. I made my way to where the sounds came from, and I saw Adriana with this scrawny-looking boy who reminded me of Beetlejuice with his scruffy hair. She was sitting there intently, listening to a story Elijah was telling her about his horses when he grew up. Now, for anyone who knows Adriana, sitting still and being quiet were skills she never displayed. In fact, it's almost like she repelled them. However, she sat there, perfectly still, listening intently. I had never seen this side of her. After a quick cough on my end, she saw me. She wasn't afraid, neither was Elijah. She simply introduced him as a very good friend of hers.

"From that day on, I did lose a small part of my sister for I saw that she was finally growing into this woman, and this so-called friend. Elijah, I knew he had everything to do with it. Not many people can say they held onto their first loves, not many people can say that it was only ever one person who has captured them. Elijah and Adriana, you have conquered love at first sight, remained true to one another after all these years. Your strength and unity as one never cease to amaze me. Your trust in each other, most importantly, has gotten you to this day, the day that if anyone deserves it, it's the both of you.

"Today, you both become complete with one another and let this be a lesson to others. Place your trust in those you love and accept their trust with the greatest of appreciation. Love like there is no tomorrow, live like today is the end, and have faith that tomorrow will come. Sometimes we are given the easy road, sometimes the most challenging, but if we can end up being as happy as both of you today, then any road taken is well worth the journey."

EIGHTEEN

CHARLIE

Lex stands and is handed the microphone. Standing in front of everyone, confident and demanding with his presence, all eyes fixate on him, including my own.

From the moment I laid eyes on him at the church, to our short walk down the aisle, then our brief encounter at the park while taking photographs, I take every opportunity possible to stare at his handsome face.

Lex has always been beautiful in a masculine way, but today, I have no words to describe how seeing him makes me feel. His presence, even though he's cautious with his actions around me, still dominates me but in a way I yearn to be owned by only him. Dressed in his black tux, a crisp white shirt with a bowtie to complement his outfit, my thoughts wander off to places they shouldn't wander off to inside a church.

I feel unholy and ready to be thrown to the gates of hell for thinking about him in a sexual way.

But now, standing in front of everyone, I block out all the noise and listen to only him, desperate for his words.

"They say love is a noble act of self-giving, offering trust, faith, and loyalty..."

Throughout his entire speech, I clutch at my pendant. My stomach flutters as his emotions speak loudly through the words he voices. He raises his glass, and everyone cheers. Adriana stands, embracing him with a tear sliding down her cheek. I memorize his words, every single thing he said.

He said...

It was a challenging road.

But well worth the journey.

And to love like there's no tomorrow.

Live like today is the end.

The MC announces the final speech for the night as Elijah takes to the stage. Sitting here, I'm unable to focus until unknowingly, I tilt my head to catch a glimpse of Lex.

Emerald eyes shine back at me, blanketing me with all its warmth and love.

And just like that, I know it will be okay.

"First of all, I want to thank you for attending this very special day of ours. Each one of you in this room holds a special place in our hearts, and it has brought us joy to be able to share this with you. I want to take a moment to thank my mother. Momma, you have sacrificed so much for me, and you gave me the strength to follow my dreams. Your love and support will forever be the reason why I am the man I am today. To my poppa, I know you are looking down on us, and as we take a moment to look up at you, just know that I love you and can feel your presence with us. You didn't miss out, Poppa... *you're right here.*" Elijah's voice slightly quivers, Adriana beside me is drowning in tears.

I pass her the napkin, grabbing my own to dab the corner of my eyes.

"To Andrew and Emily, you have done nothing but welcome me into your home and your family since the first time I met you. You have been with me through my darkest moments, given me the ray of hope that I needed. And now you have given me the greatest gift, the pleasure of marrying your daughter. I promise to spend my life making your daughter the happiest woman alive, but only if you promise to stop nagging about grandkids for a few years."

Laughter fills the room, both Dr. Edwards and Emily beaming with pride as they listen on.

"To my newly crowned brother-in-law, Lex, I just want to say that I never had any siblings growing up, but had I been given that gift, I'd have wished for someone like you. You are the strongest, most determined person I know. Without knowing it, you have touched so many peoples' lives and have never let me down. In fact, the only reason why I'm standing here today cancer-free is because of you."

I wipe the tear which falls down my cheek, the emotions of the entire day too much to hold back.

"To my beautiful wife, Adriana, my best friend and the future mother of our children, you have shown me how to love, shown me how to better myself, and most importantly, you're my reason for taking each breath. I love you, Adriana. A toast to the wonderful journey we are about to embark upon."

He lowers his face to meet hers and kisses the tears falling down her cheeks before kissing her on the lips. The applause in the room echoes as everyone cheers the amazing couple.

Lost in my own thoughts, I hadn't noticed the music filtering throughout the room as Elijah extends his hand like the true gentleman he is and asks Adriana to join him in their first dance as a wedded couple.

With a smile gracing her entire face, she stands and follows him to the dance floor. Like two perfect souls, they sway their bodies to the soft sound as the band sings 'Unchained Melody.'

It's their song, and in their perfect moment, I watch in awe as these two people have finally become one, and I was there from the beginning. Memories of them meeting for the first time at our local football game, the way Adriana would talk endlessly about him, and the way he looked at her, not like your normal high school boy. It truly was love at first sight. It's like a happy ending to a movie you spent a lifetime watching, and so I sit back and watch, willingly holding back more tears wanting to escape.

As the song almost reaches the end, the inevitable is near, and that feeling which buries itself in the pit of my stomach has tangled itself into a large knot riddled with nerves.

The MC finally announces the wedding party is to join the bride and groom as Bryan Adam's 'Everything I Do, I Do It For You' begins to play.

I can do this.

I have to do this.

Lex is by my side almost immediately. Placing my hand into his, it shoots through me again, that wild jolt of electricity which reminds me why it has always been him. But this time I don't flinch, my body craves it so very much.

I follow him to the dance floor as he stops in the middle beside the other couples. Placing his arms around my waist, he brings me close to him as my hands wrap around his neck just like I did at prom.

Our eyes meet, gazes locked like nothing around us exists, just him and me in this moment. His emerald eyes are sparkling as I study his face, every single angle, focusing on his beautiful lips which I desperately want to kiss.

Unsure if I should speak first, my nerves are overshadowed by my inability to string together a coherent sentence. What do I say? That I want him more than life itself. Should I start by saying that? His words linger in my head, and so I dance and place my trust in him.

"Lex," I murmur, his name rolling off my tongue so effortlessly.

"Charlotte, please, let me say what I need to say first."

I stare into his eyes, my movement stilling, so he has my full attention.

"For the past month, I have been aimlessly walking around wondering why I was being punished. Wondering exactly what I did wrong to be dealt so much pain. I thought I had reached low points in my life before, but they were nothing in comparison to what I've been feeling...

"A few nights ago, I sat alone in a dangerous part of Brazil. I was drunk, and the local folk were ready to rob me. I didn't care that I was close to being beaten up. They watched me, tequila in hand like a time bomb waiting to go off. It hurt so much what you had said to me, and I replayed the words over and over again in my head. Those words constantly echoed through my mind, and I question what exactly made me hurt the most... the fact that it was *his* or the fact that I wouldn't be in your life? I wanted to hurt him, Charlotte, more than you can ever imagine. I had things planned that I'm ashamed to admit. I was there ready to make that happen, but then I looked up, and I saw it, the light that shines so bright on the statue of Jesus Christ."

He chokes on his words, bowing his head in shame as I wait in anticipation.

"Just when I thought I'd lost hope, there was this little

girl a few feet away from me, her angelic voice carried in the bustle surrounding us. She spoke in her native tongue, but I understood, she asked her dad why the Christ the Redeemer was shining so bright it was hurting her eyes. I rushed to her side and asked her if she could see it, too. She nodded, and I knew it wasn't just me. Her name was Carla. It was a sign, a big fucking sign. It was at that moment I knew I missed you, that my life is nothing without you. I was no longer angry at him, but angry with myself for hurting you. You're the one having to deal with this alone, and I hated myself for making you think you had no other choice. I love you, Charlotte Olivia Mason. My life will only be complete with you in it."

My heart has been tugged every which way, and I have to finally say the words because I need him just as much as he needs me. "The baby—"

"This baby, Charlotte, is a part of you. Anything that's a part of you can't possibly be wrong. It just means that he or she will have another person who will love them more than they can ever imagine."

I pull him into me, hugging him tightly, clutching onto him for dear life. He's willing to be with me no matter what. This man loves me for everything I am, for every mistake I have ever made. I give myself a few seconds to take it all in— the enormity of love and selflessness enveloping me, and I want to return just that, give him hope, happiness, and the love he deserves.

Lex Edwards deserves the world, and I must give him that and everything beyond.

No more lies.

No more hiding the pain.

The truth needs to be told.

"Lex... this is your baby."

With his hands dropping to his sides, he steps back with an incredulous stare. In silence, he searches my face until his eyes become glassy, and a small smile plays on his lips.

"M-My baby?" he stammers.

"I doubted myself when I knew the truth. I lied, Lex. There's so much behind why I felt like I needed to lie, and I'm so sorry I hurt you, that I caused you so much pain, and I want my chance to tell you everything, Lex. Everything I've been holding back since the day it all fell apart eight years ago, but for now, for right now, I need to kiss you. I just... I just need you so much in my life... I need you, Lex. *Forever.*"

Without any hesitation, my body is flush with his, our lips only inches apart. His warm breath lingers in the air between us. I close my eyes, waiting in anticipation to feel his lips against mine, but it's his finger grazing my aching lips, tracing my bottom lip with a perpetuating touch.

My chest is rising and falling at a fast pace, my entire body shivering at the simple touch of his finger against my lips. His mouth lingers on my bottom lip, and what only is seconds but passes like hours, the anticipation mounts until he gently sucks on my lip.

Savoring this moment, everything which weighs heavily on my shoulders slowly begins to lift as his kiss spreads throughout me, shining a light on every part of me which has been encased in darkness.

He is mine, and I am his.

And together, we have started something beautiful growing inside of me.

"My baby?" he asks again.

"Yes, Lex... this baby is ours."

This time, with an elated emotion driving him, he kisses me deeper, lifting me slightly as I let out a small squeal. An eruption of clapping and whistling sounds around us. We pause, pulling apart and turn to look around us. The whole room is giving us a standing ovation, and as my face begins to blush from his family and the many strangers watching on, I turn to look at Lex. His face is beaming with pride, eyes sparkling underneath the dance-floor light. I draw him closer to me, his nose touching mine before he spins me around like a lovesick fool.

We dance, never letting go of each other. There's no other place I want to be besides right here. That is until Emily cuts in asking for a quick dance with her son. Slightly relieved because I have to pee, it serves me right for drinking four mocktails during dinner.

I quickly duck off to the bathroom which proves a little difficult in the dress, but I make it with moments to spare. As I stand there checking my makeup, Erin, one of the bridesmaids, walks in, and I can't help but smirk, silly bitch for trying to get her claws into Lex earlier during the day.

"So, you and Lex, huh?"

"Yes, Lex and me."

"You never mentioned it when I spoke about him earlier. I thought he was screwing that blonde chick... Victoria... something or other."

"Oh my God, you're joking? I didn't know that. Maybe I should break up with him?" I answer, sarcastically.

"Maybe you should... I know a lot of ladies who'd be interested in him."

"Clearly, sarcasm wasn't your major, but you should try picking up a dictionary some time. It might help you understand when it's being used."

I fix a strand of my hair and get the hell out of the bathroom, high-fiving myself for my great comeback.

The rest of the night goes off without a hitch. Several

times I was pulled into conversation with people when I just wanted to be with Lex. I dragged him everywhere with me and thank God he didn't want to leave my side, though he proved distracting when he'd whisper things in my ear.

"Can we go now?" he begged, tugging on my earlobe with his teeth.

"This is your sister's wedding. Your *only* sister. Now suck it up like the hot piece of ass... sorry, *gentleman* that you are."

"Suck what up?" His hands move slowly past my ribcage, brushing my breast slightly.

"You're evil, you know that, right?"

"Oh, Mrs. Edwards... what will I do with you?" he teases with a devilish grin.

Mrs. Edwards. Mrs. Edwards—the name is like music to my ears.

"Did you want the X-rated answer or G-rated?"

He leans in, resting his hand on my shoulder. His breath, warm and soft, lingers against my skin "X... always X."

Just as I'm about to whisper a string of dirty things I want to do with him, Emily and Andrew are standing beside us, interrupting the soon-to-be pornographic banter. Dr. Edwards clears his throat as Lex turns around abruptly.

"Oh, Charlie... I'm so sorry about everything." Emily sniffles as the tears escape her perfectly made face. Dr. Edwards hands her another tissue, somewhat unimpressed with her emotional outbursts throughout the night. I let go of Lex, throwing my hands around Emily to embrace her. This isn't just about us. There are other people entwined in our past, ones I thought wouldn't be so happy with our reunion.

"I'm sorry as well for disrespecting you. You've only ever treated me like your daughter."

We pull apart as she moves a lock of hair away from my face with a gentle smile. "You were in love, and nothing should ever stand in the way of that."

"Maybe you should tell her the news, you know, cheer the old lady up," Lex says with an amusing grin.

"News?" Emily's eyes dart back and forth between Lex and me. "And for the record, I'm not *that* old, Alexander."

"We kinda got married... well, eloped a month ago."

Emily draws her hand to her chest, shocked.

Dr. Edwards seems rather complacent.

"Well, I guess congratulations are in order," she chokes, again almost in tears.

"That's not all... you're going to be a grandmother."

Her eyes become soft, filling with an inner glow while pulling both of us into an embrace.

"I'm really going to be a grandmother?"

"Yes, Mom... a little baby to spoil."

I let go of her as she strokes my cheek. She looks at Lex, cupping his face even though he towers over her.

"My baby boy is going to be a daddy." She starts crying again.

Dr. Edwards continues to stand here watching without saying a word. Of course, he knows of the baby, helping me get the DNA results and proving Lex is the father. It had taken a lot of strength to ask him, pushing aside the shame of being with two men. But nevertheless, in the end, it worked out, and I don't regret reaching out to him.

Emily let go of Lex and performed her motherly duty, fixing his suit which crumpled slightly in their embrace.

"Son... I'm sorry," Dr. Edwards utters, bowing his head.

"Sorry for what, Dad?"

"For not seeing how you felt about each other. For forcing you both apart." His tone is soft and apologetic. Never have I seen him this vulnerable.

Emily places her arm around him, aware this is him letting go of his guilt. Sometimes these moments present themselves, and there's this uncertainty of how one should behave. It's awkward but letting go of this burden, these dark secrets, to these people, it is somewhat therapeutic.

"Dad..." Lex says, placing his hand on his shoulder. "I think I can safely say for both of us that we needed to do a lot of growing up. We can't sit here and regret our past actions anymore. We have a baby to bring into this world, and it needs someone to call 'Grandpa' who has a gray hair here or there."

In a sudden motion, Dr. Edwards pulls Lex into a tight hug. Lex lifts an eyebrow as his mouth slackens, and I gather his dad rarely shows affection toward him. Emily, of course, begins to cry. That was the onset to my own display of emotions—d*amn pregnancy hormones.*

"Wait... I don't have any gray hairs?" Dr. Edwards chuckles, pulling away slightly.

Lex laughs. "Sure, Dad."

The MC announces it's time for the bouquet to be thrown. The single ladies wait in a bunch on the dance floor. A few are pushing each other for front position, causing me to break out into a fit of hysterics as Eric and Erin begin arguing. Eric isn't shy to throw himself amongst a bunch of hungry women for the sake of the bouquet.

After Eric catches wind of Erin wanting Lex, he has a vendetta against her. He's been calling her a hick-town hoe all night and giving her dirty stares from across the dance floor.

Adriana stands at the front and, after two fake

attempts, throws the bouquet. It lands perfectly in the arms of Kate. With a look of shock, I walk over to her while laughing.

"I'm glad it was you."

"Oh, dear Lord, marriage? Please, I'm still trying to work my way up to platinum hoochie, and besides, I don't even have anyone on the radar."

"Well, now that Charlie's off the table, you are my back-up," Eric reminds her. "Remember, you said if we aren't married by forty, we'll marry each other and have blissful sex with other people, but I expect you to cook for me every night, and... what was I supposed to do again?"

"Buy a toolbox and learn how to fix stuff around the apartment," Kate tells him.

Eric cringes. "Oh, that's right, but can I get a blinged-out tool belt like the one I sent to you from the Tools R Us catalog?"

"Eric, that catalog was full of dildos and God knows what the other shit was called."

"Oh, did you buy the one with the gold sparkles?"

"Yes... and the pink one, too. Well, it was a two-for-one sale." Kate laughs.

"Oh, I've missed you guys!" I pull them both into an embrace, happy that even though my life will soon be over-whelmed with a baby, Eric and Kate have found one another.

"Stupid hick-town whore stood on my Gucci loafers," Eric complains, pulling away.

"I thought she was a hoe?"

"She upgraded to whore when I caught her mauling that redhead dude in the corner."

"Isn't that her cousin?" I ask.

Eric and Kate laugh in unison. "*Ohhh, naaassty...*"

"Well, stupid hick-town whore had her eyes on my husband."

"*Husband?*" Eric gasps, his eyes widening. "Charlie, are you telling porksies?"

"Eric, it's porkies," Kate corrects him.

"No, I'm not telling porkies which, by the way, have you suddenly turned into a British gay man? We got married," I tell him.

"*Shut the front door...* but not the back. Back Door Betty is back in style. Wait, my God, are you kidding me? When? How?" Eric spurts a million questions before turning to Kate. "And why didn't you tell me if you knew?"

"Because it's not my business to tell. I'm no big-mouth Betty."

"Guys, seriously, who cares?" I say, trying to ease the conversation away from Kate not divulging any information to Eric. "Point is... hick-town hoe needs to hoe on out and stop eyeing my husband."

I feel his arms wrap around my waist, the graze of his lips against my neck. "Who had their eyes on your man?"

Kate and Eric stare at us with stupid shit-eating grins on their faces. They hold onto each other just watching both of us. It's borderline creepy.

"Erin, the wedding whore," I tell him, not ashamed by my colorful choice of words. "Also known as Elijah's cousin."

"Oh, her... yeah, I've met her."

"When you say met, do you mean fucked?"

"Charlie!" Eric covers his mouth in shock before turning to face Lex with a serious expression. "Well, did you?"

"I'm not even going to dignify that with a response."

I squeeze him tight, very happy with his answer.

Eric is quick to pipe up. "I bet her ferret is like a wizard's sleeve. I'm sure I heard it whistle when she walked."

We all break into laughter, even Lex who's no longer immune to Eric's verbal diarrhea.

It's close to midnight when the music finally stops, and Adriana and Elijah prepare to say their goodbyes. I pull Lex aside. It's now or never.

"Lex... I need to do this now."

"Do what?" he asks, concerned.

"I need to tell you... show you... I need to finally let this go."

He doesn't ask another question, nodding his head before Adriana and Elijah make their rounds and say good-bye. After lots of hugs, a few tears, and well wishes, we both slip out of the hall and hop into my car Rocky had driven to the reception hall.

It's late, but I need to set this free. I want to wake up tomorrow and start a fresh new life with him. I tell him I will drive even though he argues with me being pregnant and tired, but I know where I'm going. I can never forget.

Twenty minutes later, we stand at the gates. Lex looks at me confused, but he doesn't ask questions.

I walk toward the small gap in the fence and move the fence slightly so we can squeeze through. Most people would be terrified being here, but it's one of the only places where I feel at peace, the solitude that I constantly crave. I haven't been back here since last year, the guilt sweeping in as the realization becomes apparent.

Somehow, I had let time pass by, but perhaps, in hindsight, it was a good thing. I needed to heal and also process Lex coming back into my life.

Outside, in the freezing air, it's pitch black with only

the slight hint of the moon. I follow the path—every step, every turn is memorized. In the corner near the sleepy willow tree, I continue walking until I see it just before me.

It sits there, the stone looking slightly worn. I place my hand on it and kneel on the ground, wiping away the snow covering the name.

ALTHEA OLIVIA MASON
IN LOVING MEMORY

"Lex, I want you to meet my grandmother because without her, life wouldn't have gone on. She held my hand through my darkest times even when her own demons were battling against her. In the end, I lost her, but I need to tell you now why I was so afraid to fall in love with you again. Why, from the moment I saw you in the restaurant, I tried to deny any feelings I still had for you. Why I pushed you away, why I lied to you that day in the hospital."

"It all started during the summer break, exactly sixty days since the last time I had seen you..."

NINETEEN

LEX

Since the moment I first ran into Charlotte at the restaurant, I knew there was more to me leaving than what she was letting on. I never thought I would be standing in the middle of a cemetery in the dead of night.

Unsettled by the surroundings, I remain silent, careful with my footsteps, allowing her to release the burden weighing her poor shoulders down.

I follow her lead to a section of tombstones sitting underneath a large willow tree. She stops and stares quietly before kneeling on the cold ground. Gently, she raises her hand and wipes her palm across the stone, its words now visible as I read them with my own eyes.

It's her grandmother's gravesite.

Charlotte shows no sign of being scared. It almost looks like she's at peace sitting on the cold, dirty ground, not at all affected by her eerie surroundings. As she begins to speak, I kneel beside her and listen to her words, the words I know will finally explain the missing piece of the puzzle.

"Lex, it all started the summer break when I moved to

Connecticut, exactly sixty days since the last time I saw you..."

I sat at the dining table, staring at the envelope in front of me. It was thick with the Yale logo stamped on the top left corner.

When I had arrived here two weeks ago, I immediately applied to some community colleges hoping my late admission would be accepted. With the help of Gran, and the fact she was a Yale alumnus and still friends with some of the head faculty, I knew this thick envelope only represented positive things ahead, and her assistance had paid off.

I looked up at the clock, it was a quarter past three. Gran said she wouldn't be home until three-thirty, so I waited, unable to do this alone.

At exactly three-thirty, she strolled through the kitchen carrying a basket of apples. She was making her famous homemade apple pie, my favorite. She saw me anxiously sitting at the table. Placing her basket down, she put the kettle on the stove. Apparently, tea solved the world's problems. With a steaming cup of tea placed in front of me and one for her, she finally sat at the table.

"Sweetie, take a sip, please. We knew this day would come. What lies inside this envelope does not define who you are."

I took her words in—she was right. No matter what happened, I would do what I wanted to do, and that is to study to be a lawyer. I took a sip of my tea and opened the envelope reading the words out loud, 'Congratulations, Miss Mason.'

Jumping off my seat, I kissed the letter thanking my lucky stars I had been accepted into Yale. Never in my

*wildest dreams had I ever thought this would happen, and
even though I knew Gran had done or said something to the
gods of Yale, I welcomed this acceptance exactly as I would
have if I had been accepted in the first round.*

"Honey, you did it. What a great achievement."

"I can't believe I got into Yale. This is... just wow!"

*"This is your path. Trust it in all its glory. Big things are
going to happen from this, you mark my word."*

*She was right, as always, and that night I lay in bed
unable to contain the excitement over where my life was
choosing to turn.*

Yale, I still couldn't believe it.

*It was one in the morning, and sleep evaded me. I was
feeling slightly ill, but I kept passing it off as excitement. It
was a new chapter of my life, and no matter what, I had to
move on. The possibilities were endless, and for a brief
moment, I wondered what he was doing. Was he with her?
What did it matter anymore? I was going to Yale. Fist-
pumping the air, I couldn't believe my lucky stars. I turned
over, falling asleep, dreaming of this new life I was about to
embark upon.*

*The next morning, I sat there quietly staring at the bowl
of cereal which looked like a pile of vomit.*

*"Honey, is everything okay? You look awfully pale
today."*

*"Yeah, um, sure... just didn't get much sleep... you know,
too excited."*

*"Well, eat up, and then let's take you to Dr. Flannigan,
just to make sure everything's okay?"* Worried, she pushed a
strand of hair away from my face.

*"Gran, I'm fine... now. Just the cereal looks... can you
please move it away?"*

It was too late, I projectile vomited into the kitchen sink, stupid nerves. Now she would definitely send me to the doctor. What was it with old people and their obsession with visiting the doctor for the tiniest little thing? I knew it was just nerves, that's all.

"Oh, honey, don't think you're getting out of it now."

An hour later, we sat in the waiting room. Dr. Flannigan, who turned out to be a she, called my name. Gran offered to wait in the waiting room, so I walked in unsure of what exactly I was being tested for.

"Miss Mason."

"Charlie, please."

"Charlie. Your grandmother tells me you haven't been sleeping well, and you've been vomiting."

"Well, the sleeping thing was due to other circumstances, and the vomiting only happened once."

"Charlie, have you been having unprotected sex?"

"Um, no... I haven't even been having sex."

"When was the last time you had intercourse?"

Oh shit, were we really going there?

I didn't want to drudge up the memory. I closed my eyes for a brief moment, trying to block out the memory of our last time on the cliff top.

"I don't know... like two months ago."

"Did you use protection?"

"Uh yeah, I was on the pill back then."

"Back then?"

"Yes, I stopped sometime after that."

I didn't like where this was going. My heart was beating fast, and I wanted nothing more than to stop speaking. I placed my clammy hands on my thighs, rubbing the palms of my hands along my jeans with a slight tremble.

Where was she going with this?

"Charlie, would you mind urinating into the cup?"

Dr. Flannigan placed a cup in front of me. I grabbed hold of it, barely making my way to the restroom just outside her office. The anxiety had consumed me as I struggled to pee. This cannot be happening. Sitting on the toilet, I knew I only had moments before she would check up on me.

I wracked my brain. I was always on the pill back then. No, we didn't use condoms, but I was on the pill. Teen pregnancy was the hottest topic in high school. I wasn't stupid. I was always mindful of taking the fucking pill every night before bed, except that one night—the night that I found out about the baby.

Back inside her office, I handed the specimen to her as she dipped a thin cardboard strip into it. I couldn't look, instead staring at a herpes chart that hung on the wall.

Oh my God, STDs?

I was so fucking stupid.

No, Charlie, don't do this to yourself.

He said he wasn't sleeping with her, and you believed him.

God knows how many other people he had slept with. I realized in that moment it was almost like I knew nothing about him. I was so naïve. I would never ever make this mistake again. Just breathe, everything was going to be okay. It had to be okay.

It felt like hours later when she pulled the stick out, her face showing no emotion. She drew her chair back to her table and reached out to a shelf beside her desk and removed some pamphlets, laying them before me.

"Lex, I took a test and it was positive... I was pregnant," she cries softly.

I sit still, shell-shocked at the revelation. Not only had I left her without saying goodbye, I left her pregnant with my child. Everything made sense now, why she was holding back, why she couldn't forgive me, recalling the clues she gave me about leaving *us*. But the baby, *what happened to our baby?* I close my eyes knowing the next part to this story is probably something I don't want to hear, something that will bring my mistakes to the surface to be laid out in front of me, a big red marker pointing out where I failed and how I failed Charlie and our baby.

"I didn't even have a choice on whether or not I wanted it, the bloodwork came back, and I was too far along. It was too late, I had no choice but to keep it, and all I could think about was the fact that I would have to look at this child every day and be reminded of you—that there was no escaping you.

"I thought about finding you, but I was still heartbroken. I had no idea Samantha's baby wasn't yours, so in my eyes, you were still the man who betrayed and left me standing alone. The one thing that I did know was that this baby didn't deserve to be second best. It didn't need to compete with the other child you were raising. I was broken, Lex, so broken and unable to pull myself out of this depression that was spiraling out of control."

As she spoke, the pain inside me grew larger, spreading throughout like the deadliest of diseases. But even in my own pain, Charlotte's is so much worse.

Taking a deep breath, she closes her eyes before opening her mouth to continue, "My grandmother was the only one who knew. We hid this from my dad. I was in a dark place, a very dark place. I struggled to see any light in this situation. What did I know about raising a baby at eighteen? This wasn't the life I wanted... at least not without you. I cried myself to sleep every night. I barely ate... I barely moved. My grandmother would rock me to sleep on our porch swing. But I was sad... so unbelievably sad that I had failed to see it wasn't only me who had demons. She was sick... very sick."

She pauses to retrieve something from her purse. It's a photograph and looks familiar. Moments later, I realize it is the same as the one hanging on her wall. But this time she didn't have the blanket covering her stomach, the bulge standing out against her skinny frame. I stare at it, shocked, unable to swallow, the pain intensifying as I study the picture in the dark of the night as we sit here.

My poor Charlotte.

How could I have done this?

But our baby, *what happened to the baby?*

I prepare myself for what I think she did, the only thing that could have possibly happened. She must have had the baby adopted. Closing my eyes to think, somewhere out there I have an eight-year-old kid. My silence masks the turmoil overcoming me. How the fuck could I have done this to her? Out of all the people in my life, I love her more than life itself. Yet, I pushed her into this nightmare, leaving her scarred forever.

"I remembered the day it all finally came crashing down, the darkest day of my life, and the day I screamed your name hoping that somewhere you would hear me and pull me out into the light."

I twisted my body, trying to get comfortable. It was no use. I couldn't lie on my stomach, so I moved to lie on my back. Great, now I had to pee again. I got up and peed for like the hundredth time that morning, then decided it was pointless and walked outside to sit on the porch swing.

It was early morning, and the sun was shining brightly on the porch, the sounds of birds and crickets chirping in the distance. I looked up to the sky, perfectly blue, except for these dark gray clouds coming in from the east. I knew they predicted heavy rain and possible thunderstorms later in the day. I wasn't surprised Gran wasn't home as she normally conducted all her errands before seven. If only I could be so productive.

My stomach grumbled slightly, oh food... again. I had no appetite despite what my body told me. I knew at my last appointment that Dr. Flannigan wasn't pleased with my weigh-in. I had lost weight. I sat there remembering the lecture she gave me.

"Charlie. You've lost quite a lot of weight. Is the morning sickness still occurring?" Dr. Flannigan asked.

"Uh... no"

"So, have you been increasing your food intake?"

"Uh... just eating the same."

"So, what did you eat today for breakfast?"

"Um... I had a glass of water," I lied. I hadn't had anything.

"Charlie, we've discussed this. It's not healthy. There are so many risks. I realize this isn't an ideal situation for you, but this baby needs nutrients which it will get if you eat a well-maintained and balanced diet."

She handed me another What to Eat When You're Expecting *pamphlet which was lucky because I threw the other one out.*

"I'd like to see you in two weeks. I expect to see these scales increase in number. Do you understand?"

"Yes, Dr. Flannigan."

. . .

Her words played heavily on my mind. I angrily got up and walked into the kitchen. Grabbing a bowl of granola, I walked back to the porch swing.

"There, you happy?" I asked the baby.

My body jerked forward as this unfamiliar feeling jabbed my stomach. I placed my hand quickly on the spot it came from, rubbing it slightly until it happened again.

It was the baby.

Unwillingly, I smiled, my first smile since all this unfolded over two months ago. My baby kicked. I placed my hand back on my stomach hoping it would happen again, but nothing. Wow, I never thought the feeling of a baby moving inside you could bring so much joy. I raced inside and grabbed more food, stuffing my face, hoping it would happen again. I waited on the porch for Gran to come home, unable to contain my excitement.

I sat there for two hours wondering where she was. It was unusual for her. It wasn't long after that a very sullen Annie, our next-door neighbor, walked up the front path. I only had to look at her face to know something was very wrong.

"Annie... is everything okay?" I asked worriedly.

She looked drained, her normally cornflower blue eyes looked gray. Her face was pale, streaks of tears staining her face. "Charlie, your grandmother. She's in... she's in the hospital. I'm so sorry, Charlie."

"I didn't know she was sick, I had absolutely no idea." Charlotte's shoulders fall as she places her palm on the tombstone again. "She had a brain tumor and had found out it was malignant. It was too late for any treatment, and she wanted to die in peace. Annie told me she didn't want to burden me as I had my own worries and adding this on top would only cause me undue stress. I still remember holding her hand—it was cold, so very cold. She was gone, but I held onto her tight, praying for some miracle. Praying that this was a nightmare I so desperately needed to wake up from."

Her skin was cold, but I didn't care. I placed the palm of her hand against my cheek. Her face looked peaceful. Her closed eyes gave me the false hope she was just sleeping like she had been doing a lot of recently. I closed my eyes, savoring the smell of her skin, the lavender scent she always wore, the one that no matter where I was reminded me of her.

This woman had always been this monumental figure in my life, but it wasn't until the end, until the very end that she became my life. She had become my best friend. This woman was more of a mother to me than my own. She nurtured and loved me unconditionally despite the mistakes I had made.

Why did this have to happen?

Why couldn't I see the signs she was ill?

The constant tears streamed down my face, the salty liquid falling upon my lips, clouding my vision and falling onto her hands. I kissed them, hoping my touch would bring her back to me. Maybe she needed a reason to live. Yes, that's it, your great-grandchild.

I climbed into the bed, lying beside her like I had done every so often. Ignoring now how she felt even colder, that her body didn't radiate that warmth, and that her skin felt clammy. I was hopelessly wishing that I could feel the touch of her hand stroking my hair, the hum of her voice filling the room.

"I felt it today, Gran..." I closed my eyes. I tried imag-

ining her smile as I told her my story, the way her eyes lit up her whole face, the big brown pools of chocolate that replicated mine. "The baby... it kicked. It was unbelievable, my baby kicked." I sobbed loudly, unable to compress the whimpering sounds that left my mouth. She was gone, really gone. Life couldn't go on, I needed her.

I called her name, my body shaking, clutching onto her tightly as I shook her body. Screaming, I demanded she come back, that life wasn't fair. She prayed to God every day—I had witnessed it with my own eyes. How could she be pulled away from this earth, this angel that was a blessing? How could God fail us all? How could he fail me?

Warm arms wrapped around me, whispering words in my ear. I turned around, letting go of her, faced with the hospital staff. I knew what they were doing, so I clutched onto Annie, burying my head into her chest, sobbing so loud that the echoing throughout the room masked the sound of my beautiful grandmother being taken away.

"Charlotte... I'm so sorry," I whisper.

In my eyes, Charlotte has always been a strong individual. For most people, not having a mother present during their late teens would prove to be difficult. Though, not Charlotte. It didn't seem to deter her from living life. She loved her dad so much, and not once did I hear her whine about the fact that her mother was living it up in Cuba with some guy half her age. I realize as she tells the story, Charlotte is very capable of hiding her emotions. Even I couldn't see that she needed a mother, someone who could guide her during this difficult stage of life, someone to smother her emotionally and physically in unconditional love, and she finally got to experience it, only now a little too late.

"They say for every death there's a grieving process, but when you are put in that position, it's the loneliest experience. It doesn't matter how many people are around you, suffering like you are, you only feel your own pain. And the grief, it comes in waves, shattering you, breaking every part of you which is barely holding on.

"I don't know how long I sat there, staring at the empty bed which was her final resting place, replaying in my mind the events... how I could have stopped this. Of course, I couldn't, but I let my imagination run away, retracing my steps," she continues.

Something was wrong, very wrong. The blood was a sure sign. Panicking, I walked to the nurses' station, the look of horror on their faces as they saw that I was covered in blood. They immediately began paging the doctors, and I was rushed to maternity when the nightmare officially unfolded.

Suddenly, everything went completely silent, like in slow motion, the panicked faces around me scurrying around the room, preparing themselves with gowns, gloves, and masks. Instruments were being wheeled into the room, the doctors discussing amongst themselves as the nurses placed a breathing mask over my face. I could feel my pulse pounding through my body, and an excruciating pain escaped as a gush of warm liquid spread all over my legs. I couldn't comprehend what was happening.

Was this still a nightmare?

Had I fallen asleep?

"Charlotte, listen to me, you need to push," the doctor told me.

I was in a blind panic. I didn't understand what was

happening. Another nurse wheeled what looked like an incubator into the room.

It was for a baby.

"Push what?" I shrieked, sucking the air that the mask provided me.

"The baby. Your water has ruptured, and the baby is coming. Charlotte, there is no time, you need to push... now," his voice raised.

The pressure built up, and unwillingly, I felt the urge to push. I held onto the nurse beside me, following her instructions, taking one last breath before I let out a scream.

"I was diagnosed with an incompetent cervix," she says, barely a whisper.

"When the baby is forced to be delivered if the water ruptures." The medical jargon isn't lost on me, but I know this story can only go one way, and I brace myself for the worst.

She nods silently.

"The bleeding... the water... he was breeched." She shuffles a little to the left where I hadn't noticed the smaller tombstone. Wiping away the snow, she leans in and places her hand on it. In the darkness of the night, it confirms what I had just thought, what I had feared.

"He died when I delivered. There were too many complications. He was too small, too fragile to even fight."

Alexander Mason Edwards
Sleep my baby angel, always and forever in my heart.

"I held him... you know... for a few moments. I saw his tiny face, and I knew he deserved a name, so I named him Alexander, after you. He was small... so very tiny." She's sobbing, her shoulders rising and falling beside me.

"It was all too much for him with everything that happened that day. I blamed myself for losing my grandmother and not taking care of myself. I thought I had killed him because I didn't want him, but I did want him... I was just terrified. The grief was overwhelming, and I called for you, screamed your name, begged you to come and rescue me, but they thought I was crazy. They watched me, even placed me on suicide watch. I wasn't going to kill myself, but I needed something to take away the pain."

The psych ward, Bryce's call. It all makes sense now.

"I couldn't see anything but darkness. There was no point anymore to life, I'd lost everything. But, Lex... I need you to keep an open mind about what I'm about to tell you, please understand that I had no other choice."

My head flinches back slightly, confused by what she is asking. Still reeling from all the information and trying to manage the grief and remorse fighting for my attention, I silently wait for her to reveal whatever it is willing an open mind.

"They wanted to place me in the psych ward. Well, they did for a day, but I begged them to call your dad. I knew if anyone understood the grief I was going through, what led to this breakdown, it would be him."

"My dad knew?" I almost choke, eyes widening as anger begins to seep in.

"He saved me, Lex. He explained my history to the acting doctors and promised to keep me under his care.

When I saw him, he asked me to do something, to promise him something. That if he were going to vouch for me, release me from this place, then in return, I needed to go live my life. Study, go to college, and live a long happy life making everyone who loved me proud. I needed to become Charlotte Mason, and I needed to find who she was and to start a life.

"So, I promised him I would. Three days later, I buried my grandmother and our son. My dad had been traveling and because of bad weather, couldn't make it back in time. It was the second worst day of my life. I promised both of them I would make them proud, that wherever they were, they would always smile down on me. It was the only thing that kept me going. It was the only way I could move on."

"*Charlotte...*" I'm at a loss for words, scared to say the wrong thing.

"That afternoon, instead of attending the gathering afterward, I went straight to the tattoo parlor. I knew what I wanted."

The phoenix.

"The tattoo, the phoenix. It symbolizes rebirth because I had to start a new life, Lex, without you, my grandmother, or the baby. As long as I was alone, I needed a reminder every day that I was still standing here and had a life that needed to be lived. I was given a second chance." She lets out a small smile through her tears. "The needle... to answer the question that you asked me, it felt like nothing, not compared to what I had been through."

"I wish you had told me," I manage to say, guilty for pushing myself back onto her. "I wish I was there with you."

"No one knew except for Annie. Not even Nikki or Eric know the truth. I kept this to myself, but now you know, Lex, why when I saw you, I was afraid. To have been left by you, to go back to that place that I promised your dad I would never go back to. After what happened in The Hamptons, I ran away trying to control the situation myself. There was no way I would listen to you or anyone, for that matter. That night I was at the restaurant with Julian, I knew he wasn't the one I wanted to spend the rest of my life with, and it pained me because I wished I did at the time. It would have made life easier. It was always you, Lex... but then you said it was over, and the pregnancy threw everything off. I lied to you because I thought if I hurt you enough, you would leave me alone. I was so scared... that it was déjà vu... *this baby*... and I knew I couldn't bear to lose it, so I did what I knew I had to do. I reached out to Dr. Edwards again. He was the only one who knew, and once again, he taught me that no matter what happens, I'm able to control my destiny. I need to fight hard for what I want. I want this baby, our baby, and I want you, Lex."

As I sit there staring at this tiny tombstone, the little inscription confirming my son lay resting there asleep, I reach out to touch it, my hands shaking as I run my fingers across the words. I close my eyes, ensuring I'm memorizing every letter, the way it feels beneath my fingertips, wanting some desperate connection with this child who was ours.

I repeat my actions, wanting something, a sign, and suddenly, in the cold, harsh night in the middle of this cemetery, a gush of warmth runs through me. I focus on it. It's undeniable the way it makes my goosebumps disappear, the way I suddenly feel at peace like a hand resting on mine. My eyes spring open only to see Charlotte has hers on the ground, and nothing is surrounding my hand. There is no other way to explain it, and I don't realize a tear has escaped until the salty liquid falls upon my lips. I've never cried. I don't ever remember crying since I was a kid, but this emotion is overwhelming in ways I can never imagine possible.

Charlotte shuffles closer to me, placing a kiss on the corner of my mouth to wash away the lonesome tear.

"You felt it, too?"

I nod, afraid yet at peace with whatever it was that happened.

"It's him, he's done this before, you know, told me he's okay. He is being taken care of. This is the only reason I was able to live my life. To place trust in God that this little boy lives on, and that although he is not here with us, he's still loved and is in a happy place."

I pull her into my arms, holding her close to my chest as we continue to sit on the cold ground. My hands move their way to her stomach where I caress our baby... *our second baby.* And while it was only moments ago I was grieving for this child I had no idea existed, I hold onto Charlotte tight, almost as if by holding her, I'm protecting this unborn child, praying it will be given the chance its older brother didn't have.

"Lex... *I'm scared...*" she cries softly.

I move her hair aside, planting a soft kiss on her neck.

"Don't be afraid. I'm sorry, Charlotte, more than you can imagine, for everything you went through alone. I can't even begin to put myself in your shoes, but I understand now. These scars that were all over your heart, your soul, I promise you that I will love you and that no measure of time will change that. I promise to spend the rest of my life mending these scars until they are healed, and no matter what happens... whatever life will throw at us, we will get through this together. Just you and me forever."

She nestles into my neck, and in this darkness, I have never felt so secure. I have never wanted anything more in my life. We have created this family. This is us, this is our family, all four of us united.

Relaxing my shoulders, I close my eyes with a calm smile. I find the strength within me, and with this strength, I promise to protect my family for as long as I shall live. The world can fall apart around us, but as long as I have Charlotte, nothing else matters.

The world doesn't matter.

We will forever be one from this day forward.

"Let me get you home," I whisper, worried she'll catch a cold.

"I am home, Lex... *with you*... wherever you are. You are home."

She turns to face me, planting a soft kiss on my lips like the world has been lifted from her shoulders.

"Well, then, how about I take you to a place that has four walls, a roof, hot shower, warm bed, and something nice to eat?"

"As long as you are there." She smiles, her eyes staring at me lovingly. "Lead the way."

I pull her up as we dust the dirt and snow off our clothes. Saying goodbye one more time, we turn our backs, holding hands as we walk down the path to the entrance and get in the car.

We drive back to the inn where many of the guests are staying. Walking Charlotte to her door, she begs me not to leave. I kiss her lips promising I will be back in five minutes after I gather my stuff from my room. I leave her behind and enter my room, surprised to find my suitcase and room completely packed with a note on top.

All your things are packed. I didn't think you would end up alone tonight. Thank you for everything. Now you go and live your happily ever after.

Love, your sister,

Adriana

I smile at the sentiment. Despite her being annoying, I really couldn't have asked for a better sister—the only person, no matter what, who knows me better than I sometimes know myself.

Pulling my suitcase, I walk back to Charlotte's room. I enter softly to hear the sound of water falling. I don't want to interrupt her, I know it has been a long day, but I do want to hold her.

Stripping off my clothes, I step inside the bathroom filled with steam. I open the glass door to find her standing, her eyes closed under the water. My eyes glide down her body, admiring each curve, imagining my hand touching every inch. Careful not to startle her, I walk in, wrapping my arms around her. She immediately sinks into me, the two of us standing together in silence. Our naked bodies mold into one, and we are perfect.

Charlotte is perfect.

With her head resting against my chest, I rub her back gently.

"I love you..." she murmurs.

"I love you, too."

Lifting her head, our eyes meet, drawing us closer to each other. Her simple stare anchors my soul, and only Charlotte, my beautiful wife, can command my heart to the beating of her own. I never want our story to end, this here

—I want to experience our unique love for the rest of my life. Without it, I serve no purpose. I will wander this earth alone, and I've been there, done that.

Nothing, and I mean nothing, will *ever* tear us apart again.

Caressing my cheek, her breasts fall against my chest making it impossible to control the urges stirring within me. With a weightless gaze, her lopsided grin catches my attention.

"What's the big grin for?"

"I hope our baby has your eyes. If it's a girl, every boy will want her, and if it is a boy, every girl will want him. I don't think you realize how powerful they are. How enchanting... like they cast a spell over you."

"Well, now you've just scared me because I don't want our daughter trying to be picked up by every player, and I don't want our son having every hoochie-mama hanging off him."

"Oh, so it's all right for you but not for him?"

"Are you calling yourself a hoochie-mama?" I tease.

"Are you calling yourself a player?"

"Checkmate, Mrs. Edwards." I let out a laugh because even in the darkest times, there is always that one person who will make you see the light, make you laugh again when you think it's impossible.

I take her mouth, trying my best to ignore the fact that we are standing here naked and wet. *That Charlotte is naked and wet.* I mean seriously, I'm a guy for Christ's sake, but I somewhat feel guilty for poking her with my cock this entire time.

"We need to get out... you need to eat."

"So do you," she teases.

"Oh, trust me, I know. I have a big appetite in case you

haven't noticed, but for now, I seriously need you to eat. It's not just about you anymore," I tell her in a serious tone.

"Yes, I did notice... it almost drilled a hole in me," she giggles, letting out a small sigh afterward. "And yes, I'm famished."

We climb out of the shower together, drying ourselves off. Charlotte places her nightie on as I find my boxers. Sitting on the bed, we call room service and order some much-needed food. With my arms wrapped around her while we wait, I kiss the crook of her neck, desperate to taste her skin.

"I can't believe Adriana and Elijah got married. Today has been so..." she trails off, moaning softly. "You're distracting me."

"Uh-huh," I breathe into her skin. "We have time to kill."

"Hey, I'm quick but not *that* quick."

There's a knock on the door. With a satisfied grin, Charlotte hops off the bed and places on her robe, leaving me on the bed frustrated. Covering my face, I let out a groan.

A young guy wheels in the food, removing the lids while eyeing Charlotte. I hop off the bed, making a slight growl, taking the bill from him. Not even checking the charges, I sign it and demand he leave.

"Really, Lex?" Charlotte stands at the side of the bed, her hands on her hips. "The guy was like, what, twenty-one at best."

"I don't know what you're talking about," I lie, motioning for her to sit and eat.

She shakes her head with a loose jaw. "Some things never change with you..."

I ignore her comment, reminding her again to eat. The

food at the wedding was okay, but there is nothing like a burger and fries after midnight.

"Oh, wow, that tasted so good," she exclaims, finishing her burger in a heartbeat.

"Have you had much morning sickness?"

"Not really. Not as much as the first time around," she mentions quietly.

"How far along are you?"

"About seven weeks now, I think."

We finish eating and brush our teeth before climbing back into bed. It is our second official night together after the night in The Hamptons which was a complete bust. Turning the lamp off beside her, she snuggles into me, only the pale moonlight filters throughout the room.

"What happens when we get back to the city?" she murmurs in my embrace.

"What do you mean?"

"With us?"

"I don't know, Charlotte. Tell me what you want."

"We're married, and I want us to live together."

"Deal."

"In my apartment?"

"No deal," I state, then quick to explain, "Well, temporarily, but we need something bigger."

"But you live in London."

"Charlotte, look at me," I beg. She turns around to face me, her fresh minty breath cooling the air between us. "I can do whatever I want... I own that company. If I need to be based in New York, then I will be in New York. You and I... this is it, baby. No turning back."

"No turning back... and Lex?" she calls my name again, softly. "You're still poking me."

"Then, we need to find a way to stop that from happening."

I lower my head to meet hers and kiss her lips, her tongue rolling against mine, soft, but the intensity is there. There is no denying I need her, and I try so much to give her the rest she needs, but it's fucking impossible.

My mind warns me to stop and let her sleep, but I need her so much. I want her to see how much I love her, how much I never stopped loving her.

Our kisses become feverish as she moans into my mouth, her body eager for more. I move away toward her neck, blowing kisses on her warm skin, her head falling deeper into the pillows as she struggles to compose herself.

Making my way down slowly kissing every spot on her chest, she begs me to go lower, and I do, taking my time. I want to savor this moment. I've been waiting to be inside her for so long and finally make sweet love to her without our usual restraints.

As I tease her nipples with my tongue, she squirms underneath my body, biting into my shoulder. I'm careful not to lie directly on top of her, reminding myself there is someone else to think about. The thought alone distracts me momentarily, but as if she knows, she pulls my head up to hers as our eyes meet once again.

I know exactly what she wants in this moment.

Never breaking her gaze, I gently slide my cock inside her, her eyes screaming out to me with pleasure. The way I slide in slowly, my cock feels every curve, guiding its way through and finding the place it calls home, then I remain perfectly still, allowing her to catch her breath.

"Lex," she whispers, out of breath still. *"Necesito que te pierdes en mí, tengo que sentir lo mucho que me quieres. Muéstrame lo mucho que me quieres, sólo a mí.* I need you to lose yourself in me, I need to feel how much you love me. Show me how much you love me, only me." Her voice is barely a whisper, but the way she speaks to me, the way the Spanish rolls off her tongue, it's our intimate way of communicating, just like old times, and she has read my mind.

So, for tonight, we do what both of us crave, what both of us need from each other. We make love until the sun rises in the morning, and it's in the light of the new day when we fall asleep in each other's arms, ready for new beginnings.

TWENTY

CHARLIE

"Welcome home, roomie!"

Lex scratches his jaw, trying to hide the smile which has been a permanent fixture since last night. After a tiring drive back into the city, we are officially home. And I officially have a live-in husband.

The whole concept of having a husband who actually lives with me is rather exciting, and I can barely contain my enthusiasm. But I also have no idea what I'm doing, never having lived with a man before, except my dad. Wait, let me rephrase that—I have never lived with an unbelievably drop-dead gorgeous man who makes me weak in the knees every single time he looks at me.

"*Roomie*... hmm, did you secretly consume some sugar on the way here? You're extremely hyperactive," he teases, placing our bags beside the couch.

"Nope, just high on love."

"Oh, that's kind of corny." He laughs

"Wow, so it turns out that I'm not one of those I-love-you-and-I'll-post-it-on-Facebook-so-   everyone-can-see-it kinda chicks?"

"You lost me?"

"Oh, I forgot you refuse to join the rest of our generation and get on the social media bandwagon," I mock with a sneer. "There are some people who constantly write on their partner's walls how much they love them. It annoys me so much so that Eric purposely does it to me all the time now."

"Firstly, what the hell is a wall? Secondly, don't think that because we are 'roomies,' I'm opening a Facebook account."

"Will you tweet with me?" I ask, batting my eyelashes.

He pulls me into him, then places his hands under my thighs, lifting me as I wrap my legs around him. Pushing my back against the wall, his lips forcefully finding mine. I still crave him, even more so than last night, wondering how this man can do this to me every time.

"It's funny how you think that you'll have time for all that bullshit," he breathes, tugging at my bottom lip.

His hands wander to the bottom of my sweater, and in a quick move, he yanks it over my head, leaving me in my bra. Like a fire raging within his eyes, they burn as they fixate on my chest, feverishly squeezing my breasts, making my body convulse. I can't possibly come again.

Not after four hours of slow lovemaking last night.

Not after the five, that turned into fifteen-minute quickie this morning.

Not after the blow job on the interstate.

And yet, here we were again, ready to explode like it's the first time we have touched in years.

He lifts my skirt, sliding his hands along my ass cheeks before cupping them firmly. His lips never leave mine, and yet, somehow, I manage to get his jeans undone. *Damn, I'm getting good at this.* I slide my hands inside and free his cock, his whimper brushing past my ear. So hard but smooth, I stroke it slowly, feeling him buckle under my touch. With shallow breaths, I tug on his ear gently with my teeth. "I could get used to it... you inside me at all times."

Lex pauses, catching his breath. His fingers now trace my lips and trail down my body until he finds that spot, the one making me weak in the knees, the one possessing every inch of my body causing it to ache until I can't take it anymore. His hand slides against my clit so effortlessly as the pool of wet drenches his fingers.

"This is how I always want to find you, soaking wet, ready, knowing that you ache just as much as I do. I want you desperate around me, I want you to want me every moment we are together."

The sound of his voice, *his dirty voice,* piling on the pleasure, drives me to the point of no return when everything dirty crosses my mind, and I want to do everything to his body in the roughest way possible.

"This is how I always want to find you," I repeat stroking his cock, its hard form throbbing against my small hands. "Hard, throbbing, knowing that you ache just as much as I do. I want *you* desperate for me, I want you to want me every moment we are together."

His eyes are wild, understanding he needs from me what I need from him. Unable to resist, he slams his cock inside causing me to gasp. He continues to watch me, our eyes on each other. This time we remain silent, but I can see it in his eyes, he's close. His movements speed up until I feel a final thrust, and he grunts my name, his grip leaving red marks on my arms. It's all I need as I follow him down this splendorous path of pleasure.

We hold onto each other, our bodies covered in sweat against the wall. Carefully, he places me down, my legs wobbly and unable to hold me up. I hold onto his forearms, trying to balance myself. His muscles are so defined, much more than I remember from years ago.

Fuck, he is so sexy.

Calm down, Charlie, he's yours, and you can bang that wanger anytime you want.

Oh, for fuck's sake, I knew Eric's catchphrase would catch on, much to my mortification.

He pulls himself out causing me to wince. "Are you sore?"

"My head is from the wall-banging, but I'm assuming you must be referring to my lady parts, and the answer is yes. You are well-endowed, my dear husband, and it's been a while since we had this much sex."

"I'll take that as a compliment," he answers with a cocky grin.

Sure, he will take that as a compliment. He's large, and my vagina is sore. I don't think any man can be offended by a woman telling them they have a big dick.

"How very humble of you, Mr. Edwards."

"We still have tonight and tomorrow and the day after, *Mrs. Edwards.*"

His words once again go straight to that place causing me to contract, and that feeling of cum oozing down my leg becomes hard to ignore. I excuse myself and go to the bathroom to clean myself up.

Wow, how on earth can he come so much... I mean, like, isn't it supposed to get less every time?

"Okay, time for the grand tour," I announce while bouncing back into the living room. "Welcome to the living room. This is how you work the TV."

"Charlotte, I know how to work a TV."

"Okay, but it's a *smart* TV."

"I'm pretty confident I can get my masters in all elec-
tronic-device handling."

"Well, let's move onto the kitchen, then."

"How about you show me *our* bedroom?"

His seductive gaze does not go unnoticed, and I can't
believe my legs quiver as he mentions *our* bedroom.

"Sure... follow me, roomie."

I pull his hand, but instead, he wraps them around my
waist, placing soft kisses on my neck. Distracted, I introduce
the bedroom but know he has other ideas.

"Take all your clothes off," he demands.

Inside our bedroom, I follow his request and strip off all
my clothes. Naked in front of him, I can't help but feel sexy
as his eyes look so desperate, fighting some sort of internal
battle. He continues to gaze at me while tracing his fingertips down my torso, the goosebumps apparent as I close my
eyes, savoring his touch.

"So fucking perfect," he whispers

I open my eyes, desperate to watch him.

"Lie down in the middle of *our* bed and spread your
legs as wide as you can."

I love it when he uses the word 'our.' How can such a
simple word have so much meaning behind it? How can one
word define a whole relationship? I follow his instructions
and lay on the bed, my head against the pillow as I half-sit
up on my elbows and spread my legs wide before him.

He stands at the end of the bed, watching me, watching
between my legs. Like a lion hungry for its prey, he licks his
lips, and I can't stop my hand wandering down to graze my
swollen clit, letting out a small cry as the two come into
contact. Placing a hand on my knee, he pushes my legs
further apart.

"So fucking perfect... always so ready for me."

Lowering himself, he traces his tongue along the inside of my thigh. My body waiting in anticipation, he knows how much I want him just to go straight for the prize, but instead, he continues to tease me, blowing softly between my legs. Tilting my head back, I lift my hips desperate for him to taste me. But no, of course, Lex is all about self-gratification, and in this case, he's happy teasing me while I go insane waiting.

"So eager... what exactly is it that you want?"

With another blow of warm air against my thigh, my entire body shakes, and I'm desperate to have him devour me, now.

"I want your head between my legs. I want you sucking every inch of my pussy. I want to hear you moan knowing you can't get enough. I want you to thrust your fingers inside me, in every hole... really hard. I want to come, and I want you to lick every inch of me clean."

He stands in front of me, his devilish grin taking over. "My dirty girl... your wish is my command."

"So, I must really suck as a tour guide, then?"

"Mmm, let's just say your audience had other things on their mind."

"Lex?"

"Mmm..." he hums.

Okay, so I don't know why I'm going to bring this up, why I decide this is a perfect time to open up a can of worms, open the dark closet, the one you dread because it's full of spiders and other scary creatures. Except mine isn't, it's just full of other men.

"When are we going to talk?"

"About?"

"Everything."

"Be more specific"?

"I don't know. I just feel like we haven't talked about other things, and I'd rather get this out now. I don't want you speculating and conjuring up your own thoughts on certain situations."

He shifts up, looking at me cautiously, but instead, I face the other way and pull him into me with my back against his chest. I can't look him in the eyes, they give away everything.

"About the past... Julian."

"*Charlotte...*" he warns.

"I get it, Lex, you're a guy. You don't need to hear this, and you have some inbuilt capability of being able to box things off, ignore, and move on. But I'm a woman. It's part of my genetic engineering to talk about these things."

He remains silent, so I continue to talk, "I did love him, Lex, but it was a different love. More like comfort love. He was everything on paper a woman would want from a man."

His body clenches, but I pull him in tighter refusing for there to be any distance between us. "Every time I got close to a man, it felt wrong. Every first date, I had a nagging feeling. I knew why, I just never admitted it to myself, but Julian made it easy, maybe too easy, but I didn't want that. When I saw you in the restaurant, it all made sense. I knew at that moment it couldn't be anyone else, but stubborn Charlie wasn't going down without a fight."

Lex restrains his words, his breaths heavy and muscles tense even in my embrace.

"I have never been so jealous in my entire life," he says in a bitter tone. "It drove me to do things so out of character for me. It cost me a lot with my business."

I pull him tighter, regretting the hurt and pain I caused him. "I'm sorry."

"It consumed me, this jealousy. It was ugly, and I was nothing but a monster to everyone around me."

"Kate?"

"Yes, Kate. She definitely was first in the firing line. Honestly, I had no idea you were her friend with the 'fucked-up love life'…"

"I had no idea you were that hot boss in love with a woman you couldn't have."

He hugs me tighter, spreading his hands on my stomach, the gentle caresses on our baby warming my heart. In just twenty-four hours, he proves to me he wants this just as much as I do.

"I never did brunettes."

"Huh?" I ask in confusion.

"You always said I preferred blondes, but that wasn't the reason behind it. After you, I couldn't go near a brunette. It reminded me too much of you, and each time it got harder to climb out of that depressive self-destructive spiral."

It makes complete sense, I just never expected him to be so affected by our parting. I honestly thought he had moved on, and our affair had become an afterthought, assuming men weren't emotionally capable of feeling such loss.

"Why didn't you look for me?"

"Why? Because I wasn't stupid. I knew how I left you, and as the more time passed, the more I knew you would move on, despite what I wanted." Burying his head into my neck, his grip around me becomes tighter. "Charlotte, this right now, this is what I've dreamed about since the moment we ran into each other in my parents' kitchen. I'm so happy right now it actually fucking hurts because I don't know what to do with myself. I'm obsessed with you, every part of you. You are my addiction, but one I never want to stop."

"Then, I'm glad I am not the only one." I smile, elated to hear him say exactly how I'm feeling too. "You are so stuck with me for life. Let's be obsessed together forever."

"Oh, that sounds like a bad eighties song." He laughs, then kisses my shoulder. "I can't think of a better way to put it, let's be obsessed together forever."

We continue to lay down, although it's only the afternoon. Shortly after, there's a knock on the door. Mrs. Landry, my neighbor across the hall, wants to make sure the noise was me and not some burglar. Unfortunately, I greet her in only my tank and bed shorts forgetting to wear a bra. It happens to be the same time my other neighbor, Mr. Garcia, walks past. I use the opportunity to grab Coco back from Mrs. Landry and thank her repeatedly for taking care of her.

"Oh, by the way, I want to introduce you to my husband, Lex."

I call for Lex to come to the door, much to his annoyance.

Standing in only his boxers, his torso shirtless, Mrs. Landry eyes him from head to toe.

"Well, Charlie, I see you've been busy."

Lex extends his hand which Mrs. Landry shakes with a flirtatious smile across her face.

"Oh my, quite a handshake." She presses her hand against her chest. "Well, I'll leave you two honeymooners alone."

As the door closes, I introduce Lex to Coco.

"I'm not a cat person."

"You're a pussy person, so I'm sure you can love Coco just the same." I mock, a smile playing on my lips.

"I'm not a *pussy* person... for the love of God, can we not compare anatomy to your damn cat?"

I cover Coco's ears. "Shh, she's sensitive and can sense your negativity toward her. Anyway, if you're not a pussy person, what are you? Tits or ass?"

"When it comes to you, Charlotte, everything..."

I wake the next morning when my alarm clock threatens me with its abrupt beeping. Six o'clock is too early. I roll over expecting to find Lex, but the bed is empty. The smell of coffee lingers in the air. I head for the shower, get dressed and ready for work. I choose a simple loose blouse, although loose being the operative word because the ladies are barely behaving themselves—d*amn pregnancy hormones*.

"Good morning, roomie." I smile while walking into the kitchen.

Lex looks so delicious in his dark gray suit. Too delicious, and I have just applied my lipstick.

"Good morning." He lifts his head to greet me, but his expression swiftly changes to angst. "Take the glasses off."

"But I need them to read?"

"Are you reading now?"

"Well, no, but it's just easier to wear them all the time when I have to work, and lately, my eyes have gotten worse."

He places his phone on the table. I'd be a fool not to notice the giant hard-on prodding through his pants.

"Those glasses make me want to bend you over this table, take your perfect, firm ass in my hands, and fuck you until you tell me to stop. But, I have an eight o'clock meeting across the city, so for now, it's easier if you just take them off."

Oh, poor baby, it sounds like someone needs attention.

"Well, Mr. Edwards," I say in my seductive I-can-be-that-hot-librarian-you-want-to-fuck tone. "How about we settle for me getting down on my knees and sucking that beautiful cock of yours?"

I unbuckle his pants, pulling his boxers down, his cock springing free before me.

His hands rest on my shoulder. I watch him watch me as I slowly slide his cock into my mouth. He groans, gripping on my shoulder tighter, his breaths uneven as I take him in deep, relaxing my throat muscles to allow him to go further.

"Fuck... take it in deeper."

Knowing he wants more, knowing he is coming undone drives me on. It makes me want him to remember this moment for the rest of his day when he sits in meetings trying to concentrate on important matters. I want this image ingrained in his mind. Placing my hand on his shaft, I pull his cock up and down while moving it in deeper. His body shakes before he grips the table causing a glass of water to spill followed by, "I'm coming... I'm fucking coming."

With warning, I suck harder, enjoying the taste of him filling my mouth. As his body slows down, I slow my movements, licking the tip of his cock clean.

"Jesus, you know how to give head," he utters, breathless.

"Well, it helps that you have the most perfect and deliciously inviting cock in the universe."

He zips his pants and buckles his belt making himself presentable again.

"Come here," he commands.

I sit on his lap, placing my arms around his neck before running my nose against his skin. He smells so damn good I catch myself closing my eyes and inhaling his scent.

"Did you just sniff me?"

"Uh... umm, yep."

"I don't want to be away from you for the next ten hours." His voice remains still, but I can see he's struggling.

"I love you. Nothing will change in the next ten hours, especially that. We need to get back to the real world."

Stroking his face, I lean in and plant a soft kiss on his lips.

"I want to see the baby."

I pull away, slightly confused by his request. "Sorry, sweets, but you kinda got to wait until it comes shooting out of my vagina."

His expression tightens like he's trying to find the right words. "I mean, I want to see the baby... you know, in an ultrasound. I want to hear the heart beating."

I continue to gaze at him, trying to figure out what he wants, what exactly is bothering him. "What's wrong?"

"I need to know this is real, that this isn't a dream. I want to hear our baby's heartbeat. I need to confirm with my own ears that it's beating strong."

Bowing his head, it takes a moment to click. He's scared that first of all, this is the only reason we are together, and second, if anything happens to this baby, that I wouldn't want him.

"Lex... look at me."

He lifts his head, looking like a little lost boy, afraid and unsure. "I love you, Alexander Matthew Edwards. Whether it's with or without this baby, we still would have found a way to be together. No matter what happens, I'm here.

Remember, obsessed together forever? I want to hear the baby's heartbeat, too. I will book it. Now promise me you'll try to be productive today."

"How can your simple words calm me?"

"Because that's what we do, calm each other during a storm or mini-meltdown."

"I love you, Charlotte."

"I love you, Lex. Now, please get to work because I need that coffee. It's been torturing me all morning."

With a smile, I hop off his lap as he places his laptop in his bag. He kisses me goodbye, promising to call me throughout the day. I pour myself a coffee, and with much delight, take a sip. In an instant reaction, I spit it back out.

"Oh, by the way, it's decaf," he yells before closing the door. "Sorry, no regular for you."

"That witch! She got to you, didn't she?"

"She got to everyone." He laughs as he walks out and leaves the apartment.

There's something comforting yet odd about sitting at my desk. This has been my home away from home, but today it feels slightly off. It's because I miss him, and it is only eight forty-five. Ten hours is a long time.

I make my way to the boardroom for our weekly Monday meeting. I'm not surprised when Eric drags me into the most random conversation with Emma, but I have to admit it makes me laugh and takes my mind off this separation anxiety consuming me.

After the meeting finishes, I look up the number and book in the ultrasound. Sitting back at my desk, I open my text messages, not surprised one bit there's already one sitting in there from Lex.

LEX

I'm sitting here listening to why we need to sell our shares in another division, but all I can think about is your morning breakfast feast. This is driving me crazy.

ME

Hmm, by morning breakfast feast, I'm assuming you're referring to my protein shot? Yes, it has crossed my mind, too... Okay, maybe like a million times. Do you realize it's only 10 am???

LEX

Yes, I do realize that. Time has never dragged so slow. Was the stock market always this boring?

BTW... your glasses will be the death of me.

ME

I think you need to get your mind out of the gutter and back into the boardroom, Mr. Edwards. A productive CEO always sets positive examples for his staff. By any chance is Kate free for a coffee at 2 pm? And BTW my glasses actually serve a purpose, not just for your pleasure.

LEX

My employee says hello and that she is free for coffee at 2 pm if you are. And yes... I said you will order tea. FYI, this is the last message I am passing on between the both of you.

ME

Tell her I said GREAT. And Boo! You're a
party pooper. I've got a client who just
arrived. Love you, Mr. Uncooperative
Edwards.

At two o'clock on the dot, I sit in the coffee shop in front
of Kate. It's so good to catch up with her now that everything's out in the open. I just didn't know how our friendship would work when all I want to talk about is Lex
fucking me a dozen times in the past forty-eight hours.

"So... how's everything going?" she asks while taking a
sip of her latte.

"Is this going to be weird? You know, talking about
him?"

"As long as you stay off the subject of anatomy, I think
it'll be fine."

"Please, I'm not Eric."

"Ahh, touché."

"I guess it's been great, I mean, you know like it's
surreal. All of a sudden, I'm living with him and pregnant
with his baby, but you know, it's only been like a day. We
both have busy schedules, and it's going to be hard for us to
find time just to chill in this moment."

"Right, Mr. Edwa... I mean Lex is a workaholic, but I
know he is making time to clear his schedule. Just this week
is crazy with a business summit being held downtown. We
have a merger riding heavily on a few discussions, so Lex is
really under the pump trying to get this all finalized. I'm
surprised he let me have coffee with you. Then again, he
probably wants me to check up on you."

"Well, you can tell him I'm fine, and I won't shy away
from having a catch-up with a good friend."

Kate smiles. "Yes, a very good friend."

"This is weird, though, right?"

"Totally weird. I get it, he is Lex to you, but to me, he will always be Mr. Edwards. Blimey, he is a lot to handle."

"You're telling me. I can only imagine what he's like in the office."

"Uh, let's see... control freak... obsessive... to put it mildly."

"Mmm... kinda hot, though. Tell me what's going on with you."

"Hmm... bugger all, I haven't gotten laid in like two months. I believe I've been re-virginized. The men in New York suck. Seriously, I cannot find anyone decent."

"You won't find anyone going clubbing with Eric, that's for sure. In fact, if you want to go on a manhunt, do not involve Eric. Since my manhunting days are over, I'm more than happy to accompany you, just for support."

"Oh, please, and get fired in the meantime? Lex would kill me for dragging you along. No, it's okay. I wish to live a long, healthy life. Just without mind-blowing sex. Seriously, though, how long before I become a virgin again?"

"I don't know... a year? Can we google this?"

So that's what we do for the rest of our time, look at Google images of ladies who believe they are virgins again. I can't stop laughing, it's one of those things that Eric would never do, and just looking at a vagina sends him into heaving vomit-like symptoms. We say our goodbyes, and I head back to the office to drown myself in work so time can pass quickly.

The afternoon becomes busier, and I barely find myself able to catch up on emails or even Eric. I look at my schedule. It's jam-packed this week, but hopefully, it will settle by next week. Christmas is just around the corner, and I haven't even begun to think of what to buy for everyone. I mark in my calendar to organize a shopping day with Eric. He's been quiet today, not his usual flamboyant self.

Before I know it, darkness falls outside my window. The office is quieter, and I realize I've buried my head in this brief for the last four hours. I quickly check my emails before closing the office and heading home.

It's after eight when I sit on the couch, reading over a case, waiting for Lex to come home. Coco is in her element beside me, probably wondering why I'm fully clothed since yesterday had me walking around the apartment naked.

With my eyes heavily focused on a witness statement, my phone chimes, the loud sound startling my focused thoughts.

LEX

Sorry stuck downtown. Won't be home till late. Sleep well beautiful, I promise I'll make it up to you.

My shoulders drop as I fall back into the cushions, disappointed at the text. I know Lex has work commitments he can't get out of. This is Lex's life. I don't know why part of me expects it will be different now—that we will both be home by six every night, cook dinner together, and have a lovely meal followed by hot sex and mindless television.

He is a fucking billionaire for God's sake and obviously worked hard to get to that position.

That night, I climb into bed and take out my *What to Expect When You're Expecting* book, but fall asleep soon after conception.

It's dark, but I feel him slide in beside me. His body smells amazing, freshly showered, and with heavy eyelids, I open them slightly to see my clock. It is just past midnight. I stir, trying to wake myself up.

"Shh," he whispers.

"It's late."

"I know. I'm sorry."

Struggling to maintain any sort of conversation, I fall into a deep sleep until the morning light creeps into the room. I'm awake again, but this time his lips are all over me, his cock pressing hard against my thigh.

"Good morning," he murmurs into my ear before sliding in.

I gasp, unprepared for the pleasure to spread throughout me since I just woke up. Plunging further into me, he fucks me hard before I call out his name, riding out the orgasm which only takes me two minutes to reach.

Catching my breath, I clear my throat to speak. "That's a nice way to wake up."

"I'm sorry about last night."

"It's okay, Lex, you work. I get it."

"But it's only our second night together here."

"We'll have plenty more nights."

He pulls himself off me and lays by my side, resting on his elbow. "I have some bad news."

"What?"

"I have to go to California on Saturday but just for a day. I'll be back on Sunday night."

Of course, I'm disappointed. I mean, it will be our first time apart, and it hasn't even been a week. I try my best not to show it, but my damn hormones are all over the place.

"Okay. Will this happen all the time?"

"No... I mean, occasionally. I'm sorry I can't get out of this one. Look at me, please."

I turn to face him, trying not to cry. I blame the hormones—always blame the hormones.

"This is an adjustment for both of us. I'm not used to

having to factor someone else in just like you aren't. But I'm learning the word *delegate*... please be patient with me."

"Of course, I'll be patient with you. This is a huge adjustment for me, too."

He wraps his arms around me, burying his head into my chest. Stroking his hair, I remember the ultrasound appointment, scolding myself for forgetting to text yesterday.

"I booked in the ultrasound, it's at midday. I'm sorry I completely forgot to tell you. Will it be okay, or should I reschedule?"

"I'll be there... wouldn't miss it for the world."

At midday, we are in the ultrasound room as the sonographer moves that wand-looking thing around my belly smeared with lube. Oh gross, it so reminds me of Eric's endless KY stories.

"Okay, so I'm just going to take a few measurements first." She continues to click on buttons and type as Lex sits beside me, resting his hand on my forearm. Both of our eyes are glued to the screen, waiting in anticipation for her to finish the important stuff.

Having a medical background, Lex is analyzing the image, his face serious as he watches her do her job. Secretly, I think she is intimidated by his persistent stare.

"So, this here is your baby," she says, pointing to this little pea-shaped thing on the screen.

"And judging by the size, you are about nine weeks along."

"Nine weeks already?" I ask, stunned.

"Give or take a few days. Now time to hear the heartbeat."

She turns up the dial on the monitor, and I wait, holding my breath until the loud thumping sound echoes through the room. It's like music to my ears, the tell-tale sign that our baby exists, but this time I treasure this moment. This unbelievable life-changing moment consumes me so much I'm ready to burst into tears.

My eyes refuse to leave the screen as I watch our baby, in its tiny form, move up and down on the screen. It may be black and white, making absolutely no sense, but that little pea is our baby, and I cannot take my eyes off it.

"You have a very happy baby inside there."

I glance over to Lex, who is unable to hide his happiness, his eyes dancing so bright as if the emerald lights up the dark room. His grin is infectious as I watch him experience this moment he has been so desperately waiting for.

"Do you hear that? Our baby is happy." He beams.

The sonographer hands us a picture of the baby, my hands shaking as I stare at the image until Lex asks to hold it for a moment. He takes out his phone, snapping a photograph of it.

"What are you doing?"

He shows me his phone, the wallpaper is now our baby.

"Doesn't matter where I am, I can see our baby anytime now."

It's his heartfelt words that cause a single tear to drop down my cheek. Wiping it with his thumb, he kisses the spot where it falls. I pull him into me, sobbing into his perfectly pressed suit. He gives me a moment before lifting my head, so our eyes meet.

"I love you. Obsessed together forever," he whispers, rubbing his nose against mine.

"Obsessed together forever."

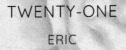

TWENTY-ONE

ERIC

This is the thing about change—I don't like it.

Contrary to what people might think, I'm happy never having to think about changing jobs, apartments, or friends. The only change I do welcome, however, is my wardrobe, but even then, I've been known to hoard certain pieces, something my mother says has been inherited from her side.

Waking up on Sunday morning, the day after Adriana's wedding, I know it's all changing, and that sinking feeling sticks with me. I just can't shake it. If I were honest with myself, it's the whole Charlie and Lex hook-up thing.

I mean, if anything, I encouraged it. Getting Charlie to After Dark the night of the charity ball, sending the janitor in to interrupt them, you always want what you can't have, right? So, I sent the janitor in, made sure they didn't fuck all the way, and *bam*, of course, you could see her desperation in the days which followed. At the time, it was all fun and games, but now I'm losing my best friend, and it hurts like fucking hell.

"Eric, we're checking out in thirty minutes, shall we

interrupt the lovebirds?" Adriana winks as she opens the mini-bar to determine whether or not I went on a late-night binge.

"Um, isn't that kind of awkward? What if they're in the middle of, you know... some wham-bam-thank-you-ma'am?"

"That's why you go in first. I can't experience any family scarring on the first morning as Mrs. Evans. Better yet, send Kate. I'm sure she's seen Lex in far worse situations."

"You're such a loving sister, Adriana." I smirk.

"Well, duh."

Fifteen minutes later, the four of us stand in Lex's and Charlie's room.

"Seriously, get the fuck out," Lex snaps as he goes back to snuggling his head into Charlie's neck. The good news is they aren't fucking, *but* the room reeks of sex. Plus, they are both naked under the covers. That kind of kills my buzz, although I can honestly stare at Lex all day. Okay, that was kind of creepy, and, well, I don't know if it constitutes me as being a bad friend considering he is her husband.

"As much as I love you, big brother, you have to get your naked ass out of here. The inn booked a traveling polka group, and well, unless you want to have polka tunes stuck in your head all week, it's time to leave."

"How long do we have?" he asks.

"Fifteen minutes, at most," Adriana responds after a quick glance at the clock.

"Then get the hell out of here and let me enjoy my woman for five minutes," he barks, climbing on top of her as she giggles under the sheets.

"Okay, my cue to leave... see ya outside." Adriana waves.

"Five minutes? Really, Lex, is that all it takes?" Elijah teases.

"Okay, you two peeping Toms, let's get out of here." Kate grabs our arms and pulls us outside into the hallway.

"You're not classed a peeping Tom if you are invited into the room," I point out.

"But you weren't, *Mr. Tom.*"

I pouted as we leave the room, following Kate and Elijah to the lobby where we are supposed to wait. Spotting a large mirror near the reception desk, I walk over to examine my hair. What the hell is happening today! Strands are poking out everywhere. It almost looks like I have bangs, *God forbid.* Damn, this is what happens when I switch hair products. Annoyed with my uncooperative hair, I sit in the fancy armchair which looks like it belongs in Buckingham Palace, practicing my royal poses until Kate questions me.

"What the hell are you doing?"

"Practicing my royal wave."

"Why?"

"This chair... it's fit for a royal."

She lets out a small laugh and calls me a fruit loop before burying herself in her phone. Bored waiting, my mind goes back to the charity ball when all this unfolded. Emma and I had no idea who this guy was and how he was able to bring Charlie's world to a complete standstill.

"So, that was weird, right?" I asked Emma.

"Uh, yeah, Charlie is never shy or quiet around guys, and did you see his eyes?"

"Oh, honey, that wasn't the only thing I saw."

Emma laughed as I continued, "Okay, so I've never heard her mention him. Have you?"

"No, but I haven't known her as long as you, and she's like your BFF," she pointed out.

"True... but it's like this guy had a spell on her, you know. Like everything about her changed when he stood in front of her. We need a plan."

"A plan for what?" Emma asked worriedly.

"A plan to get these two together."

"Eric, she's with Julian."

"So what! Hugh dates five girls at a time. Once he had nineteen!"

"Okay, but Charlie is not Hugh Hefner, thank God, and well, maybe if they were together, it ended for a reason. We shouldn't meddle in her affairs."

"Oh, stop being a party pooper. Wake up and smell the jizz. He is Lex Edwards, billionaire CEO, more gorgeous than... God. Look, I'll say it... more gorgeous than David Beckham."

"Eric, how dare you say that." She chuckled. "Okay, you have a point, he is the most beautiful man I've ever seen, but please do not ask me to smell the jizz again."

"Deal. Now, where do we start..."

So, this is how it all began. I'm Billionaire Matchmaker, and with my talent, I could start my own reality television show.

When Lex asked me some questions at the bar, I knew he was interested, so naturally, I was going to get Charlie to After Dark. I had no idea how to get rid of Julian, but thank God, he was caught up with something. Not that I didn't like him. I mean Christian Bale lookalike, I was foaming at the pants looking at him. I was goddamn jealous of Miss

Mason's male followers, and for once, all the hot guys were straight.

A week later, everything started to unfold. She was distant, on edge, extremely high-strung. She kept trying to bury herself in work but failed miserably. I knew she wouldn't talk, the stubborn bitch, so I decided we needed some Eric and Charlie pamper time.

I sat there in the chair as the lady filed my nails. It was Charlie's birthday, and we were having a day of pampering. After spending a day on Fifth Avenue maxing out my three credit cards, we decided to have a light lunch followed by manis and pedis at our local salon. I was flicking through a back issue of US Weekly *as Charlie rambled on and on about how she busted Nikki and Rocky in Nikki's office two weeks ago. I dropped the magazine in the water as Charlie broke the news of the last part. The manicurist cursed me in her language, and all the manicurists turned to face me, shaking their heads. I couldn't help but crack up laughing. Geez, I'll replace the three-dollar back issue with a pregnant Angelina Jolie on the front.*

"Charlie, are you fucking serious?" I started coughing as the laughing became uncontrollable. The manicurist was annoyed with both of us as we couldn't hold still. She eventually stabbed me with the filer which calmed me the hell down.

"Sorry," Charlie apologized to the manicurist. "I'm not lying. I mean, why is it always me? Why do I always have to catch them? And the worst part is that they are never embarrassed! They just say sorry, then carry on."

I laughed, struggling to get my words out. "Charlie, please, like you can talk."

"What's that supposed to mean?" she asked nervously.

"Um, like, hello... Lex rocking up to your office on Monday night. You don't think I believe nothing happened, right?"

"I don't know... I mean nothing happened," she stammered.

"So, how do you explain a cufflink with the initials LE engraved on it that was lying on the floor underneath your desk?"

"Uh, he was... um, fixing my chair."

"More like slurping on your lady door."

"Eww, E, did you just say 'slurping on my lady door?'"

"Well, he was, wasn't he? Don't deny it, girl. You've been tapping his ass nonstop since then, I can tell."

"How on earth can you tell that?"

"You're walking funny... kinda lopsided. My guess is that you are getting some back-door action as well."

"Eric!" she gasped.

The manicurist snickered, which caused Charlie to turn bright red. It was so true. I had a radar on people who had just gotten laid. Plus, I could smell sex like a mile away. Hmm, maybe this was my gift.

"Not in front of the..." she continued to spell out the word manicurist.

"Um, Charlie, you know they can spell, right? So, how was it, and how big is he? My guess is huge 'cause you haven't worn your really high pumps all week."

"Holy shit, Eric, do you have some sort of sex radar? His size is... well, it's... perfect."

"Damn, girl, you got it bad."

"I do not!"

"I mean, not even I have found a perfect one. Some were small, some were big, some leaned to the left, some leaned to

the right, and there were some that were so covered in bush you couldn't even find it if you sent a search party with heavy-duty torches and a hedge trimmer—" I continued on as she cut me off.

"Okay, okay, I get it. You haven't found the right one. Can you please not go on about large bushes? I want to maintain an appetite for tonight's dinner."

"You're the birthday girl..." Smirking, I went back to reading the magazine next to me, issue date December 2009.

It's times just like this that I miss already. I don't know if they will still happen. She's gotten back with the love of her life, has a full-time sex schedule on top of being pregnant. I don't know why it gets to me so bad. I should just talk to her, right? I mean she is my BFF. I confide everything to her, but what about now? This is way too much thinking for a Sunday. Thank God, Kate agrees to hit up Barney's when we get back into the city later today. Retail therapy is just what I need.

"Do you think things will change now?"

"How so?" Kate asks as she tries on a red strapless dress but gives up trying to squeeze her boobs into it when she realizes she has no chance in hell of zipping it up.

"With Lex and Charlie..."

"Well, of course. I mean they have each other, they are practically moving in together, and *hello,* they're having a baby. Plus, holy shit, can you believe they got married!"

"But do you think Charlie will still, you know... hang out with us?"

In a huff, she pulls the dress off, standing there in only her lacy purple thong and matching bra. "Eric, what's going on?"

I hesitate, which is unlike me. I always have something to say. I've been told on numerous occasions that I have no filter, like none whatsoever, but Kate hasn't known me that long, and she doesn't know this is out of character.

"I just... you know, she's my best friend. I don't want to lose her," I shamelessly say, my head bowed, trying to understand why this gets to me so much.

"Doll, look at me?"

I glance up, Kate staring at me with this look of pity on her face, but goddamn, seriously, she has a great pair of tits. I mean like Halle Berry great.

"Are those real?" I ask, sidetracked.

"What? *Yes*! And I don't mean look at my tits. Eric, Charlie treasures her friendships. Yes, life is changing but for the better. She'll always be in your life."

"I guess. Can I touch them to make sure?"

"Wait, you're serious. Are you sure you aren't straight?"

"Honey, please, vaginas scare me. It like reminds me too much of that movie *Innerspace,* you know with Meg Ryan? All pink and mucus-like."

Shaking her head in disgust, she puts her jeans back on. "Never say mucus to me again. Honestly, Eric, your vagina lingo needs to step up a notch. And yes, you can but make it quick."

After confirming they are, in fact, real, we decide to head on out for a really late lunch before catching a movie. Kate is fast becoming my favorite person to hang out with. I just love the British sense of humor plus, aside from Emma, she is the only single friend I have.

"Will you still call Lex 'sir'?"

"I don't know... yes... I think. I can't call him Lex in the office, you know?"

"Did you ever want to spank him when you called him 'sir'?"

"What? No... never. I have never looked at him that way. Trust me, back in the day, I saw way too much of his not-so-good side."

"Did he ever try to come on to you?"

She laughed out loud "No... apart from that minor comment with joining him and Victoria. Honestly, Eric, it was never like that. He's my boss, and yes, now we run the same social circle, but I love my job and admire his intelligence. I have learnt so much from him. That's all. Now, get your mind out of the gutter and let's order because I'm hank marvin."

"Hank marvin? What the hell is that?" I need a translator for Kate but enjoy the new catchphrases.

"Derr, starving!"

Monday morning rolls around faster than you can say 'doggy style.' *Fuck, I need to get laid.* It's exactly eight-thirty, and I have everything prepared for our meeting. Coffee is brewed, and an assortment of breakfast pastries is centered on the large meeting table. The projector is ready as Nikki is going to present an update on a case the firm has been tangled in. At eight fifty on the dot, Emma walks in.

"Hey, chica, what's happening?"

"Nothing," she answers quietly.

Huh, odd. She bows her head, pretending to be immersed in paperwork.

"Spill."

"Spill what?"

"Why you acting all 'something up my puss'?"

"Eric, nothing is up my puss."

"Well, maybe that's the problem, then. So, spill it now, or I'll nag you for the rest of the day."

She sighs, knowing there's no way out of it. When it comes to extracting information from people, I'm a born nagger. Either that or I will manipulate the conversation so eventually, the truth will reveal itself. My mother says it's a hidden talent of mine amongst other things. Taking her glasses off for a moment, she reaches for a tissue, attempting to clean the lenses.

"So, I kind of did something, it's embarrassing. I can't even think about it without wanting to crawl in a hole and die."

"OMG, you peed on him?"

"No! How mortifying. Although this wouldn't be far off. I kinda um..." she tenses her body, unable to get her words out, "... I kinda, um, farted during sex."

She buries her head in her hands as if that's going to erase this. Poor Emma, when it comes to screwing around with co-workers, she sure lacks knowledge in the sexual department.

"Like asshole farted or pussy farted?"

"*Eric,* I can't believe you just said asshole farted." Her cheeks burn while she crumples into the chair. "Well, I'm not sure, but I don't think it was that."

"Okay, so walk me through it, but make it quick before someone walks in the middle of this conversation, and God forbid it be Tate. He'd cut my dick off and serve it to the mafia."

"Okay." Taking a deep breath, she continues, "So, he wanted to do it from behind, and it was great, right? But as he came and pulled out, I farted... and it was loud like echoed-in-the-room loud."

"But isn't that normal, the air escaping from the vag?"

"I don't know, is it?" Emma asked, exasperated.

The door creaks and trying to pretend like we aren't talking about this, I straighten the coasters in front of me. Thank God, it's only Charlie.

"Okay, it's just Charlie. She'll tell ya it's normal."

"Tell who what's normal?" She looks at us suspiciously, placing a pile of manila folders down in front of her.

"Tell Emma that fanny farting is normal," I blurt out.

"What the hell is fanny farting?"

"Oh, Kate says that's what Brit's call it. You know, after a guy pulls out, and your vag sounds like it's farting."

Charlie nods her head, not at all surprised we are talking about this topic at this time of the morning. Over the years, Charlie has immuned herself to the stuff that comes out of my mouth. Exactly why she is my best friend.

"Oh... I see. Yeah, it happened to me once in college. I was mortified, left his dorm room, and avoided seeing him at all costs."

"Great... that's just the advice Emma needed."

"Sorry, Emma... but true story," Charlie admits with a sad smile.

"What are you doing here, anyway?" I asked, knowing Lex had spent the night at Charlie's, and according to Kate, they are now living together. "I thought you'd be knee-deep in Lex's love juice?"

"I still have to come into work. You think I can neglect this?" she questions, picking up a blueberry Danish, then devouring it in like two seconds. "Besides, I was knee-deep about an hour ago."

Emma lets out a small laugh, but it only lasts a few moments before Nikki walks in, followed by Tate and Becky. Emma walks around to the other side of the table directly opposite Tate, who looks somewhat hurt at her distance. Am I missing something here? I thought they were just secret work fuck buddies.

Note to self—*interrogate Emma tonight at spin class.*

Nikki begins the meeting, and like nothing has changed, I sit back with a big smile on my face, taking down the minutes, enjoying this moment before anything else decides to change.

The rest of the week is pretty much the same, except for Tuesday night. I'm well aware that Charlie is distracted and tries to seek comfort in others, and when I say 'others,' I mean I screwed my ex again.

Okay, yes, what the fuck was I thinking?

I mean, I caught him blowing another guy, and let me tell you, I have no idea what he saw in him. He has a dad bod—isn't cut up at all. In fact, I may have seen a hint of man boob. Nevertheless, it still was a blow to my ego, excuse the pun. As soon as he shot all over me, I knew I had made a massive mistake.

So, to get over a bad mistake laced with complete regret, I blow Miguel, this gorgeous waiter I'd been eyeing for a while at Tapas on Tenth. Now, when I say gorgeous, I'm talking Henry-Cavill-spank- you-in-the-face-with-his-cock gorgeous.

But there's one problem. It's huge, and I don't mean his cock. That's huge, of course, like he puts donkeys to shame, but this one problem is, well, let's just say not appetizing. Normally, I'd be straight on the phone to Charlie dissecting this particular situation, but tonight, Lex is taking her out to dinner, and well, I don't think he will appreciate me calling up Charlie to discuss my epic blow job fail.

Again, change is definitely not my friend.

So, the week from hell sees me hitting up social media

more. Same old desperados trying to grab any sort of attention they can. I find myself tweeting a few hotties. One, in particular, is this guy 'The Bone Ranger.' He's funny, his profile pic is of this cowboy hat. Ding, ding, ding. I'm picturing this guy wearing only chaps sitting naked on a horse. He's into role play. It's just fun, right? Until he sends me a direct message, and we get to chat more. He's into the same stuff I like, is a *giver*, and so I find myself obsessively messaging him every spare moment I have.

I'm yet to get sight of the goods, but let's face it, I'm shallow.

This will be a deal-breaker.

"Good evening, Master Kennedy."

Seeking solace in the familiar, I decide to visit my mother. Entering the building, I greet Gerard, the doorman, and make my way to the elevator. As soon as I exit, Malcolm, my parents' butler, greets me at the door. I love Malcolm like a grandfather, but honestly, the whole 'Master' thing should be kept in the bedroom alongside a crop and ball gag.

"Hey, Malcolm, Mom and Dad home?"

"I believe your father is at a board meeting, your mother is in the den, and your brother is also accompanying her."

Great, my brother is here. Insert sarcasm times a million. I walk to the den to find my mother and brother discussing an article about religious changes in the Middle East.

Boring with a capital B.

"Hey, Mom."

"Eric! What a lovely surprise." She stands and walks

over to me. In familiar fashion, she hugs me tight, her signature scent of Chanel No. 5 lingering in the air.

"Hi, Dom." I wave.

"Hello, Eric. It's been a while," he answers stiffly.

Okay, so this is the thing about my brother. He's from another planet, *like seriously*. He is eight years older than me, a computer geek, I mean like he wins awards in excellence and shit like that. He isn't gay, although I can't confirm that because I've never seen him with a girl. He is quiet, lives alone in his apartment in SOHO, and well, much to my mother's disappointment, we have nothing in common and don't get along.

He dresses well, actually really well for a straight guy. Occasionally, I ask him where he gets a certain sweater vest, but he always answers in one-syllable words annoying the fuck out of me. He is tall, like way taller than me. From what I can see, he works out some, but he's always covered up. He wears glasses, these thick black-framed nerd ones.

Dominic doesn't look at all like me. His hair is almost jet black, and he has a very masculine jawline, not at all like mine. I may be twenty-two, but I swear I could join Disney because I look so baby-faced. Dom looks like a man, a real man, but too bad he has the personality of a wet mop.

"So, what's been happening, you still doing that computer stuff?"

He huffs, only slightly under his breath, "Yes."

And that's the end of that conversation.

He ends up leaving, and I spend the night on the couch watching *Pretty Woman* with my mom. God, I love my mom. She is so beautiful, so refined. She was born in China, grew up there until her parents sent her to study here when she was eighteen. She met my dad not long after, and, well, from the bits I've heard, they spent the next few years trying to convince my grandfather why he should let her marry an American. They have fifteen years between them, and my dad was a colleague of my grandfather at the time. It was messy, like really messy. My mom broke every culture rule possible, but in the end, I guess it was all worth it.

I snuggle into her side as we both sit quietly and watch a whore turn into a princess.

By Wednesday, I'm experiencing major hump-day issues. *God, I just need a good hump.* The Bone Ranger is a great distraction, but it isn't the real thing, *yet.* The only thing that makes my day somewhat interesting is an email Nikki and I received from Lex in the morning.

> **To:** Eric Kennedy; Nikki Romano
>
> Eric & Nikki,
> Can I request you join me for lunch today at George's on 7th at midday?
> I have some urgent matters I would like to discuss with both of you.
> Your attendance will be highly appreciated, and I ask that this not be mentioned to Charlotte. I will explain why during our lunch.
> Lex Edwards

Okay, so, kind of weird because I have no idea what this is about. Nikki thinks the same, but anyway, we make up some lame-ass excuse when Charlie asks if we want to go out for lunch.

"Where are you guys going?" she questions.

"I don't know about Nikki, but I... um, am meeting up with a friend for lunch."

"Which friend?"

I don't work well under interrogation. I think sweat beads are forming on my forehead. Oh my God, that means I'll need to get another facial! My T-Zone is so high maintenance.

"A friend of my brother's."

"But you hate your brother."

"I don't hate him, *Charlie,* I just think he is a thirty-year-old geek who needs to be taught how to get laid and maybe then he can hold a conversation with me."

"Well, I offered to do him. Remember last year at your parents' Christmas party? He may be a geek, Eric, but he is a hot one. Glasses and all."

"Lex would so kill you for saying that."

She laughed. "Probably, but don't you worry about him. I've got him whipped and at my feet."

"He would definitely kill you for saying that, and when you say 'feet,' do you mean he is a toe sucker?" I ask.

Yep, there's my no-filter again.

"Oh, E..." She kisses me on the cheek. "Have fun with your secret lunch date, and for the record, Lex loves everything." She winks before walking out of the room.

Nikki and I sit at the table and she orders a Long Island iced tea. The waiter is cute, so as he walks away, I tilt my head to check his ass. *Hmm, a little too wobbly for my liking.* Since we have time to kill, I bring up the subject of Miguel because I need to bitch about it. Let's face it, he's great apart from the whole funky spunk thing.

"I mean it was that bad, I had to use a goddamn chicken rag beside his bed to spit it out in. Thank God, it was in the dark. I don't think he noticed."

"Look, Eric, I'm telling you. Wheatgrass is the trick."

"What am I gonna say, Nikki? 'Hey, have a shot of wheatgrass juice so I don't have to feel like I'm swallowing expired milk?'"

"No. You need to go to one of those health bars. Suggest it and mind you, they do taste like shit, but you'll need to have one, too."

"But my jizz is fine!"

"Okay, I'm not even going to ask how you know that, but the reason I suggest that is so you both are doing it, and it won't look like you are targeting him," she tells me.

"Oh, right, I get ya. So, what, Rocky has bad spunk?"

"Please, my man tastes just fine. Like sweet candy juice if you care to know."

"Yeah, TMI. That guy's a tank. He must blow a bucketload."

"It's about quality, Eric, not quantity."

Lex arrives halting that conversation. As usual, he looks like sex on legs. I mean, I totally get why Charlie is hooked on him. He's like some walking sex god, and women around him almost swoon in his presence, except for Nikki. I swear that woman has one wound-up cooch when it comes to Lex.

"Good afternoon, Eric, Nikki."

He sits, motioning for the waiter to come over.

"No offense, Lex, but I've seen you practically bang my best friend in front of a group, a 'Hey, what's up' will be fine…"

"Duly noted," he responds with a nervous laugh.

He seems fidgety, very unlike him. For a few moments, he

remains silent like he's thinking about what to say. I don't mind, it gives me more time to look at him. Geez, he has great lips. I bet he sooo goes down on Charlie like every day—that's why she's got that damn glow. I wonder if she showers beforehand. Look, I'm no vagina expert, but don't things get all stuck up in there? Fuck, seriously—vag thoughts are grossing me out.

"What do you want, Edwards? Apart from stealing our best friend to satisfy your sexual gratification," Nikki reminds him.

He takes a sip of his water, and suddenly, he appears calm, smiling to himself like he knows a secret we don't.

"Here's the thing... I love Charlotte more than life itself. You two are her best friends, and what I'm about to ask means a lot to me and will to her one day."

I sit, waiting in anticipation. Please tell me it has something to do with getting us Celine Dion concert tickets. They are sold out, but I know he can pull some strings. Like maybe he can even get me backstage.

"I realize Charlotte has plenty of important people in her life who mean the world to her, but both of you have been there for her through thick and thin, and, for once, I want to do things properly. I want to throw her a proper wedding in Carmel with our family and friends. Now, before you both say something, we have to keep this under wraps because I don't want the media all over Charlotte. Not during this stage in the pregnancy."

I gasp, covering my mouth soon afterward, slightly disappointed I won't be watching Celine.

"So, what exactly are you asking?" Nikki questions.

"You plan the whole wedding," he answers bluntly.

He grins back, and damn, my man bits do back-to-back somersaults. Nikki sits there quietly like she has to think about it. I kick her with my foot to be met with a why-the-fuck-did-you-do-that stare.

"I'll do it! But I swear to God, Lex, if you hurt her in any way, shape, or form, I will cut your balls off into tiny pieces and feed them to the wolves. You got me?"

"Yes. Thank you, Nikki." He forces a smile, struggling to keep his composure around Nikki. "Now, just the finer details... it's next month. Charlotte and I are flying to Carmel to spend some time with her dad."

"Excuse me?" Nikki and I blurt in unison. I continue, "But it's in four weeks?"

"I realize that, so I will give you two assistants." He motions over to another table where Adriana and Kate are seated. I hadn't noticed them there at all. They walk over with huge grins on their faces.

"Adriana is a... well, a freak with anything wedding-related. The four of you can put your pretty little heads together to make our day memorable. Kate will be all yours for the entire week. She is an expert at organizing anything last minute and can also help you with any coordinating that needs to be done."

I sit there in an out-of-body experience. I can't believe this is happening. I turn to look at Nikki who surprisingly has a huge smile on her face.

"Okay, so that's it. I've got an important meeting, so I'll leave you to it."

He stands up and pulls his wallet out of his pocket, throwing his black Amex on the table.

O.M.G!

"Oh wait, Lex..." Adriana calls.

He turns around one more time to face us at the table.

"Do we have a budget?" she asks with a deviant smile.

"It's Charlotte, no price can be put on marrying her." He winks before walking off.

Catching the breath I have been holding in, this is no doubt the best thing ever to happen to me. Planning a wedding with no budget, and I'm talking billionaire money here. Holy fuck!

"O... M... G!" I gasp, fanning my face with my hands.

"Right?" Kate laughs

"This will be epic," Adriana nods.

I nod, agreeing.

Nikki is silent, which is odd coming from Miss Opinionated.

"Nikki?"

"This day is going to be the wedding day of Charlie's dreams. The fairy tale beginning, even though I still think he's a jerk. No offense, Adriana."

"None taken. Any ideas, though?" Adriana begins scribbling notes into a journal-looking thing.

"Of course, I've got ideas. I've been waiting for this moment since the night Edwards had my baby in jail. Leave the bachelorette party up to me..." She rubs her hand with a devilish grin.

By Friday night, I've hit a slump in my so-called life. I sit alone in my living room wearing sweats and my hoodie, much to my disappointment. In my life, I don't think I have ever stayed in on a Friday night, except that one time when I got mono. I curl up on my couch, checking my socials. Same old bullshit, and I'm disappointed 'The Bone Ranger' is offline.

I throw my phone over to the other chair, so I won't be

tempted to check it again. Flicking through the cable channels, absolutely nothing's on. I settle for an infomercial on
this miracle face cream.

Fuck, do not get out your credit card.

After forcing myself to change the channel to MTV
because I'm this close to buying the face cream as well as
the bonus hair remover, I hear a knock on my door. I stand
and quickly grab my fry pan in case it's some ax murderer
before noting the price tag is still on it.

Well, duh, I have no idea how to cook.

"Open up, *E*, it's me."

I unlock the hinges because I recognize the voice.
Standing there is Charlie in her sweats, carrying Chinese
take-out, pizza, and ice cream.

"Geez, Charlie, a little bit early for cravings?"

"This isn't all for me, now scoot." She walks in and
places the food on the table, heading into the kitchen to put
the ice cream in the freezer.

"What are you doing here? Shouldn't you be spread out
in bed getting your waterhole filled by snakey Edwards?"

She laughs, grabbing plates and bottles of water to take
back to the living room.

"Friday night is our night," she simply replies.

"Charlie, it's okay, I get it. You've got this great man now.
I don't mind that Friday nights are now spent with him."

She pauses before grabbing both my hands. "Eric, life is
moving so fast for me. Never in this lifetime did I think that
I'd be in a relationship with Lex again, let alone pregnant
with his baby... *again.*"

"*Again?*" I ask, shocked.

"Long story... we need more ice cream for that. Look, as
I was saying, while this feels like a dream come true, it's also

a little frightening. There are parts of my life that will never change, and that includes my friendships. I need you in my life more than ever now, E."

I hug her tight because just like me, she feels it too, and here I was thinking I'm the only one going through this. She's my best friend and needs me, probably more than ever.

"What did Lex say when you told him you were coming here?"

"He understands what my friends mean to me. That won't change. Besides, I made him read *Fifty Shades of Grey,* well, at least start it. He wants to know what the hype is about and, well, I said read it for yourself."

"OMG, Lex Edwards takes on Christian Grey? I couldn't think of anything hotter."

"He doesn't understand why a woman would want to be with such a control freak." She laughs again.

"Oh, holy hotness. I need a detailed daily update on this. Damn, I'm jizzing in the pants."

"*Eww...* and you're in sweats? What is the world coming to?"

"Oh, you're right, me in sweats can't possibly be a sign of good times ahead."

We sit on the couch and eat while gossiping about Adriana's wedding. The food is delicious. I do a mental calculation of how much extra gym time I need to do to work this off. Ooh, it means I can see Simon, the cute college dude who makes that grunt when he does squats.

"What are we watching?" I ask while shoving an eggroll into my mouth as Charlie loads Netflix.

"*Bring It On.*"

"Nice... the cure to Friday-night blues."

The movie starts, and we sit there watching, occasionally commenting at our usual places.

"Hurry up, get them out," Charlie reminds me.

I race to my closet and pull them out, throwing a pair over to her just in time.

"Give me a T!" We cheer in unison.

We laugh as we do our usual skit. Pom poms in hand, we mimic the movie just like we always do. When it comes to cheerleading, it's a secret obsession.

After the movie finishes, we somehow get stuck watching infomercials again until Charlie wants to buy a steam mop. Seriously, even I want the mop, and that's saying a lot since I already have a cleaner.

I sit there, snuggled into my best friend. Like nothing has changed, but everything has.

I know life will be different.

As I glance over at her, I notice how different she looks.

Apart from that I've-been-fucked-like-crazy look, she's glowing, and her smile, it's flawless. She looks over at me and winks. Charlotte is happy. I finally know now what it means when people say that another person's happiness is essential to your own. It makes me think maybe I should give Miguel another go. I mean, he was happy because he came. I should be pleased because he's happy. My body shudders as I think about the funky spunk again.

"You okay? Swallowed something bad?" Charlie asks, innocently.

I let out a loose laugh, nearly choking on my wonton. *Serves me right.*

"Actually, I did. Let me tell you about my Tuesday night, but first, dip that wonton straight into that vinegar mixed with the fishy lemon sauce thing."

She follows my instructions, scrunching her face and

sticking out her tongue as she realizes how bad it is. Grabbing the water, she tries to wash it down but ends up gargling for a moment.

"Fuck, E, that was..." she lets out a cough, "... that was fucking sour."

"Right, so now that you have tasted it, let me tell you about my night with Miguel..."

TWENTY-TWO

LEX

Our first two weeks as a couple are pure bliss, well, at least that's what I tell myself. The reality is, we argued over the pettiest of things, but arguing leads to one thing, and the only thing that's on my mind—hot, off-the-charts animalistic raw sex. The kind of sex which does nothing to satisfy my erection. If anything, it makes me want more and more to the point where I have to remind myself we still have to function as human beings outside the apartment.

It isn't the first time I lived with a woman, but eight years living in a bachelor pad has me set in my ways. I'm not a slob, quite the opposite, in fact. I'm extremely anal, and it turns out so is Charlotte. The problem is we have different ways of doing things, and we don't always see eye to eye.

"The toilet paper should face forward, over," she argues.

"I disagree."

"Why on earth would it be under?"

"Because it looks tidier this way."

She looks at me, the argument far from over. Bathroom politics are not hot, although Charlotte standing there in her tank top showing her erect nipples and cute-ass panties is, which leads to me fucking her in front of the mirror, and so that was Monday.

On Tuesday, we decide to eat McDonald's, much to my horror. I can't even recall the last time I ate cheap fast food. Charlotte's cravings are all over the place, and being the great husband that I am, and so she won't feel so bad, I eat what she eats.

"Did I just see you dip your fry into that chocolate fudge sundae?" Cringing, she waits for my response with a clear look of disgust on her face.

"Yes, Adriana and I used to do it as kids."

"*That is gross!* Fries and dairy?"

I dip a nugget in there, and the look of disgust intensifies.

"Lex! Who does that? I bet you that you're the only one doing that. Prove to me someone else does it?"

"If I do, will you flip the toilet paper my way?"

"I'm that confident that, yes, we can have the toilet paper your way."

I reach for my phone and google 'fry in sundae.' Video after video appears. I hit play, and a very annoyed Charlotte huffs. "Whatever."

I won the toilet-paper-roll battle, the compulsive neat freak side of me metaphorically sits in its smoking jacket with a pipe and slippers. It also results in me licking chocolate fudge off her erect nipples. I hear no complaints from her, only two screaming orgasms.

Wednesday is our first official real-couple fight. After much persuasion, Charlotte agrees to go apartment hunting with me as we need something bigger. We talk about whether we should move to the suburbs, but both our offices are in the city, so it makes sense from a commute perspective.

Surprisingly, something perfect comes up almost immediately, and I'm ready to put in an offer. The apartment is located on Fifth Avenue, a rare find with sweeping views of Central Park.

With Charlotte's hand in mine, she walks around the apartment with her mouth wide open. I have to say, it's impressive, and so is the thirty-five million-dollar price tag.

"Can we afford this?" Charlotte whispers beside me. "I mean, I could sell my place as well as the one in Connecticut, but I don't think—"

"Charlotte, we're not selling anything," I tell her. "And yes, we can afford this."

"But... I want to contribute. I don't want to freeload off you."

I lower my head, shaking it with a small laugh. "Charlotte, that should be the least of your worries. If you love it, it's ours, okay?"

We continue the tour of the place and stop inside the grand kitchen.

"The kitchen is fully equipped with everything a professional chef will need. I assume, Mr. Edwards, you would have a full-time chef?" Anita, the realtor, asks.

"Yes, as well as a live-in housekeeper and possibly a nanny," I boldly respond.

"*What?*" Charlotte asks, her pitch high.

I sense she's annoyed. *Why? I have no idea.*

"Charlotte, please, I won't have it any other way. If you're worried about the money—"

"I don't care about the money. What makes you think I'm going to be one of those women who sits around with hired help? I wasn't raised that way and don't intend to raise *our* child with hired help, either. I'm not like that, and I don't give a shit about your fucking money."

I asked the realtor to excuse us. Attempting to control my temper, I clench my fists, remembering that this is the woman I love, and she's carrying my baby. *Fuck, women are so unpredictable!*

"Was that really necessary in front of the realtor?" My voice is low, trying my best to remain calm.

"Probably not, but right now I don't care. I understand that you are wealthy, but you don't control everything we do, do you understand that? I don't want money to dictate our life. If you want me, then you need to learn to consult with me about things like this. I may like clothes and shoes, but I don't want to be known as some stuck-up New York housewife. I have worked very hard to get where I am, and I'm proud of what I have achieved. It was never my intention to work hard and have others serve me, it just doesn't sit right. You want a woman like that, perhaps you need to go back to Victoria Preston."

Where the fuck did that come from?

Charlotte knows I was never with Victoria. This is so left field.

"Is this your hormones talking?" I ask, confused.

Shit! I went there.

Her face contorts into pure rage until she storms out, slamming the door behind her. I apologize to the realtor who no doubt will run to the press with a '*Lex Edwards on the Verge of Break Up*' headline. God, what the fuck is that? Why can't Charlotte see how difficult it is for me to factor someone else in. I'm used to making my own decisions. I can't be so fucking accommodating all of a sudden.

I walk outside to be met by the icy winter breeze, and that is just from Charlotte's glare. Sitting in the cab, she remains silent staring out the window, avoiding me. Not wanting to push her, I allow her some time to calm down, choosing my words very carefully.

Inside the apartment, behind closed doors, she throws her keys onto the table and motions for Coco to come to her, still ignoring me.

"Charlotte, I assume that having help will allow you to focus on your career. I know that's important to you."

"Sometimes I feel like I don't know you. This money and wealth have changed you," she admits. A more rational Charlotte now appearing. Thank God.

"It has, for the better."

"No, Lex, that's where you're wrong." She places Coco down on the floor, crossing her arms in defiance. "I fell in love with *Alex,* this unbelievably beautiful and smart man who isn't hung up on money. A man who is happy to live in a tiny cottage in a small town, who pities those who are so fixated on material possessions. Tell me, am I looking at that same person now?"

"Charlotte..."

"Don't you get it? Money can be a curse rather than a blessing. I want to be the one who cleans our bed sheets, knowing that I'm making *our bed.* I want to look at that and smile, reminiscing about all the wild sex we're having on it. I want to be the one who cooks our meals, places the cutlery on our table knowing that it's you who sits across from me at the dinner table, chatting about our day, and most importantly, I want to be the one raising *our* baby. I don't want to miss a single milestone because it's assumed the wealthy need a nanny. I want all the *normal* things, Lex. White-picket-fence type normal. A long time ago, I pictured you and me and our children. We led a simple life, and we were a family."

"I pictured that, too, a long time ago."

"Then, you know." It isn't a question, rather a fact.

I pull her into me, letting out a sigh. "Yes, I know. I'm sorry, Charlotte. I promise to be less controlling. We're a family now, but there's one thing you have to get used to."

"What's that?"

"We, and I emphasize *we,* are wealthy. It's our money, Charlotte, not just mine, and because of that, we'll always be in the public eye so outbursts like that need to remain behind closed doors."

"I'm sorry. I forget you're famous," she mocks.

"Not famous, more high-profile, Charlotte, but there are a lot of people who want to see me fail, and that includes my relationship."

She quietly runs her hands down my chest, past my abs until they linger at the buckle of my belt. Beneath my pants, I begin to stir. *This woman will be the death of me.*

"You are mine, they can all fuck off. Your cock belongs to me. It fucks *me* every day, sometimes twice a day, maybe three if I'm lucky. They can wish all they like, but this..." she says, sliding her hands into my pants, "... belongs to me."

"Well, then, get down on your knees and suck the fucking cum out of it because I swear to God, Charlotte, it will only ever belong to you. And for the record, people in white-picket-fence houses don't fuck like we do."

"This makes us dirty, oh *so* very dirty," she teases, while sliding down to take me all in, her eyes never leaving mine as her mouth wraps around my cock, and finally, we're back to pure bliss.

After meeting Eric and Nikki and informing them of my intention to marry Charlotte, Adriana has doubled her annoyance level if that's even possible.

ADRIANA

Are lilies OK?

Do you prefer French script or Calibri for the font on the table cards?

Lex, I really think you should invite our cousins from Australia.

This is only the tip of the iceberg.

At that point, I had my mother intervene, and then when that failed, I called in the big guns—Nikki. According to my secret spy, Eric, Nikki's in charge of the bachelorette party. Payback is on her agenda. However, I'm always one step ahead of her. Despite her evil ways, she manages to control Adriana, and thankfully the messages stop.

The hardest part is trying to keep this all under wraps from Charlotte. I told her I needed to fly out to California for work, a partial lie which ends up being postponed because work takes priority. The purpose is to see Mark Mason and ask for his daughter's hand in marriage. He doesn't need to know we are already married. I do value my life, especially now that Charlotte is in it.

Who would have thought Lex Edwards—the traditionalist.

But so the guilt doesn't eat away at me, I decide to finally have a meeting with one of the top production companies in LA looking for an investor.

We are sitting on the couch watching mindless television when I sense something is off with Charlotte. "Is something wrong?" I ask, placing my laptop aside.

"I'm fine."

Fuck, typical woman response which means something.

"Okay, then... we can waste time by me dragging it out of you, or we can talk about it and then get naked all night."

She lets out a small laugh, the smile enough for me to know that it isn't something major.

"I'll miss you," she simply says.

So that's it—*separation anxiety.* I don't blame her. We have only been officially together for two weeks, and I'm already heading interstate.

"I wish I didn't have to go..."

If only she knew the reason why.

"No, I get it... I really do. It's just... I'll miss you."

"I'll miss you, too." I part my lips and lean in, her mouth soft and warm, inviting me, but the desperation as always lingers. What starts as a slow burn turns into a frenzy, and now I feel the same anxiety, knowing I won't see her, knowing I won't touch her for two whole days.

There hasn't been one day since the night in the hotel where we haven't fucked, and it isn't once a day, either. It's the moment we wake, the moment we climb into bed, and if work schedules permit, a few times in between. Charlotte is insatiable, and I take advantage of whatever the hell it is, pregnancy hormones or not, I'm getting laid by the woman I love.

"Right, dinner time," Charlotte chimes.

"Um, hello? Are you forgetting something?" I ask, grabbing her hand and placing it on my cock.

"I'm sorry, sugar cakes, but it's not me who's hungry."

"Fine, go make dinner. I need to make a phone call, anyway."

She makes her way to the kitchen, singing some annoying jingle from a commercial, my perfect opportunity to make sure I have everything covered for the weekend. I pull out my cell and dial his number.

"Dude, I was waiting," Rocky complains.

"You got better things to do while you're in the doghouse?"

"No, and how do you know I'm in the doghouse?"

"Women talk, Rocky, in case you haven't noticed."

"Yeah, well, what the hell was I supposed to do?" he asks with a raised tone.

"How about *not* have lunch with your ex?"

"We didn't have lunch... and she's not my ex. I slept with her one time like a billion years ago, way before Nikki. I ran into her downtown, and she asked me to join her for a coffee. She drank coffee, and I had green tea. End of story."

"You ordered green tea? Maybe that's why you're in the doghouse for being such a pussy."

"Fuck you, Edwards, hurry up and get pretty boy on the phone."

"Hang on a sec." I hit conference and dial Eric's number, and he answers almost immediately.

"Okay, here's Eric," I announce.

"OMG, guys! Are we having a three-way? This is so hot, it's like one of my wildest wet dreams," Eric squeals.

"Dude, keep your tiny Tim to yourself," Rocky states. "I reiterate, I'm all about the pussy."

"Rocky, that is so racist, just because I'm half Asian doesn't mean I have a tiny Tim. In fact, I have a medium Tim, apparently not as big as some." Eric coughs as he says it.

"Can we end this disturbing penis talk? Listen, I need you both to watch Charlotte on the weekend while I'm gone."

"Why? You think she's gonna run off with that Baker dude?" Rocky chuckles.

"Oh, snap!" Eric snickers.

"No, I don't think that, but I don't feel comfortable leaving her alone."

As if I would think that!

"Damn, this was not the three-way I envisioned. Okay, well, I'll take the night shift—"

"Eric, no taking her to any clubs, you understand?"

"Dude, talk about possessive. We got your back, Edwards. Now let's go before tiny Tim starts charging us by the minute."

"Rocky, as if I would ever charge for phone sex. Mind you..."

I hang up the phone, the two of them can enjoy their random conversation. I have better things to do. I need to devour every inch of Charlotte before my flight takes off tomorrow.

I remember the first presentation I did in front of a whole auditorium of business associates, investors, and political parties—I was a nervous wreck. But within the first minute, I found my footing and never looked back.

I sit on the sofa belonging to Mark Mason, cautiously watching him in case he pulls out an assault rifle from behind the recliner he's sitting on. While being back here brings back memories, he makes me feel unwelcome. His resistance to my request to meet with him only confirms one thing—I have a hell of a lot of persuading to do.

"I hope you didn't come into my home to tell me the

reason why you are here is because you want to marry my daughter," he threatens.

Fuck!

"With all due respect, sir, I did come to ask for that, but not before you hear me out."

"What could you possibly have to say that will make me believe you can take care of my daughter? Did you invent some sort of time machine so you can erase all the pain you caused her?" He pauses, allowing me to speak, but for some reason, I hesitate. "I didn't think so."

Here it goes. *C'mon, Edwards. One man, you can't wimp out.*

"I love Charlotte. I always have since the moment I came back that summer, maybe even before. I was a kid, and I made the wrong decisions and hurt everyone around me, but mainly the one who mattered the most. I can't erase that, and to forgive myself took years of destructive behavior, but in the end, it was Charlotte's forgiveness I needed the most. I don't know who is looking down on me, but I thank my lucky stars that somehow, something brought us back to one another. She is my life, and I want to give her everything she desires. Perhaps I'm not asking you for your permission as such, because let's face it, Charlotte will do what she wants to do, anyway..." I pause thinking about what to say next. "What I'm here for is to reassure you that Charlotte will be taken care of. Aside from financially, I'd move heaven and earth for her. I will do everything in my power to give her the life she deserves. All I ask in return is that you support us on this journey because, without your support, Charlotte won't feel whole, and I can't let that happen. I cannot watch her experience hurt and pain, not if I can help it."

He grazes his beard with his hand. Just like my dad, he has a poker face. *What the hell is he thinking?*

"I know you won't hurt her again, for anyone who has ever met Charlie knows Charlie is to love her. No one would purposely cause that girl pain."

"Wait," I'm shocked at his answer. "Does this mean..."

"I'm not stupid, Edwards. I do know what it's like to love someone. I get it, you love my daughter, and you want to marry her. You think Charlie would allow me to disapprove of this relationship? Please, she and Debbie alone would gang up on me with all their I-am-woman-hear-me-roar mumbo jumbo. And to top that off, my ex-wife would be on the next plane over probably stabbing a voodoo doll with pins chanting *destroy Mark.*"

I laugh unexpectedly. What else can I do in a situation like this? He understands. He wants the best for his daughter, and I am the best for his daughter.

I ramble on about my intentions, the exact plan. Yes, finally, I have a plan, and it's perfect.

"That's a lot of stuff going on for one day. How the hell do you expect to pull it off?"

"I have our friends working on it. All I need from you is to pretend this conversation never happened."

I said *our friends.* Is this what it's like to be normal?

Shit Lex, you fucking soft cock, I think to myself.

"Deal, but you're sleeping in separate rooms while you are under my roof."

"If Charlotte agrees."

She will never agree. She is a walking horn-dog, but, hey, who am I to complain?

He stands up and walks over to his desk, pulling out a drawer. He reaches in to retrieve something. It's his checkbook. "Tell me how much the wedding is, and I'll pay."

"Sir..."

"Cut the 'sir' crap, Edwards. I'm still getting laid three times a week with my girlfriend. I ain't that old."

Right. *Awkward.*

"Okay, Mark... listen, you don't need to pay a cent. It's all taken care of."

"It's tradition, the father of the bride pays."

"I don't mean to sound arrogant, but I can pay for the wedding with an hour's worth of work. I don't want to offend you, but it's peanuts to my bank account."

He looks hurt, which I fail to understand since it means he doesn't have to take out a second mortgage on his home. "If you want to help, there's plenty to do like explaining the whole thing to your ex-wife and making sure she gets here in time."

"Fuck, that's a lot to ask. Maria and Debbie in the same house? God, what if they start comparing my technique and shit?" he complains.

We both laugh at the same time before he holds out his hand, and I shake it.

I leave Mark's house, pleased I have him on board 'Project Marry Charlotte Mason.' There is one more person I have to see before I leave Carmel—Finn Rodriguez.

I knock on the door, taking a deep breath as I know this will be a battle. An attractive lady answers who I remember from prom.

"May I help you?" She looks at me intensely, certain she recognizes me.

"I was after Finn."

"Alex? I mean Lex? I mean... sorry, I can't remember what Charlie..."

I smile, she relaxes almost instantly. "I prefer Lex. Sorry, I didn't mean just to show up unannounced."

"Sorry! Excuse my scatterbrain, please come inside. I'm Jen, by the way." She holds the door open.

"We met at prom. Are you sure? It might be best that I wait outside."

"Oh, Finn won't be home for another half an hour. Please come in, but I'm warning you, the kids won't leave you alone."

I follow and take a seat in her living room while Jen offers me an array of beverages. Minutes later, a little girl walks in. She's maybe five.

"This is my daughter, Mikayla. Mikayla, this is Charlie's boyfriend."

Boyfriend—the word sounds juvenile. Even more reason to announce to the whole world she is my wife.

"You're pretty," Mikayla says as she stands in front of me.

"Why, thank you. So are you, Mikayla."

"My daddy says that Mommy isn't allowed to talk to pretty men because they might steal her."

"Mikayla! Excuse her, please, it's a 'Mommy and Daddy' joke. Oh, and sorry about calling you her boyfriend. I'm not sure what word to use."

"Hopefully not for much longer," I reveal.

"Are you serious? Wow! I spoke to Charlie a few days ago. She's so happy, Lex. I'm glad you two found your way back together again."

"How much has she told you?"

"Just that you were living together, but tell me, Lex, do you have a death wish by wanting to speak to Finn?"

As soon as she says the words, the screen door slams, and Finn yells out to his family. He enters the room, his eyes suddenly turning to me, the rage clearly visible. His tall stature overshadows a short Jen, and his clothing looks bulky. I guessed by them he's a firefighter. I'm not one to be disrespectful to those who help our community but...

"Jen, *what's he doing here?*" he asks in a bitter tone, almost spitting out his words.

She stands before him, placing her hands on his chest to calm him down. I guess now would be the best time to give him the reason. I'm not afraid of this jerk, never was. In fact, I despise him for obvious reasons.

"Finn, I wanted to speak to you."

"I got nothing to say to you, Edwards. Charlie may have forgiven you, but I don't forget so easily," he shoots back.

"I'm not here to cause trouble, especially in front of your family."

He asks Jen to take the kids to the backyard.

"You have some nerve showing up here. You think people won't start talking shit again?"

"Finn, I don't care what people think. I'm here because, for some reason, you mean something to Charlotte."

"Damn right, I do! She's my fucking best friend. What are you gonna do? Buy me off?"

Why didn't I think of that idea? Except, now I'm that Lex and apparently, I am compassionate according to Charlotte.

"Yes, because that would make Charlotte happy." My words are laced with sarcasm.

"Then tell me why you want to show your face in this town again?"

"I'm asking Charlotte to marry me... properly."

Without warning, he throws a punch at me hitting me right in the jaw. *Fuck!* I'd been hit in the ring, but I'd expected those punches. I touched my jaw, the pain spiraling throughout me. I lift my hand to my chin, the slight tang of blood lingers. *Fucking dickhead.*

"*Finn!*" Jen enters the room, pushing him to the side, scolding him for punching me.

"I'm sorry. Lex... let me get you an ice pack." She returns moments later, and I place the cool pack on my face.

It helps. God, I'm so ready to hit him back.

Why did I fucking let my guard down?

"What makes you think Charlie will say yes?" Finn's nostrils flare, the adrenaline spiking as he tries to push Jen aside.

This time I'm ready.

"You're her best friend, I'm sure you can answer that," I shoot back.

Jen motions for me to sit, and I do on the large couch and begin to speak. I explain to them my intentions and the fact that I need their help to pull this off. Jen rushes to my side, hugging me, and I sit there feeling somewhat uncomfortable. Not knowing what to do, I hug her, this stranger I barely know.

"You broke her, you know... she was a damn mess," Finn speaks quietly.

"I know," I simply answer, always so acutely aware of my actions.

"I've wanted to do that since the moment you left town."

"I know, I deserved it." It's the truth, even I have to admit that.

I look at my watch. My driver will be here in a minute. I hand the ice pack back to Jen, and she squeezes my hand and gives me a sincere smile.

"Listen, I need to go. It would mean a lot if you could do this for me, and in return, how about I forget the fact that you broke Charlotte as well... sexually. Truce?"

"I'd hardly call that a break... more like a slight tear." Jen laughs.

"Fine." I hold out my hand, and he reluctantly shakes it.

"For the record, guys, that fight was totally hot."

"Edwards, leave my home now. *You...*" he motions to Jen, "... put those kids to bed. I'll show you what's hot."

I close the door behind me, ready to take my bruised face back home.

It's just before midnight when I arrive home on Sunday. I enter the bedroom, and although Charlotte said she would wait up for me, she's fast asleep.

I'm eager to be inside her, but instead, I stand and watch her—her tiny snores barely audible, her eyes shut tight, her face nestled into her pillow. Her complexion is glowing, and I can't help but bask in her beauty knowing that *our* child will mirror her beauty, it's impossible not to. I pull my phone out of my pocket for like the hundredth time today and stare at my home screen. *Our baby.* It's one of those moments where I take a minute to appreciate everything good in my life, and all of it is lying in our bed, fast asleep.

It overwhelms me, and my desire to have her kicks in. I strip at a fast pace and climb into bed. She makes a whimper, and as much as I know she needs her sleep, selfish, horny Lex needs her more. I nestle into her back, and without warning, I slide my cock inside of her, maybe a little too fast, but after a few strokes, I feel the moisture build up, and her moaning increases.

"*Lex...*" she murmurs, reaching behind to pull my head into her neck.

"It's me, baby, I missed you," I say while slamming into her harder on the verge of an orgasmic finish.

She cries out, her body tensing.

I don't want it to end—I never want it to end.

"Come with me, Charlotte. Please... together..."

And just like that, I pull her into me tight and tug on her erect nipples causing her to scream my name, her walls contracting around my cock. I hold onto her hip trying not to hurt her.

"Fuck," I growl loudly, enough the neighbors and possibly the whole apartment block can hear.

With our breaths shallow, she turns around to face me.

"It's late. I missed you, too."

I stroke her cheek and kiss her, unable to hide a smile as my mind wanders.

"What's the smile for?" she asks, smiling in return.

"Just happy to be home."

For the first time in my life, I find it—not a place but a person to call home.

TWENTY-THREE
CHARLIE

As I stand on the porch staring blankly at the door, Lex holds onto my hand and squeezes it tight.

I'm beyond anxious, my palms sweating as I begin fiddling with the rings on my left hand. When Lex suggested we fly back home to Carmel and finally announce the news to my dad, I tried my best to come up with every excuse under the sun.

It turns out, every excuse has a solution.

Nikki assures me she can hold down the fort at work, and the doctor told me it's safe to fly since I'm only in my second trimester.

Lex even plays the I'm-offended-you-won't-come-out-in-the-open-with-our-relationship card. It comes across like he's mocking me. Maybe it's my imagination.

A week later, and I'm standing here on the porch at the place I once called home. It isn't that I don't want to tell my dad I'm back together with Lex, I'm just anxious his gun collection may have tripled in nine years, and the last thing I want is a wild goose chase all over town.

"It'll be okay. It's been nine years, Charlotte," Lex says, calmly.

"I don't feel well," I moan.

"Morning sickness again?"

Whoever came up with the term morning sickness must have been a male. It should be called all-day sickness. The list of food that repulses me is growing longer by the day. On the plane ride here, I officially added oranges to my list. The man across from me had the need to eat three of them in a row, and I had the need to puke three times in a row in the tiny-ass restroom.

There was a week or two where it disappeared, but for some unknown reason, I caught a second wave of it, praying this is short-lived and won't carry on during the entire pregnancy.

"Yes... err no..." I muster up the courage and knock on the door.

Seconds feel like hours, my heart rate picking up the longer we stand here. But then I remember little bubba inside of me, and placing unnecessary stress on the baby is not good. Taking deep breaths, I talk myself into calming down. Lex is right, nine years is a long time.

The door opens, my dad stares at me in shock.

"Charlie?"

"Daddy!" I cry, running into his arms.

It has been a year since I saw him last, but unlike every other time I've seen him, this feels so much more emotional. I'm here, no longer his little girl, but a woman pregnant with a baby to the man I love.

I hold onto him, allowing his smell to embrace me, a mixture of Old Spice and laundry detergent—a sign he has a good woman taking care of him. He pulls away, no smiles, but a stare so cold I swear the birds flew out of the trees like a sixth sense as to what is about to go down.

"What the hell is Edwards doing here?" he raises his voice.

"Dad, please. We need to talk."

"He's not welcome here."

"Dad! Can we please act like mature adults and talk?"

"Mature adults? He was an adult, Charlie, when you were a teenager. An adult who took advantage of you," he shoots back.

"Dad..." The walls of my stomach weaken. Covering my mouth, I push him out of the way. "I need the bathroom."

After a nasty let's-see-what-I-had-for-lunch situation in the bathroom, I stand at the basin, splashing my face with cold water. Seriously, when the hell is the morning sickness going to stop? I open the door and hear my dad and Lex speaking, the voices are muffled, and I can't really hear the conversation. However, I'm guessing it isn't pleasant.

I enter the kitchen and interrupt what looks like a heated debate.

"Charlie—"

"Dad, if you're talking about the small-minded folks in this town, I really don't care what people say, they can talk about us as much as they want. I know who I am. I'm a woman who fought hard to put my past behind me. I studied and graduated from Yale Law School. I opened up a law firm in New York City. I have been given a second chance with the only man my heart has ever belonged to, and now... now... we are having a baby."

There, I blurt it out, no sugarcoating—this is the real deal. I decide to hold onto the information about us getting married on a whim in The Hamptons.

One piece of information at a time, Charlie.

His face changes, a look I've never seen before. I glance nervously at Lex who shrugs his shoulders, obviously just as curious as I am.

"I'm going to be a granddaddy?" he asks with a slight croak in his voice.

I nod, and instantly he pulls me into a big hug. Thank fuck! The tension eases, and right on cue, my stomach grumbles. *Oh, shame.*

"Time to get some grub in you... doesn't mean you're off the hook, Edwards," he warns.

"Dad, let it go. And please don't use the word 'grub.' That sounds like something you find dead on the road and decide to grill it."

"I was thinking your favorite Buffalo chicken wings," he says proudly.

"Nothing with wings," I answer queasily.

"How about Debbie's pot roast?"

"Uh, too meat juicy like."

"Well, what do you want?"

I think about it for a moment, and like a lightning bolt it hits me.

"A peanut butter and jelly sandwich with a side of ketchup," I announce proudly, the thought making my mouth drool.

"What?" they both ask in unison.

We all laugh, and Dad gets straight to it. Ten minutes later, I sit in front of their disgusted faces and dip my sandwich into the ketchup. It tastes like heaven and hits the spot perfectly.

"So how long are you here for?" Dad asks.

I turn to Lex, unsure of how long he expects us to stay in Carmel.

"Four days," Lex answers.

"And where will you be staying?"

"Um... we were hoping here, but if it's a problem, we can find a hotel."

"You know you're welcome to stay here... in separate rooms," he adds.

"Uh, hello, Dad... I think the jig is up. Unless, of course, you think this baby was immaculately conceived?"

Lex laughs as my dad cringes.

We speak a little bit more about life back in the city when Debbie arrives home. I'm excited to see her. She is possibly the best stepmom you could ask for. Lex heads out, saying he needs to pick up a few things from the store.

I shout out, "Hey, if you're heading that way, anyway, how about you pick me up a tub of vanilla fudge ripple ice cream?"

With Dad cleaning up and Lex gone, it gives Debbie and me a chance to catch up in the living room.

"Honey, I'm so glad you've come back to visit. We've missed you."

"It's actually nice to be back. I probably wouldn't have been able to say that a few months ago."

It's the honest truth, and I thank my lucky stars the nightmare is over.

I tell Debbie all about Julian and how Lex and I ran into each other, including every insane thing that happened since then, excluding the nuptials, the angel on my shoulder whispering, *"Your dad will kill you with his bare hands."* Debbie nods and listens intently, and by the end, she's hugging me so tight that I can feel her tears drop onto my shoulder.

"Oh, Charlie. You deserve to be happy... and a baby? What a blessing. Your dad has been waiting to be a grand-daddy. We both knew it would be you before your sister."

"Aww, please, Melanie? Unless a baby can travel in her backpack, there's no chance in hell." I laugh.

"It'll be nice to have a baby around," she says with a smile on her face.

It dawns on me that Debbie is also waiting in anticipation for this moment. She never had kids, and by the time she met my dad, they were both too old to start a family.

"Well, lil' bubba can't wait to be spoiled by its grandma, too," I mention softly as I place my hand over hers.

Her face lights up, and with ease, she pulls me into a tight hug, not letting me go for what feels like an eternity.

Lex has some work he needs to catch up on, so I take the opportunity to head down to the local fire station. The building looks exactly the same, its worn-out brick gives it history, built sometime in the early 30s if I remember correctly from history class. The bright red trucks sit horizontally in front of the building and coming from inside are the sounds of rowdy men yelling and cussing at the television.

"Talk about productivity," I say out loud.

They all turn around to look at me. Finn's face lights up as he runs over and grabs me, lifting me high in the air as if I were light as a feather.

"Charlie, are you kidding me? Is it really you?"

"In the flesh." I grin.

"How... why?"

"We need to have a long chat. When are you off?"

"In about two hours... I'll pick you up, say, around three?"

"It's a date."

Smiling, I say goodbye and head back into town.

Exactly two hours later, the doorbell rings. I couldn't have run any faster, Lex and my dad scolding me for almost tripping down the stairs. As I open the door, I'm met with a goofy grin belonging to my childhood best friend, Finn Rodriguez.

"Hey, girl." Finn wraps his arms around me. I miss his suffocating hugs, although I don't miss his man sweat.

"Mark, Alex," he nods.

Oh, he called him *Alex*. Lex doesn't correct him. In fact, Lex smiles at him, which is weird. Am I missing something here? Mr. She's-mine-and-no-one-can-touch-her-including-that-Rodriguez-kid?

"You wanna grab a bite to eat?" Finn asks, eyeing Lex.

"Sure, let's go." I kiss Lex goodbye, and thank God he understands I need some alone time with Finn. Last night when I raised the topic, I thought he would go crazy demanding he be there, but much to my surprise, he shrugged it off and said to have fun. Have fun? Okay, seriously, something was up with the universe.

As we sit in the local coffee shop, I know there's no better time than now to let it all out in the open.

"Go, ask me your million questions," I say while shoving the most appetizing chocolate cake into my mouth.

"I have no questions. You broke it off with Julian, and you're back together with Lex."

"Yeah, I guess that's the main... wait, did you just call him 'Lex'?"

He shuffles his feet but laughs it off. "Sorry, I heard you call him that once, and it must have stuck."

"When did I call him that?" I ask, confused.

"Must have been Jen, then, I don't know. Anyway, so *Alex* and you are back together."

"Don't you want to know what happened?"

"Charlie, I'm a guy, we don't care for sordid details. Unless it's dirty, but since I look at you like a sister, that's just plain wrong. Actually, it's just plain wrong that I called you a sister when we did it twice."

"Foot-in-mouth disease, welcome to my world." I chuckle.

"Okay, so what I mean is, if you're happy, Charlie, then that's all that matters."

"I'm pregnant, Finn," I blurt out.

He almost spits out his strawberry milkshake. His face reddens and his eyes go hard. *Shit, did I just ruin our happy reunion?*

"Don't tell me you're with him because of that?"

"Finn, really, do you think I was raised in the 1950s?"

He remains silent, and I allow him a moment to let it sink in.

"You know babies cry all night," he informs me.

"I know."

"And you need to change their diapers like thirty times a day."

"I'm aware of their bowel movements, yes."

"And you can't have sex for like six weeks after the birth."

"Yes, I know..." Realization of what he's said hits me like a sledgehammer. "Wait! *Six weeks?*" I ask a little too loudly, and the old lady behind Finn turns around.

He smirks, *bastard*. Nikki never mentioned that, probably because she was doing something else to compensate. Mental note—*ask her later*.

"It'll be okay, Finn, and besides, you're only a phone call away. An experienced parent like yourself should be able to answer all my questions."

"Congratulations, Charlie." He smiles.

I place my hand over his and squeeze it tight.

"Hey, I got an idea, you up for some law-breaking fun?" he asks with a mischievous look on his face.

"Sure, why not. I can always represent myself."

"When you said 'law-breaking fun,' I didn't think you meant breaking into Carmel High," I sigh.

"Charlie, don't you miss high school? We had so much fun," Finn reminds me.

We stand in the hallway as I give myself a moment to take in my surroundings. It is surreal to be here again, walking the same hall I used to walk down every day. Not much has changed, the lockers are still the same, but maybe the walls have been painted. The trophy case still stands there in all its glory. Unconsciously, I make my way to my old biology classroom. The door is unlocked, and without hesitation, I find my old desk, the one sitting beside the window near the fish tank. I run my fingers over the desk-top, remembering how many times I'd sit here and stare out the window daydreaming about Lex. After prom, I would sit there and daydream about how he fucked me on *this* very desk. I carefully lift the lid, and low and behold, there it is engraved in the corner where only I could see—the initials CM 4 AE. It was all very juvenile, but I couldn't help but feel nostalgic over this tiny reminder.

"Finn, we should get out of here before we get busted."

"Yeah. But let me take you to one more place."

He holds my hand and leads me down the corridor until we are standing in front of the gymnasium. God, I hated this place. The number of times I was hit by the dodge ball has left me scarred for life.

"No offense, Finn, but sports wasn't my thing back then... we aren't going to re-enact gym class, are we?"

"Will you just shut up for just one second?"

I roll my eyes as he opens the doors.

"Welcome to prom night," he announces.

My eyes widen at the scene in front of me. The gymnasium has turned into prom night exactly like prom night nine years ago. The disco light shines around the room, the spotlights focusing on the massive Eiffel Tower standing in the corner, just like I remember it. The Parisian street signs are arranged throughout the room. *Adriana must have had something to do with this.*

And standing in the middle of the room is the most perfect man dressed in a black tuxedo.

I walk toward him, trying to catch my breath and take it all in.

"Charlotte."

"Lex, what is all this?"

"Before you say anything else, I have a dress and shoes waiting for you over there."

He points to the locker room. I'm still confused as to what the hell is going on, but I follow his instructions. I walk over and enter the restroom. Inside, hanging on the door is a beautiful emerald green gown, almost a replica of my prom dress, with a pair of silver Manolo Blahniks. I change into the gown, which fits like a glove even though my stomach has begun to show, then walk back outside feeling extremely self-conscious. Why? I have no idea.

"Charlotte... you look breathtaking," he whispers.

"I believe you've said that to me once before."

"But this time I hope you don't abandon me on the dance floor."

"Lex, what is all this? I mean it's beautiful, you're beautiful."

"We didn't get to have our prom dance in front of everyone to see. I didn't get to hold you close to me, and I wasn't able to look at you the way I'm looking at you right now."

"I kinda don't want to ruin the moment, but it's only us."

"Is it?" he asks with a mischievous grin on his face.

I turn around, and walking through the door is Rocky and Nikki, Adriana and Elijah, Eric, Emma, Kate, Finn, and Jen. All nine of them are dressed formally in suits and gowns.

"Are you kidding me?" I laugh, unable to comprehend this moment.

"And I didn't get to do this..." He cups my face and gently places his lips on mine. It's *the* most perfect, gentle kiss, the kind of kiss that travels down to the pit of your stomach, smothering it with butterflies.

With my head nestled on Lex's shoulders, I watch as the others dance. Each one of them dressed impeccably, smiling, laughing, enjoying this trip down memory lane. Having the closest people to me in this one room tugs on my emotions, and I can't help the tear that falls upon my cheek. Where the hell did Hard-Ass Charlie disappear to? I'm seriously crying over the most nonsensical things these days.

"I have to confess something..." Lex speaks.

My stomach churns a little. *Oh, for fuck's sake, Charlie, he is yours, he married you!*

"What is it, Mr. Edwards?"

"There is another reason why I did this."

"Oh?"

He removes my hands from around his neck and places them in his own hands.

"If I had known all those years ago in the treehouse that you were the one, I would have saved myself a shitload of misery. No matter what life has thrown at the both of us, here we are, standing here... together. Charlotte, you complete me. For eight years, I believed I had met my fate. I have been punished for my actions, but somehow, someone gave me a second chance at life, gave me a reason to breathe again. Charlotte, you are my reason that I stand here with a heart bursting full of love. You are the reason that in five months from now, my wildest dreams will come true. I want every part of you, and I need to do this properly. Will you do me the honor of making our family complete? Will you marry me, *again?*"

He kneels on one knee and opens a small black velvet box—an emerald ring is nestled perfectly inside. The diamonds almost blind me, but I shift my gaze and stare directly into his eyes, his beautiful eyes, and for some stupid reason, my tongue is tied. Am I supposed to respond? I already said yes when I married him. *C'mon, Charlie, don't leave him hanging.* Gosh, if only my brain would shut the fuck up. *Wait, what?*

"Yes," I blurt out.

With his eyes dancing, he gently slides the ring on my finger, kissing it softly before he stands back up and embraces me.

"You know I couldn't say no, right? I'm legally Mrs. Edwards already," I tease.

"Legally, yes, but emotionally, I needed to do this. This makes it real to me."

A loud round of applause follows, along with some whistling. Rocky, of course, echoing throughout the room.

One by one, each of them comes up and congratulates us. Eric grabs my hand before hugging me, rambling on about carats and diamonds, followed by more OMGs.

"It's so great that you guys are here. Are you planning on staying long?" My words are neglected, there's a hush, and all eyes are on Lex. Am I missing something?

"The reason why I called them here is because we are getting married tonight," Lex adds.

"Huh? As in tonight, tonight? But we're already married?"

He nods.

"I don't get it..."

"Tonight, at the stroke of midnight, you will become Mrs. Charlotte Edwards again, but this time in front of all our family and friends. A wedding, Charlotte. We never had a wedding."

"But... but... what?"

"Everything is taken care of. I won't see you again until 11:50 p.m., Charlotte. Apparently," he says in an annoyed tone, "... I have a bachelor's night to attend."

"Yes, and dear Charlotte here has hers," Nikki responds, much to Lex's displeasure.

"Okay, I'm confused, really confused, but I don't care. I trust you, Lex."

His hands find their way back to my face, placing his lips on mine, this time with more pressure, and I know, without a doubt, he's anxious. It's the same kiss he always gives me before we'd say goodbye each day before work.

"Six hours until you're my wife... in the eyes of our family, friends, and the whole world."

"That's a long time." I smile back.

"Thank God, you are thinking the same thing," he murmurs, rubbing his nose gently against mine.

"Okay, show's over, we need to get down to serious business," Rocky announces.

Nikki and Rocky pull us away from each other. I mouth 'I love you' before being hustled out of the gymnasium and into a Range Rover waiting at the entrance of the building.

"Wow, nice ride. So, what's next?" I dare to ask. I still have no idea what's going on.

"Your dress, silly... finally, I get to reveal my creation." Adriana beams as she clutches my arm and rests her head on my shoulder.

A wedding dress.

When Lex said we didn't have a wedding, I thought he meant the reception. My insides are doing the cha-cha, dancing on the ceiling, singing from the tops of their lungs. It's every girl's dream, and why I thought I deserved anything different is beyond me.

It's all systems go—I'm prepared and ready to marry the man I love in front of everyone.

What I'm not prepared for is this bachelorette party, and if Nikki had anything to do with it, I am in trouble.

Deep trouble.

TWENTY-FOUR
LEX

"I t's a boat."

"It's a boat, would you get a load of this guy? Dude, it's a Lady M luxury yacht for fuck's sake," Rocky says, overly excited as he stands beside Elijah and me on the dock.

"Excuse my ignorance, *yacht*, why are we staring at it?" My head isn't clear but rather in a warm, fuzzy haze as my girl just said she will marry me in front of everyone. Of course, I know it's a fucking yacht, I also know the builders after my stint last year which saw me yacht shopping.

"Because we've got five hours to celebrate your freedom before you're tied to the ball and chain *again*," Rocky explains, clearly impatient to get aboard.

"I highly doubt Charlie is a ball-and-chain kinda gal, Rocky. Perhaps you need to find your balls again. Should I call Nikki to see if she has them in her purse?" Elijah snickers.

"Dude, aren't you supposed to be on your honeymoon? I thought you'd be porkin' your new wife like the cowboy you claim to be."

"Rocky, not all Texans are cowboys..." Elijah points out.

The conversations around me become a distant sound as I stand still watching the ocean. The waves calmly lap against the piers, the heavy scent of salt lingering in the air. The sun's setting on the horizon, a reminder that in five hours, Charlotte will walk down the aisle and say "I do" in front of our family and friends.

My mind refused to let go of that moment where I stood waiting for her to walk through the door of the gymnasium. I always knew how I wanted to propose, it was a no brainer. I promised her things back then I couldn't deliver, and if I had a time machine, I'd go back and act on them, but this was the next best thing.

Adriana was thrilled she was in charge of recreating the prom scene. It's the reason she decided to stay in New York instead of taking me up on my offer for her and Elijah to spend their honeymoon in the Virgin Islands.

"Adriana, c'mon, you deserve a honeymoon. You don't need to help me."

"Lex, I'm Mrs. Evans, nothing will ever change that. I don't need a tropical island to enjoy my husband. Please let me do this, you are marrying my best friend, and I don't want to miss a thing."

It was all set. Finn texted me at the café warning me they were about to leave. Everyone had flown in. Kate made sure all flights and accommodations were booked accordingly.

Eric and Nikki had picked out the emerald green dress Charlotte was to change into courtesy of an associate's close friend, Vera Wang.

It was time.

The moment she walked through the double doors, she

was completely stunned by the scenery, her eyes scanning the room. I knew she was taken back to a time and moment that held a lot of promises for us.

When her eyes found me standing in the middle of the dance floor in my tux, she ran to me. Her kiss smothering me, not allowing me to get a single word in, but I couldn't help it. I allowed it to linger because I knew at midnight she would be officially mine, and that thought alone made me not want to let her go.

When she emerged from the restroom, I couldn't help but be in awe of this beautiful woman walking toward me.

My words came out perfectly, exactly how I pictured them, having rehearsed it a million times in my head.

She said yes to marrying me... again.

"Look at this pussy-whipped fucker, all daydreaming and shit. C'mon, we only have five hours to partay!" Rocky hurries us along onto the yacht.

We climb on-board, the other guests are somehow already here. As well as Rocky and Elijah, there is my dad, Mark Mason, Finn, and my Uncle Hank. With a stunned expression, Eric has also joined us. I'm wondering why on earth he wants to hang out with the men unless Rocky had plans to turn this yacht into some Mardi Gras celebration.

Anything is possible with him.

Standing beside them is also one of my long-time friends from London—Bentley James Woods.

"Well, look here, if it isn't my long-lost mate, Lex Edwards," Bentley speaks loud enough so everyone onboard can hear.

"BJ, where the hell have you been?"

"Not getting engaged and having babies. You've gone arse over tit for a bird? Who would have thought?"

"BJ?" Eric quizzes. "Do I dare assume?"

"Mate, the initials are an instant pick-up line, and my instincts tell me you ain't gonna get a kick out of the pussy on parade tonight," BJ insinuates.

"Oh, hell no, I'm all about the tallywacker!"

"Dude, you've been spending way too much time with Kate," Rocky mentions as he walks by.

BJ's face lights up. I know what he's thinking. "How is my good ole chum, Kate?"

I pinch the bridge of my nose, not wanting to delve into the history of Kate and BJ. Kate's personal life is exactly that—personal. But when she started screwing BJ, it became my business, much to my dismay. I'm almost certain Eric's texting Kate already wanting her version of this story which makes me think he has joined us to report back to the women.

I quickly greet everyone, Mark pulling my arm in for a moment.

"Listen here, boy. No touching anything that comes on this boat. I'm watching you," he warns.

"Not with a ten-foot sail, Mark."

Such terrible boat humor.

I head to the bar where BJ stands. The music has started, not so loud that I'm not able to hear him speak. He orders a round of shots, ignoring his signature drink—rum and Coke.

"It's been four months since our last pint at the Yorkshire Grey, and you're a changed man." BJ coaxes me to take the shot which the bartender places before us. We count down, and in unison, drink the nasty liquor threatening to compromise my judgment on anything which may take place tonight.

"Changed for the better. I may have spoken about her once." The shot is almost like swallowing acid, and I let out a loose cough.

"*Once?* When you got on the piss, you would always ramble on about her... Char... something or other. Bugger, this shot is strong. I can't even remember her name."

"Charlotte."

"That's right. So that's it, Lex Edwards is off the market? You were my wingman."

"It's best you don't bring that up here," I caution.

There are memories I want to erase, the endless nights of fucking random women. Bentley James Woods is trouble, trouble that I don't want near Charlotte. We all have a past, right? It's just that I did things I'm not proud of, and unfortunately, BJ was a witness to it all.

"Look, Lex, I won't fart arse around the topic. We had fun, I get it, buddy, you're gonna be a daddy. Just don't forget about little old London town. I assume you'll be moving to New York?"

"Yes. But quit the Mr. Nice Guy act. Who invited you here?" I question.

"Your lovely sister, Adriana. Relax, will ya, buddy ole pal? Adriana thought you should have a least one friend here. Look, I'm here to have fun, I won't go bringing up your colorful past with anyone, okay?"

He pats me on the back, switching the topic to business. Now, I'm in my element. BJ was born into a rich family like every other pretentious bastard in London. His family owns property all over Europe. However, BJ is heavily into the real estate game, which made him a fucking millionaire in his own right. Money can buy you a lot of things, but appar-

ently not class. He's known for being a womanizer—
marriage and babies definitely are not on his agenda.

Without warning, Rocky yells out, "It's showtime,"
interrupting our conversation.

Fuck.

Eight, and I mean *eight*, strippers come out to the
makeshift stage and start dancing. I can handle this, it's
pretty tame. Besides, it is just tits. Panties are in check, for
now. *I will be fine.* I have a beautiful woman waiting for me,
ready to marry me, but who right now is probably being
smothered by sweaty manwhores dressed up in uniforms.

Fuck, fuck, fuck.

I motion for Eric to come over. I need to ease my jealous
mind.

"Okay, so do all vajayjays look like that?" He points to
the girl dancing butt naked, his head tilting sideways
cringing at the sight.

"Her lips are out of proportion," Rocky interrupts.

"Lips can be out of proportion?" Eric gasps, clutching
his hand to his chest.

"Eric, what are the girls doing? Surely, Charlotte or
Kate would have texted you?"

"Uh, uh... Nikki banned all phones. 'What happens at
the party, stays at the party.' Her words, not mine."

Fucking bitch!

Finn and Elijah sit beside me with smirks on their faces.
I know enough to know that something is about to go down,
but I have absolutely no idea what.

"So, you enjoying yourself?" Finn asks.

"Cut the bullshit, Rodriguez, why are you two looking
at me like that?"

"No reason. Just want to make sure you are enjoying
your night," Elijah follows.

"Listen to you bunch of pussies sitting around yapping when you should be watching that." Rocky points to three of the girls practically having an orgy with each other. Eric's facial expressions are priceless. One minute he's intrigued, the next minute he cringes and covers his eyes.

"Guys, relax, have a drink." Finn hands us shots, and we all drank fast.

I remind myself to slow down. I'm getting married in a few hours. My mother will kill me if I turn up drunk at the altar.

We sit around drinking while the girls dance in front of us. They are not half bad, fake tits and all. Uncle Hank is having the time of his life, and I officially declare him a clone of Rocky. The similarities are uncanny, and they get along like a house on fire. Several times I catch them in the corner getting their own private lap dance.

"You shouldn't be looking at that," Finn growls, trying to act all tough. "You're marrying my best friend."

"When I look at you, I'm reminded that you've been with my Charlotte," I slur.

"You called a truce on that. Besides, I was fucking seventeen, I knew nothing about pussy."

"Please do not use that word when referring to my future wife."

"Get over it, Edwards. It was dark, so I didn't see anything, just fumbled around for stuff, you know."

"Are we still talking about this?"

"I guess we aren't. So, tell me, how did you finally get her to break up with Batman?"

"Who?"

"Julian."

Great, Rodriguez had to go there.

"My friend, let me tell you this... I didn't make her do

anything, he got what was coming to him. Let's be honest, he never had her to begin with."

"Nice play, Edwards. For a moment, I believed you. However, I know your type. Dominating and shit. Like that stupid book that Jen and Charlie always talk about... something gray, I don't know, but it's a load of shit."

"It ain't that bad." I chuckle.

"Yeah, well, I guess I can't complain. Jen's a wild one. Fuck, she'll kill me for saying that."

"Your secret is safe with me, plus it explains why you have four kids."

"I'll tell you now, Edwards, once that baby comes along, say goodbye to any pussy you're getting."

Is that the truth? It had crossed my mind, and I'm conscious when I'm fucking her, but luckily, I studied this in med school and know my dick can't get anywhere near the baby's head.

"Don't listen to him, son. You and Adriana never ruined—"

"Dad, I love you, but please, please, please do not mention your sex life *ever* again to me."

Amused, he places his arm around me. Is he drunk? Shit, I decide no more for me since I'm getting married in less than three hours. Control, Edwards, you're fucking used to this.

Rocky claps his hands and motions for me to take a seat on the chair sitting in the middle of the room. I get it, striptease. I can handle this. It won't be my first, but it will be my fucking last. The girls mean nothing, tits in my face do nothing for me unless they are Charlotte's.

Eric places a blindfold on me. He gets some sort of pleasure from doing it. *In your dreams, Eric.* It becomes pitch black, and I try to focus on the shuffling around me. The music starts, 'The Thong Song,' and I sense a body close to me and feel a slight brush against my leg. Her fingertips barely scrape along my thigh, stopping just below my dick. I want to laugh, it's a pathetic act to turn me on.

Her warm, minty breath lingers near my neck followed by her meager attempt to rub her pussy against my cock. In the distance amid the beat of the music, I hear snickering, and I swear I hear Eric say, "This is disturbingly wrong on so many levels."

The music is close to finishing, and as a finale, she grazes her teeth along the outside of my pants against my dick. Without control, I feel a slight stir. *What the fuck?* I wasn't turned on, but now I'm conscious of the familiar feeling, the tingling throb impossible to ignore.

No. No. No!

"Take it off! Lex has a boner," Eric shouts with such enthusiasm.

Slowly, Eric undoes the blindfold, and I almost fall off my chair, the shock of the granny standing in front of me in a purple corset and thong enough to make me dry heave.

Everyone in the room breaks out laughing, and I'm unable to find the hilarity in this, given the huge wood I'm sporting. Seriously, why the fuck am I turned on? And why the fuck won't it go down?

The granny winks at me, her false teeth visible. *Oh fuck, the false teeth grazed my dick.* I'm gonna beat the shit out of Rocky. I turn to look at him, his face cringing. Why the fuck is he so mortified? He booked the granny escort to strip for me!

I can hear BJ in the back shouting, "Get yer gums around my plums."

"That was hilarious!" Eric roars, slapping his hand on his leg, unable to contain himself. The granny walks away, saying goodbye to everyone, her saggy ass tainting my poor brain. There are just some things that can never be unseen. Rocky is still looking odd, something's wrong. He isn't taking as much pleasure in watching me suffer as I expected he would.

"What's wrong with you?" I ask him.

"Dude, did you spike my drink?"

"What? No, why?" My eyes divert to his pants where a huge boner is sticking out. "*Oh...*"

"Fuck, then what the hell?"

It clicks, and as I stand there, I watch the other men noticing they all have a similar expression. BJ is happily getting a dance from two girls in the corner, so his wood is expected, and the same goes for Uncle Hank. Elijah and Finn keep adjusting their pants, squirming uncomfortably and attempting to avoid eye contact with the girls who dance around them. My dad is at the bar with Mark, both of them with their legs crossed, having what looks like an incredibly uncomfortable conversation. Eric stands next to us as quiet as a church mouse, his face barely able to hide the mischievous grin, and I know, without a shadow of a doubt, he's the reason why there's enough blood pumping on this yacht to fuck all the women of America.

Viagra.

"What's up, guys? Or should I say, who's up?" Eric bursts out laughing.

"You're dead meat, Kennedy," Rocky threatens

"All I can say is thank God! For a second, I thought the granny gave me that boner." I breathe a sigh of relief, unable to contain myself for minutes on end.

I walk through the rose bush, cussing at the thorns scratching my arm until Rocky turns to look at me, warning me to shut the fuck up and quit wailing like a baby.

We left the yacht, boners and all, with an attempt to spy on the women.

Elijah declines giving us a lecture about trusting the woman you love. The rest head back to the hotel to get ready for the ceremony. We still have two hours, plenty of time to get in a sneak peek.

We run behind a tree and dart for the playhouse. The party is at Finn's place, and he knows exactly where we can get the best view.

"Okay, we made it. Open that window, and we'll be able to see," Finn whispers.

"Ow, what the fuck is this?"

Finn warns Rocky to keep his voice down.

"You're sitting on a teacup."

We remain still as we watch them on the porch, the three of us shocked by what we see. Apart from the dick paraphernalia overload, the waiters are dressed in nothing but a leather thong, collar, and mask. One of them even has a chain which Nikki is not afraid to use. I search for Charlotte, and she's laughing uncontrollably as Eric animatedly talks. No doubt it's about the granny story.

It doesn't take him long before he shouts that the entertainment's here.

Entertainment?

And then we hear the sirens go off, and low and behold, Eric yells, "Does anyone here have burning loins?"

Nikki cheers loud along with Kate as three bulked-up men appear in firefighter costumes. *Ridiculous.*

"Do not look at me, okay? They're not actual firefighters. In fact, I wouldn't be surprised if they are gay or some-thing," Finn mutters.

I pray to the gay God of Dorothy that they are.

Ginuwine's 'Pony' plays in the background as Nikki persuades Charlotte to sit on the chair. Now, I think she will be mortified, but she seems to enjoy it, her hands waving like she's in some nightclub as a single woman. *Fuck!*

"That's it, I'm going in," I announce.

"Relax, would you? She's not doing anything wrong." Rocky attempts to diffuse the situation, but I'm ready to stop the entire party.

We watch on, and this time Jen stands and starts dancing with one. He pulls his suspenders off, bumping and grinding with Jen. She places her hands against his chest, running them along his torso.

"That's it, I'm going in," Finn grits.

"Relax, would y*o*u? He's still in his boxers." Rocky rolls his eyes. How he remains calm is beyond me.

And so, we continue watching until the music changes. They don't get fully naked wearing only thongs. I relax. I mean, what's the big deal, right? Until Nikki rips off a thong and a dick flings out in all its glory. She shrieks in delight, rubbing herself up against him until Rocky yells, "That's it, I'm going in!"

We attempt to hold him back, but he's determined, that is until he pulls us up, and the three of us pummel through the door, falling flat on our faces. The music stops, and the women gasp, followed by laughter.

"*Nicola Joanne Romano*, you better have a damn good explanation for what I just saw!" Rocky is furious, his normal laid-back attitude a far cry from the jealous streak on parade.

Finn looks scared, probably from breaking the playhouse.

And me?

Charlotte gazes directly at me, giving me a wink, and just like that, I know I have nothing to worry about.

Nothing at all.

TWENTY-FIVE

CHARLIE

I run my fingers along the intricate beading and the fine lace designed so beautifully down the sleeves.

My eyes gaze at the soft pattern of the fabric, so delicate and unique, yet a timeless classic design. Adriana really outdid herself. She stands beside me waiting impatiently for some sort of reaction from me, but I'm literally speechless. My dream has somehow morphed into reality, and I need to pinch myself to make sure it is real.

Unfortunately, Adriana does that for me.

"Okay, you haven't spoken for like ten minutes. You hate it, don't you?" Adriana sulks.

I motion for her to be quiet as I continue to stare at the dress.

"She's having second thoughts, I know it," Nikki complains.

I ignore their comments, my eyes fixated on this exquisite creation. I'm not the type of girl who has her wedding all planned out since I was five, nor do I go to sleep at night imagining the dress I will wear. The truth be told, when Lex and I got married the night in The Hamptons, I was somewhat happy to skip the formalities. It isn't until five minutes ago that the desire to wear this perfect dress, walk down the aisle, and say the 'I do's' in front of everyone has consumed me.

I want it, I want him, and I want every woman in the world to know Lex belongs to me. Call me a selfish bitch, but when God hands you the smartest, most delicious and unbelievably caring guy in a box with a giant red bow, you say thank you and take it with the utmost appreciation. I should wrap a bow around his beautiful cock too. *Mmm, great thinking.*

Lost in my perfect little Lex's cock-bubble fantasy, I haven't noticed Nikki is still rambling on about me getting cold feet. Please, my feet are boiling hot. That's how sure I am.

"*Paciencia,* let her take in this moment."

The voice is oddly familiar, a voice I've heard a million times before. I turn around slowly to see my mom standing behind me with her hands cupped to her heart.

"Mom?" I break out of my moment and run into her arms, the overwhelming familiarity of the warmth of her embrace comforts me more than I thought I needed.

I don't dare to let go, holding onto her tight, not realizing the tears are streaming down my face. When I gather myself enough to pull away, I wipe my eyes able to see her clearly. My mother has always been a beautiful woman, and I have to admit as a child, I used to be jealous. I wanted to look exactly like her, and I remember scrutinizing the features I inherited from my dad.

My mother was born and bred in Cuba, a hot-tempered Latina as my dad would say. Her skin was nicely tanned all year round, and her frame naturally toned, but I would say that was because of her love of dancing, especially salsa. She has these mesmerizing hazel eyes, eyes her mother once told her were full of wisdom from the moment she was born. She hasn't aged one bit—her secret papaya and something-or-other concoction clearly isn't bullshit.

"*Mi corazon,*" she pauses, lifting my face to meet hers.

I'm met by her concerned stare, the one I witnessed several times when she would do readings for her friends.

"*Estas con niño?*" she asks, shocked.

Fuck, she asked if I'm with a *child*. I can't hide the pregnancy any longer, especially since everyone knows besides her.

"Mom, please, we need to talk, and before you ask, no, I'm not marrying Lex because I am pregnant."

She continues to examine me, taking her time to study my face. I know what she's doing, trying to get some sort of insight as to what the hell is really going on. I remember what she once told me, so I stand still, smiling and reminiscing about all the happy times Lex and I shared—the past, the present, and to the future. Like an open book, she reads me. I see the look of concern fade, and once again, I can see that slight sparkle in her eyes, along with the shimmer of hope.

Placing her hands on mine, she squeezes them, and so much of me just wants to curl up in her embrace all night long as I did numerous times in my childhood. It used to be because I was scared of the tales she told, the ones without a book in her hands. They were stories she spoke from her heart, like a glimpse into a diary, and finally, in this moment, I understand. They were her tales. I look into her eyes, and I can see an aura of gray surrounding her, a dark cloud hovering over her beautiful soul. My mind's on rewind, frantically trying to remember the stories. The dark angel, how he came in the night and took her to the woods where he stole what she was holding onto. Sometimes she called him the big bad wolf, depending on her mood.

But standing in front of her as an adult, I finally understand the ending of her story. Her heart had been stolen, by who, I have no idea.

"Mom... we need to talk. Who was he?"

"*Corazon*, we will. First, we have to celebrate your last night as a single woman."

As soon as she says the words, Nikki pulls us along onto the back porch of Finn and Jen's house. Colorful lanterns hang from the patio roof, above a long table decorated with hot pink flowers. But on closer inspection, they aren't flowers, they are penis-shaped candies, and as my eyes dart to the tableware, I notice penis-shaped straws which sit in the glasses alongside penis-shaped plates. *Where on earth did they get this from?* I look above and hanging from the beams of the patio is a penis-shaped piñata. *Oh, dear Lord.*

"Um, Nik, there's a hell of a lot of dick in here," I complain.

"Woman, please, there can *never* be enough dick in here, at least for now. Here's to the best bachelorette party *ever*." She grabs her penis straw and takes a sip of her Long Island iced tea. "Ooh... nice."

We laugh, and I make my way over to the buffet table. It had been teasing me since I arrived, more so than the penis-shaped candy. The candy is strangely satisfying, and I can't help it if I have more than one in my mouth.

"Effing hell, there's corndogs. I tell you what, if there's one thing you Yanks do well, it's corndogs." Kate piles them onto her plate and starts talking about some American football player she is obsessed with when a group of men standing at the door catches my attention.

"Kate," I whisper.

"Like you need to google the words 'locker room pecker' because I tell you what, Charlie, Eric knows where to find the..."

"Kate!" I interrupt.

"What?"

I'm trying not to be conspicuous as I tilt my head to make Kate look at the men.

She bursts out laughing like a private joke plays in her head. "Oh, dear... Nikki went all out."

"Why are they dressed like that?"

The three men are dressed only in black leather thongs, dog collars, and leather masks. *Please don't tell me they are doms.* It's fun reading about them in erotic fiction, but standing only a few feet away from us makes me extremely uncomfortable.

Nikki is aware I'm pregnant, and obviously, I can't participate in their naughty games unless they are for her. *Horny bitch.* I wonder if Rocky gave her that hall pass they always joke about.

"Nikki! Your subs are here," Kate yells.

Nikki abruptly turns, her game face in place as she walks over, and without saying a word, she pulls the chain, and the subs gets down on all fours. *It so explains why she's wearing black patent 8-inch pumps.* So, I'm wrong, they are subs, and Nikki clearly is the dom and loving every second of it. Kate doesn't hesitate either, mouthing off to one of them who just stands there tolerating her abuse.

I, on the other hand, am worried about the other guests. I rush over to where the older ladies stand chatting, hoping they will understand the hilarity of the situation. "Mom, Debbie, Emily, I'm *so* sorry."

"Sweetie, it's just a bit of fun. The one on the right looks like he may need a good spanking." Emily giggles as she drinks her cocktail, her constant swaying hinting she's just a teeny bit intoxicated.

Okay, yes, I'm jealous. It sucks I can't drink.

I realize as I stand among the three of them that I haven't really introduced Debbie and my mom. They have been chatting quite animatedly, so I assumed they know of each other. This is awkward. How do you introduce two people who have shared a lover?

OMG, did I just refer to my dad as a lover? Stop Charlie, just stop.

"Mom, this is Debbie. Have you guys met?"

"No, but I know you are Mark's girlfriend," Mom clarifies with a pinched expression.

Is there a hint of jealousy in that remark?

"Mom, please..."

"Hi, Maria, it's nice to finally meet you." Debbie smiles.

"Aren't you going to tell me Mark has said many wonderful things about me?" Mom asks, laced in sarcasm.

This is terrible. "Mom, are you jealous? Seriously, because you are banging a hot thirty-year-old model from Brazil. Need I say more?"

Debbie and my mom laugh, smoothing over any differences.

Mom holds out her hand which Debbie squeezes. They begin chatting about doms and subs, so I decide to leave because I swear they are heading down to a conversation about my dad and his bedroom skills. *Oh, I'm seriously ready to hurl.*

I'm having such a great time chatting with Emma and Kate until it dawns on me as I look around the room that my sister is missing.

"Hey, Adriana, how come my sister isn't here?" I ask, disappointed.

"She's in Ghana doing a trek of some sort and was unable to get out of it. I'm sorry, Charlie."

Typical Melanie. She lives such an adventurous life, and to be honest, I don't expect anything different. Maybe a phone call now and then wouldn't hurt considering I haven't seen her in four years, since the last time she was on American soil.

The night is off to a great start.

We dance, sing karaoke, laugh, and enjoy each other's company.

The subs serve us, and I have to admit it's kind of *hot*. I mean, I'm not into that shit, but hell, who am I to criticize a cut-up man serving me on command? Yes, I know, maybe once or twice during the night I demand he do things. Nothing naughty because God forbid if Lex finds out. I wouldn't be surprised if he installed video surveillance in here.

Eric makes his grand entrance two hours later, his presence drawing attention as he yells, "I feel right at home." Enthusiastically, he grabs a drink and sucks on the straw before saying something about a small dick to Kate. I rush over to his side, wrapping my arms around him. It isn't a party without Eric—you don't need entertainment if you have him and his non-filtered mouth.

Adriana takes over the microphone, slurring her words as she says something about the piñata. Jen brings out a stick in the shape of a penis and explains how we play.

"So basically, we just beat the cock with a cock?" I question.

"I'm officially in party heaven! Charlie, I saw a vag... like a weird, flappy-looking vag." He cringes, explaining what went on at Lex's bachelor party. I listen attentively until Kate whacks me in the face with the cock stick.

"Did you just turkey slap me, Kate?"

"Please, like that's the first time you've ever been slapped around the chops with a tallywacker." She chuckles.

"Nothing like a good old turkey slap," Emily pipes in.

"Mom! I'm not letting you drink like ever!" Adriana cries.

"Adriana, you have to accept the fact that your dad and I are very sexually active. In fact, just the other day we bought this—"

"*Lalalala...*" Adriana covers her ears.

No doubt Lex would have pulled the plug on this conversation a long time ago. I let the two of them get back to their family woes as I have a more important task ahead of me.

I whack the piñata as hard as I can, but much to my disappointment, I barely make a dent in it. Eric is up next. He whacks the piñata like a maniac until it breaks, and little white fish-shaped candy flies out. Nikki, Jen, and Adriana, in their intoxicated state, fling themselves onto the floor, fighting over the candy.

Nikki yells out, "I can swallow the most, have you seen my husband."

I cringe. I have seen her husband. *Gross.*

"Okay, so I know you can't drink, *but* I know what will cheer you up," Eric tells me.

"What's that?"

"I spiked all the ladies' drinks with Viagra," he admits with a proud grin.

"*E!* What? Is there Viagra for women?"

"Yes, kinda... well, sorta."

"Like everyone?"

"Well, not you, silly, but yes, everyone else."

"Emma?"

"Yep."

"Emily, Debbie, and my mom?"

"Ahh, yep."

He holds out his palm, and I high-fived him before he runs back to the dance floor and joins them like the crazed lunatic he is and wrestles the microphone off Adriana who is doing a rendition of 'Islands in the Stream.'

Eric announces the entertainment is here, and uncomfortably, I'm forced to be the center of attention. I'm not surprised one bit when strippers strut their goods around me, these bulked-up, hot guys dressed in their fire gear. Holy shit, they are hot, not as hot as my man, but I swear I can see Eric's drool hit the floor.

Nikki is bouncing around like she has ants in her pants. Emma's long gone, and would often yell out comments like "Fuck you, Tate, and your mafia whores!"

Gosh, I so need to find out what the hell that's about.

Emily is whistling really loud, enjoying herself. Debbie and my mom grab champagne, each drinking straight from the bottle.

At this point, I want to grab my confiscated phone to text Lex and say I had nothing to do with this, but knowing Rocky, there's probably pussy galore parading in front of them right now, so I don't feel so bad.

Eric is in gay-man heaven, groping one of the stripper's butts, who surprisingly doesn't flinch at Eric's touch. Okay, so that kind of kills my buzz—*they are gay*. Nikki and Jen don't seem to care, though, tugging on the G-strings trying to peek inside. They soon grow impatient, and the strippers go the full monty.

So, here's the thing—a naked man is standing in front of you, and much like the giant elephant in the room, you can't help but look at it. Times that by three, and I feel like I'm in a zoo. I swear they are looking at me, the penises, that is. Is that even a word? Plural penis? *God, I feel so dirty*.

Nikki is rubbing her body up against the blond stripper, his semi-hard cock impossible to ignore. A loud bang forces me to look away. *What the hell?* Rocky has fallen to the ground in the backyard outside the pink playhouse, and the shadows of what look like others disappear into the dark. He yells her name, and she laughs at a very angry Rocky. I know somewhere Lex is standing watching us. I don't know where, but I feel him. His stare is on me, and I know he won't show his face, but if Rocky is here, then so is he. I smile because I wish that if he is looking at me right now, he can sense how much I miss him and how the next two hours seem like a lifetime away.

Behind the big oak tree, I see him, his silhouette and gaze permanently fixated on mine. I wink and watch as the silhouette of my beautiful man relaxes.

"I wish I had what you have." Emma sighs as she stands beside me, looking at the stars.

"What's going on, Em? Tate giving you a hard time?"

"Nope, the opposite. He doesn't care about anything. He has his other skanks to worry about."

I place my arm around her, trying to ease her pain. *Men suck.*

"I'm sorry, Em, I didn't realize Tate was like that. Plenty more cock in the coop."

She giggles. "Did Eric teach you that?"

"Who else?"

"You nervous?" Adriana asks as she fixes my train.

I'm reeling from the fact that in less than twenty minutes, I will see Lex again.

"Not a single bit." I beam.

Adriana announces she is finally done. Standing back, she watches me. Barely above

a whisper, all I hear is, "There are no words," as I watch her wipe a falling tear from her face.

"Mascara, Adriana," I gently scold.

She laughs, dabbing her eyes with a tissue. "It's showtime."

According to Jen, the girls planned a simple wedding. No bridesmaids or groomsmen and a simple, short ceremony. The only thing I have to do, which I couldn't have wanted any more at this moment, is to walk down the aisle with my dad.

My dad holds out his arm as he whispers, "Charlie, you sure about this?"

Without taking a single breath, I respond, "Never been so sure of anything in my entire life, Dad."

He pats my arm, a slight build-up of tears in his eyes. *I'm so ready.* The violin begins to play 'Can't Help Falling in Love,' the sweet melody prickling my skin with goosebumps.

On the cliff top, a place we had called ours, a new memory is about to begin. As I turn the corner, my eyes are immediately drawn to him. His emerald green eyes shine so bright, brighter than any light I have seen, and so without any hesitation, both my heart and feet walk toward him, finding their way to a place called *home*.

TWENTY-SIX

LEX

In life, we strive for perfection. Whether it's emotional, physical, or material, and time and time again, we are reminded perfection is only momentary. Our natural instinct is to crave something greater, explore our want, our thirst, or our desire to find something superior.

As humans, our brains are programmed to think this way, but tonight at the stroke of midnight, my brain has been reprogrammed because perfection is walking down the aisle toward me like an angel of purity in all its beauty.

Charlotte's smile radiates. A few more steps and she will finally be beside me.

Mark kisses her cheek before handing her to me and then, as I expected, as I craved, *the jolt*. Electrifying every single part of me, a constant reminder only *she* has the power to make me feel this.

I know without a single doubt she feels it too, and I know I shouldn't have done it, but I lean in and kiss her lips, caught up in the moment.

"Charlotte, you are beautiful," I whisper softly against her lips.

The celebrant interrupts us, and there under the pale moonlight, three minutes past midnight, I begin to say the words.

"Charlotte Olivia Mason, I promise to cherish you and love you unconditionally for the rest of our lives. I vow every breath I take and every beat of my heart belongs to you and only you."

I slide the ring on her finger, once again kissing it before it's her turn to speak.

"Alexander Matthew Edwards, I take you to be my constant friend and my loving partner. I promise to be faithful and devote myself to you, only you and our marriage. I give you my hand, my heart, and the air I breathe for as long as we both shall live."

Charlotte slides the ring on my finger, *again*.

I don't wait for the words, I kiss her. Five hours apart feels like a lifetime, and now in front of our family and friends, we are officially Mr. and Mrs. Edwards. There's a roar, whistling, and clapping amongst our nearest and dearest. A soft violin piece plays in the background, and without warning, a burst of thunder rolls in on the horizon, but Charlotte doesn't flinch one bit. She used to be terrified of the sound, never giving me an explanation as to why.

"How come the thunder didn't scare you?"

"Because I have you to protect me." She smiles, placing her arms around me as we continue to lose ourselves in each other, our lips unable to unlock until Rocky tells us to stop because it's bordering on pornographic.

We pull away as the music starts, and right here, on our spot, we dance to what was once our song.

"I love this song." Charlotte rests her head on my shoulder.

"I know... I wasn't sure if—"

She interrupts me by placing her finger against my lips. "I don't care what happens after. No one can ever erase the moment in time when we sat side by side playing the piano and singing. Whatever the hell happened after, I don't care. That moment stuck with me, that song stuck with me, and, Lex, it is our song. It's not tainted, and thank you for choosing it today for us to dance to."

Charlotte is eerily calm, a perfect calm, and I feel my body relax, allowing myself to enjoy this dance with my wife.

The girls planned a simple ceremony followed by an even simpler reception here on the cliff top. Our loved ones surround us as they talk to each other and dance beside us. It's to be followed by cutting the cake, my speech, then straight to our honeymoon where I get to enjoy Charlotte for a month. A month of fucking my beautiful wife all day, all night. *Now that is heaven.*

During our dance, people come to congratulate us, but I manage to hold onto Charlotte tight because my fucking boner is standing out like an eyesore. Eric, the fucking idiot, is obviously amused by it all. I have the right mind to kidnap him and have women rub their pussies all up in his face just to teach him a lesson. The throbbing pain is unbearable, and I need a release, but how awful it would be if I was caught jerking off at my own wedding? For some reason, the others don't have a problem. In fact, I can't spot the others apart from Rocky, who looks pretty smug. I suspect he's had his release already.

I motion for Charlotte to come with me. Without asking a thousand questions, she lifts the hem of her dress in her hands so it won't get caught on the ground. With her hand in mine, I take her down the path, but along the way, we hear rustling in the bushes followed by a giggle. I stop and place my fingers against my mouth, motioning for Charlotte to be quiet, so we could hear who it is.

"Andrew... right there..."

Oh, fuck, no!

I grab Charlotte's arms with force as she covers her mouth unable to contain her laughter, knowing all too well the idea of my parents having sex is the biggest nightmare of all time. Yet, somehow, the general is so pumped with Viagra that his saluting is relentless. As I continue to lead her down the path, I find the isolated cave and pull her inside.

Against the rock wall, I smash my lips against hers.

"Lex, we have everyone waiting..."

"Don't worry about them, Rocky has it covered. I need to fuck you now as my wife. I promise to make sweet love to you when we get back to our hotel room, but right now I need to fuck you."

There is no objection as I lift her dress and plunge into her, the sound of her small cry echoing in the cave.

"I saw you with the firefighters, Charlotte. It made me so fucking jealous. This, the way I'm fucking you, is to show you that you belong to me. *Obsessed together forever*, we said the words. I am obsessed with you, every move you make, every stare at another man, I'm watching."

She doesn't say a word, only pulling me in tighter and begging for more.

"And did you see me touch the firefighter? Did you see me look at his cock?" she asks, teasingly.

Oh, she fucking knows what she's doing, allowing my jealousy to consume my raging testosterone. I grab her ass, gripping it so tightly knowing my nails are digging into her. I can't get in deep enough. *Calm the fuck down, don't hurt the baby.*

"Yes, I did, and I wanted to rip you off that stage. You are *my* wife, *my wife*..."

My words warn her in exactly five seconds I will come undone.

It rips through me brutally and with so much force, my legs begin to shake, struggling to keep my balance and gripping onto the wall for support.

Around me, she clenches while whimpering. My entire body jerks forward, sensitive to the slightest touch. We stand for a moment, catching our breaths until Charlotte admits she knows about the Viagra.

"Charlotte, I can guarantee even without it, I would have fucked you into oblivion. Oh, and have I already told you that you look beautiful tonight?"

"Yes, but only like a hundred times. I may need to hear it again to be sure."

"Hmm... I married such a smart mouth. Charlotte Edwards, you look beautiful."

"That's better, and you, my husband, look like sex on a stick. I'm sorry, you know you look handsome, but this tux is making me insanely horny. There, I said it. Inappropriate for wedding speak, but hey, that's me."

"I think our lack of consideration for the sacred wedding celebration was displayed minutes ago, and I'm more than happy to remind you *again,* should you need it."

"Now, that's the Viagra talking." She giggles.

We head back, and as we resume activities, Rocky is quick to pull me aside. He sniffs my collar like some fucking weirdo.

"Dude, I said ten minutes. What took you so long to

blow?" Rocky complains, narrowing his eyes. "I had to do a rendition of Chicago *and* Barry Manilow."

"And the crowds are still here?"

"Dude, you smell like pussy."

I'm ready to smack him in the face when Charlotte drags her mother over to meet me. She clears her throat, and Maria waits patiently for my full attention.

"I know you've met before under different circumstances, but Mom, I want to introduce you to my husband, Lex Edwards, *and* before you start sending him bad karma or shit like that, remember he is the father of our baby as well. So there," she says matter-of-factly.

To be polite, I lean over to kiss her hello, but exactly like the first time we met, she places her hand over my cheek. I'm trying my best to be respectful, but the resentment toward her is hard to ignore for she is the one who spun her lies about Charlotte moving on. If it weren't for that, who knows what might have been? Maybe I wouldn't have wasted eight years wandering the earth like a nomad.

Certain she senses my bitterness toward her, she pulls her hand away immediately. Her face looks disheartened, and she must know she fucked with the universe big time by feeding lies to Adriana and me.

Charlotte is called by Kate.

Before leaving, she whispers, "Let it go."

How can I let it go? This woman fucking angers me.

"Cometemos errores cuando estamos tratando de proteger a la persona que amamos. We make mistakes when we are trying to protect the person we love."

"We do make mistakes when we are trying to protect the ones we love. I should know that since I spent eight years trying to fix mine," I answer bitterly.

"Then, you must understand how I feel."

"I'm trying. That's the best I can do."

"I see things, Alex..."

"Lex," I correct her.

"You are still Alex in her eyes. You may think you have this new persona, but Charlotte still sees you as Alex. The one she fell in love with. This 'Lex' you speak of, he is only capable of hurting her. He became a man lost in a world of deceit and self-destruction. Perhaps you need to look at yourself, find who you really are," she warns.

"You think I would hurt Charlotte again?"

Who the fuck does this woman think she is! I don't give one goddamn fuck she is Charlotte's mother.

"I don't think, I know," she tells me.

"Well, you're wrong, okay?"

"This gift has been passed down from my great aunt. Its force is strong and unbeknown to me at times. The vision is there, blinding me and warning me to inform those in its path."

"I don't believe your mumbo jumbo, Maria. I don't care that you're Charlotte's mother. Sounds to me like you're jealous of your daughter because she found something you haven't. Don't poison her mind. Leave her alone and let her make her own decisions."

Staring blankly into my eyes, her gaze wanders to where Charlotte is standing with Kate. Charlotte is laughing, happy, and content. Nothing, and I mean nothing, will ever change that again.

"I'm not here to poison her mind. Her path has been decided upon. You, on the other hand, still have the chance to change yours." They are her parting words before she walks away.

Unable to mask my anger toward her, I'm unaware

Mark is now standing beside me. He places his hand on my shoulder, patting it.

"Don't listen to her nonsense. Nothing's decided, what stuff like that does is implant a vicious seed in your head. I've had years of hearing that garbage, I should know," he rambles.

It's too late. Her words are seeping into my conscience, slowly planting a seed. Am I capable of hurting Charlotte again? How? I know I can't exist without her, so the thought of pushing her away inflicts pain upon myself.

This isn't what I want to be thinking about on my wedding day. Shake it off, Lex, jealousy is an ugly trait, and that's all this is.

I scan the area looking for Charlotte, needing her touch to reassure me that it's just us for a lifetime. She's standing beside BJ and Eric, laughing and carefree as BJ drapes his arm over her. He's a sly bastard, and without even thinking, I move toward them.

"Mate, why haven't you introduced me to your lovely Mrs. yet? I had to hunt her down myself, and I tell ya what, this one sure is a keeper." He laughs, holding onto her tight, *too tight for my liking*.

"BJ, you're only saying that because I gave you a run for your money," Charlotte chastises.

"You're a top bird, Charlie. Now tell me where I can find my good friend, Kate. She did a runner on me."

"How about you keep your dick in your pants and away from Kate?"

I burst out laughing, pulling Charlotte's arm toward me. BJ lets go, and with a pout, continues to ramble on about Kate being a cold-blooded bitch until Charlotte puts him in his place. Another reason why I love her.

"Kate's never mentioned you, BJ. Surely, if she had, I'd

know your length and girth by now." Eric smirks.

"Eric..." I warn.

Our conversation is interrupted as Adriana pulls me aside. "Are you ready?"

I nod, it's speech time. I don't have to write anything down on a piece of paper. I'm going to wing it, that's how much confidence is behind the words I'm about to speak. As Adriana calls for attention from the crowd, my dad whispers something in her ear, forcing her to look at me, asking me to hold on.

My dad has prepared a speech, much to my discontent.

"I'm a man of few words, but I hope the words I say carry depth. This day was inevitable for anyone who knew Charlie and Lex nine years ago." His gaze shifts to my mother as she smiles reassuringly, and he continues, "Charlie, you came into my life as a little girl and became my daughter's best friend. Life threw some curveballs, but here you are, standing as the strongest woman I'm honored to know. You became my daughter twenty years ago, and only today have we celebrated this milestone."

Charlotte holds onto my mother, clutching a tissue, the two of them wiping their faces. My dad pauses, his voice quivering slightly.

"Lex, I know we have our differences. I know we don't see eye to eye on almost anything, but, son, *you have done me proud.* Every day I relish in the man you have become. You fought me tooth and nail to follow your dreams, not mine, and I stand here today thanking you for challenging me and for making me see that you are your own man. I love you, admire you, and thank you for making me a better person."

Damn, he hit that fucking spot I've been avoiding, the weakest part of me which yearns to be accepted by my father. He walks toward me and hugs me tight. I don't let go for what seems like minutes. Rocky's voice rings in my head about smelling like pussy which makes me pull away faster than the speed of light.

Everyone claps, and now I feel slightly nervous, scared I will fuck up, and she won't believe me. *C'mon, Lex, that's impossible.*

"For those of you who wonder why I call Charlotte by her full name, it's because many moons ago I told her I wasn't like anyone else. I was a man who saw this beautiful woman and wasn't going to stop until she was mine. Others tried, and they have failed, and even after all the mistakes I have made, I know that when Charlotte walks into your life you can never look back."

Reaching out for her hands, she places them in mine as I allow the warmth to spread throughout me.

"Charlotte Olivia Edwards, you are my wife, my reason for taking my breath every morning. I ache when I'm away from you, and I ache when I am near you. I see the light, and you are there, making it shine. I am complete now that I have you, and soon, you will give me the greatest gift a man can ask for.

"I promised to be your husband, but as I stand here, I promise to also be a father. I promise to cherish and love our children like I have been shown by my parents. Once upon a time, I was dying a slow death, and I will forever be in your debt for making me come alive again. Charlotte, my beautiful wife, I love you for not only who you are but for who I am when I am with you."

As a tear falls so gracefully onto her lips, she mouths 'I love you' before kissing me softly and sealing the deal.

We are officially one.

In front of everyone who matters the most to *us*.

TWENTY-SEVEN

CHARLIE

I sit still while staring out the window with my hand entwined in his.

There's nothing but light shining over the clouds. We're heading to London after spending a month traveling through Europe. Nikki and Tate were gracious enough to let me go, especially knowing it won't be long before I can't travel.

I've never been so relaxed yet excited in my whole life. The worldwide destinations I got to experience, tropical islands to historic architecture, and since I was constantly reminded it was our honeymoon, the sex never stopped. Lex was insatiable, and here I thought I was bad. There were days when I was sore, and those were the days we ventured out of the room to sightsee, but it only ended up with us back in the room for more hot sex.

As the plane touches down at Heathrow, I can't contain my excitement. It's my first time here, and all I can think about is meeting the royals. *Yeah, like that is going to happen, but everyone knows the Queen of England, don't they?* Lex, on the other hand, looks tense. I offered to give him a blow job on the plane, but he kindly refused, much to my disappointment.

I take out my phone, snapping photographs of Big Ben as we drive past. It reminds of the Griswolds' futile attempt to exit the giant roundabout which, in turn, makes me laugh out loud. Eric is so jealous and gave me a long list of places he wanted me to visit, including some hot gay club. Why am I not surprised?

It doesn't take us long before the driver pulls up at Lex's apartment. He rarely speaks about his home, almost avoiding the topic every time. I was shocked when he agreed for us to come to London, but according to Kate, he needs to tie up some loose ends in the London office before finally making the move to New York. I'm annoyed he failed to mention that to me resulting in a mini-fight followed by some hot sex on the beach in the Greek Islands.

We ride the elevator up until it reaches the penthouse. He keeps his hands to himself, something is definitely wrong and Lord almighty, he is as stubborn as a mule.

As the doors open, my jaw drops.

"Holy shit, this is your digs?"

It's almost four times the size of mine, and now it makes sense why Lex complains about us buying something bigger in Manhattan.

The design of the apartment is an open-plan loft with dark wood floors, and the furniture is mainly white. It doesn't look lived in or very homey, to be brutally honest. The building itself is modern compared to some of the older structures around it.

"So, are we just going to stand here, or will you take me to your room and fuck me? Because I'm still annoyed you didn't accept my blow job which, might I add, was served to you with no strings attached," I point out.

He relaxes, and that beautiful smile as always melts my insides. Placing his arms underneath my legs, he lifts me, carrying me up the stairs.

"Our room, Charlotte, not mine."

Lex opens the door to the bedroom, and before us is a king-size bed. I'm giddy at the thought. It's like seeing your boyfriend's bedroom for the first time, except we aren't in high school, and he is my husband.

He places me gently on the bed. No doubt if I weren't pregnant, he would have just thrown me. I wait eagerly as he removes his jacket, throwing it over the chair before climbing onto the bed and over me.

"Do you know how many times I've imagined you in this bed?"

"Probably the same amount of times I've imagined being in this bed."

"I'm warning you now, I won't last long. Expect me to fuck you, and fuck you hard, and then I'll make sweet love to you all night long," he whispers while nibbling at my ear.

"Well, I..." He forces his lips onto me, his body pressing against mine, but somehow, he manages not to put pressure on my stomach.

"I hope you're not attached to this blouse."

I'm just about to speak when he rips it open, the buttons tearing apart as he buries himself in my breasts. My body caves, pushing out the image of Eric having a heart attack because the blouse was vintage Valentino.

His hands slide up my skirt, gripping my ass so tight making me squeal with delight. I try to wiggle out of my panties, but Lex has other ideas, pushing them aside and ramming his cock into me.

Whoa, steady on.

Lex is like a magician because I didn't hear the buckle of his pants. Sliding himself in and out, he pushes in deeper, his mouth sucking hard on the base of my neck until he runs his tongue along my collarbone, and I'm coming undone.

"Good morning, Mrs. Edwards."

I can barely open my eyes, the jetlag has worn me down as well as the constant lovemaking. I turn to look at the clock, seven-fifteen. Where the hell does Lex get all his stamina from? That will make it what, New York time, and count back five.

"It's two in the morning in New York if that's what you're trying to figure out."

"You look very handsome... edible..."

I feel the pool form between my legs. God, my husband is so yummy in his perfectly styled outfit. He sits on the edge of the bed, and I can't help but admire his vest with his gray tie tucked beneath it. Fuck me sideways, backward, and forward. This man knows how to dress, and vest porn is where it's at.

"Did you know a suit to women is like lingerie to men," I tease.

He yanks the bed sheet off, admiring my naked body.

"Like a naked body to men," he leans forward, sucking on my nipple. I squeal with delight because the sensation is so much more intense while I'm pregnant. My breasts are almost double in size, and I am finally showing enough to field a stranger's question as to whether I'm pregnant or just ate a burrito.

"But I can't be late," he tells me, pressing his lips tight. "Rain check?"

I pout. I know he has to work, and that it has been eating him up while we were traveling. "Go, I'll see you tonight."

"How about you drop by the office before lunch, then we can grab something to eat?"

With a smile, I nod, still excited by the fact I'm in London. There's so much I want to do today as long as I can muster up the energy to get out of bed.

"I need to go. I'll leave you alone to snoop around. If you're looking for my secret porn stash, it's on my computer. The password is Charlotte69Edwards."

"Are you kidding?"

"Would I kid about you and 69s?"

He kisses me goodbye and heads out the door. I linger in bed for a while, checking my phone before my stomach rumbles, and the kitchen calls. I take my time looking at his books, his wardrobe, running my hands along his perfectly pressed suits before I make my way to his computer. Okay, so I'm curious. *I mean, who wouldn't be, right?*

I log on, and in the Documents area of File Explorer, I find the folder titled 'Private.' I roll my eyes—how creative—but as I search, I'm not prepared for the folders to be categorized, so I send him a text.

ME

> I never figured you to be so anal about anal.

I laugh at myself. Where is Eric when I need him? He'd have totally enjoyed that comment.

Having fun, I see. I'm very anal over your anal.

Oh damn. Your own fault, Charlie. I decide to shut down and head out. There will always be porn. I'm dressed in jeans, knee-high boots, and my fancy jacket I bought back home. My hair is let out loose, and the weather has cooled overnight. New York is cold, but London enters the freezing-my- tits-off zone.

I make my way over to Lex's office and arrive at the top floor. All at once, his staff runs in circles. They are mostly blonde, a few redheads, and ebony hair, but not one brunette—*what a control freak.* I walk up to the desk, and a young twenty-something-year-old greets me. Quite possibly, everything about her is fake from tits to nails. I smile, asking to see Lex.

"I'm sorry, ma'am, do you have an appointment?"

"Firstly, I'm probably only a few years older than you, sweetheart, so how about we skip the 'ma'am' crap? And second, Lex is my husband."

"Excuse me?"

"I think you heard me, now will you call him or..."

I hear my name being called. It's Kate. As soon as I see her, my face lights up. She runs over and hugs me tight.

"Sod off, Christine, you've been warned about being rude to clients before."

"She isn't a client, she claims to be Mr. Edwards' wife." She laughs.

"You're damn right she is. Come with me, Charlie. The stupid, stuck up little..." she mutters to herself. "I'm so happy you're here. Eric is running around like a headless chicken without you. He texted me like five minutes ago reminding me to remind you to buy some fancy hand towels to go with his tea towel?"

"Gross. He said he wanted to have a royal hand towel by his bed in case of emergency."

"Oh, my days, so he can squirt on the queen's face?"

We laugh together as Kate holds the door open for me. Lex sits at his desk. Looking up to see me, he smiles. Someone is on speakerphone, but he motions for me to come in. Kate leaves me, and I stand by his desk unsure of what to do. He pulls me into his lap, and I sit there, uncomfortable, listening to some guy trying to convince Lex it's a breach of contract if he were to pull out of a deal.

Lex merely states he isn't pulling out, but is only able to complete the work from New York. I grab his Post-it note and scribble some legal advice and his rights. I pass it to him, and he reads it out loud. The jerk on the other end let's out a loud sigh before agreeing with Lex. In a polite way, Lex tells him to go fuck himself before hanging up on him.

"Are you sure you don't want to head up my legal division?"

"We've had this conversation, and besides, I don't want to report to you. I don't want to report to anyone, hence, why we own the practice. But, if necessary, I can call you *boss* in the bedroom?"

He kisses me deeply. The few hours we were apart sucked balls big time. Speaking of which, I can suck his balls right now. *Charlie, you horny bitch, seriously just chill.*

"I can't do lunch. If I work through, I can be home around six? I need to get some proposals drawn up."

"Fine, fine, but if I max out my credit card at Harrods, it's all your fault."

Reaching into his pocket, he pulls out his wallet and hands me his Amex.

"I've been meaning to give you this."

"What the hell for?"

"To use. What do you mean what for?" he asks, annoyed.

"Well, for starters... I can take care of myself. I don't need your Amex."

"Why do you have to be so stubborn all the time? Take the fucking card. I feel like a broken record. My money is *our* money now."

"Yeah, and I sound like a CD with a scratch. I'm not ready to accept that. Give me time."

He tries to do that intimidating glare he does, the one that makes his staff hide in their cubicles but I'm not having a bit of it. I am a goddamn lawyer, and I know he hates the fact I am trained to ignore this type of intimidation.

After the 'showdown,' he manages to stop being a prick and kisses me goodbye. He promises to meet me back at home after I enjoy London and manage to hunt down Eric's royal hand towel, which will now be referred to as the royal chicken rag.

I'm barely able to press the button on the elevator as my hands are so full of shopping bags. Yes, I became some sort of shopaholic, buying beyond-adorable British baby attire.

As the doors open, I drag my tired feet through the living room, dumping the bags on the sofa. I'm exhausted, the jetlag still tiring me as well as this shitty weather. Pulling my scarf off, I walk toward the bedroom until the sight before me stops me dead in my tracks. The blood drains from my face, my heart beats erratic as I drop my scarf trying to make sense of what I'm seeing.

"Sorry, sweetheart, thought you were Lex."

The woman lets out a disturbing laugh, and yet I'm still tongue-tied, trying to think of something to say. *C'mon,*

Charlie, wittiness and comebacks are your specialty. Yeah, maybe not when a woman is practically naked and hand-cuffed to your husband's, no, *our* bed!

"How did you get in here, and who the hell are you?"

Interrogation, okay, let's start with that.

"My name is Roxy, and I have a key. Lex gave it to me years ago during the time when he couldn't keep his hands off me," she answers calmly.

"Past tense. What makes you think you can still barge in here and expect the same?" I try my best to control my tone, but this is personal, and I'm not in the courtroom defending a client. My feelings are hurt. Lex is a fucking jerk, and any sense of rational thoughts go right out the window along with any pride I have.

"Sweetie, Lex likes his regulars. You must know that, just like the way he likes his sex. Rough and dominating. He likes his women to take him all in. He likes it when we let out a cry as he slams his cock into us, the way he takes you from behind, face down, arse up. He likes to finger our arse, not one but sometimes two..."

What the hell am I listening to!

The tears are on the verge of slipping, but I put on my poker face. *Don't let this bitch get to you.*

"If you think this bothers me, then your loss. It's the past, Roxy. We all have one..."

"No one can tame Lex, let that be a lesson learned."

"Well, I'm the one wearing the wedding ring, doll face," I struggle to say, hoping my nerves won't betray me.

The sound of footsteps echo throughout the hall, and I turn around to see BJ inside.

"Roxy, what the fuck are you doing here? Take that beastly fanny of yours and leave them the fuck alone."

"BJ, what a pleasant surprise. You want to do a tag team

again?" With a shrill in her voice, she licks her lips. It's impossible to ignore her fucking vagina as she purposely spreads her legs.

"Belt up, Roxy. You're not welcome here anymore. Now get your shit and leave before I drag you out of here," he warns.

He walks over and hugs me as I'm barely able to hold it together. I allow myself to be comforted by him because my mind's going crazy with so many questions needing an answer. We are interrupted as Lex runs through the door, out of breath, his eyes darting between Roxy and BJ, then a look of sorrow as he focuses on me.

"Roxy, how the fuck did you get in here?"

"Lex, baby, remember... you gave me this key? The night both you and BJ had your cocks in my pussy."

This is too much.

I pull myself out of BJ's embrace and head out of the room.

I can't cope.

The sordid image is now ingrained in my brain, and I want to erase it, but no, I can't fucking drink!

"Charlotte, please wait!" Lex grabs my arm, but I manage to slip out of his grip.

"Don't touch me..." I warn.

"Please don't leave me, Charlotte. Remember, you were fucking Julian. You were even going to marry him."

My head spins back to face him. *Is he fucking serious comparing my once-loving relationship with Julian to this whore who took in two dicks at a time!*

"I'm not going to leave you. However, I need to be alone right now. And since you want to bring Julian up, how about I tell you about all the times he fucked me in my apartment, on my bed, on the kitchen table, on the couch, in the shower... maybe now you will understand how I feel." I storm out of the apartment so fast not realizing BJ is trailing me.

"Charlie, wait!" he calls out.

Stopping in my tracks, I wait because I have no idea where I'm going alone in a city which holds so much of Lex's past. "C'mon, love, let's take you somewhere and talk."

BJ is fast becoming my favorite person to be around, purely because he knows I'm pregnant and can't drink. He does the next best thing—he takes me to a chocolate café. Now, the chocolate fondue fountain in the window alone is enough to make me forget for a few moments that Lex is a big-ass jerk.

We sit in a booth near the counter as the waitress reads out the menu to us. BJ tells her to give us the sample plate. My body is battling with my mind, the anger slowly subsiding, and the scent of sweet confectionaries lingering in the air.

"They make all the chocolate in that kitchen." BJ points to the back somewhere.

"You come here often?"

"Ahh, cat's out of the bag. Let's just say I'm a regular, and women love chocolate when they need consoling."

My shoulders shake as laughter finds me. It's his go-to place to bring pathetic, depressed women, and no doubt after he fills them full of chocolate, he fills them full of sperm.

"BJ, why don't I expect anything less from you, and I've only known you for like two minutes?"

"Listen, Charlie, back there—"

"He was single, he enjoyed sex, dirty sex. I get it."

Fuck, it hurts like hell, though.

"Okay, I won't argue that, but you gotta hear me out. I've never met a chap who was as miserable as Lex. You've changed him, Charlie, for the better. Don't listen to Roxy, let it go, and move on. Christ, that Roxy makes Pamela Anderson look like a virgin."

I let out a small chuckle, momentarily distracted when the sample plate of chocolate, including the mini fondue fountain, is placed before us. We sit in silence while I allow myself to get lost in chocolate heaven.

"BJ, tell me what happened... with Roxy?"

"Aww, c'mon, love, you don't want to hear that. It's done, and Lex ain't gonna go back."

I remain silent. I'm going to push him, stupid guy code what-happens-in-London-stays-in-London bullshit.

"So, tell me, have you brought Kate here?" I smirk, switching topics.

"Blimey, Kate is a tough bird. She ain't one to break down in tears and talk a donkey's ear off about her relationships. No, Kate and I met through Lex. He won't let me talk about it, but basically, I shagged her a few times. Quite a gun in the sack, that one," he chuffs.

"Kate would cut your balls off for saying that."

We laugh together as we dig into the fountain. My God, it truly makes me forget all the shit that just went down. "Thank you, BJ, for bringing me here and allowing me to vent, but just so you know, my pants belong to your best friend, so there's no getting in there."

"Anytime, love, you know where to find me. And listen, send my regards to Emma."

I raise my brows. "Emma?"

"Yeah, Viagra's one hell of a powerful motherfucker."

I leave the café still in shock that BJ screwed Emma. I want to text Emma, but I have even bigger things to deal with as I walk into the apartment and find Lex sitting on the couch, slumped over with a drink in his hand. His eyes are bloodshot as he turns and looks my way. We sit in silence as I try to find the right words to say. We are both hurting, and I'm not the innocent one here, either, after I shot my mouth off about Julian fucking me everywhere under the sun.

"We both have a past, but I don't like secrets. Tell me what happened?" My voice is calm. It's my court voice, the one I use every time the opponent is on the stand trying to get away with some ridiculous alibi.

"What's the point, Charlotte? It's done." His voice is croaky. *Has he been crying?*

"Because if you don't tell me, then my imagination will run wild. However, my imagination is probably in for a rude awakening."

He remains still, pouring himself more liquor.

"We fucked her several times. Yes, what she said is right. Most of the time I was out of it on coke, but sometimes I was well aware of what I was doing."

Ouch! Do I need to ask any more questions? Why the fuck are women built with this stupid need to know every vile detail of their partner's past when they are well aware of the hurt and pain it causes when they hear the words.

"Once, in college, I got really drunk at a frat party and let a guy grope my boob while I was Frenching his friend."

Lex's shoulders move up and down. I'm confused as to why until I realize he is trying to suppress his laughter.

"True story. There, I give you my almost threesome encounter."

"Charlotte," he murmurs, the emerald green in his eyes clouds as he reaches out and touches my wedding ring. "When Roxy sent me a text saying she was in our bed, I thought I lost you."

I ache for him.

All of him.

This isn't his fault. I know he can't control the past coming back to bite him on the ass. I was callous, and the Julian stuff was uncalled for, but I do have one more question to ask.

"You said you never did brunettes. She had the same hair color as mine?"

He gazes at me, confused. "She was blonde. I barely recognized her today."

Forgive him, Charlie, stop being a fucking cold-hearted bitch.

"You hurt me with what you said about *him.*" Lex barely manages to get the word 'him' out, the pain killing him, and I contributed to that.

"I'm sorry I said those things. Yes, they are the truth, but I said them because seeing her and the way she spoke to me about what you did to her left me absolutely gutted."

The truth is out, and it's impossible not to notice his body recoil. I wait for a sign for like ten minutes, and then slowly, he places his arm around me and pulls me into him. I find my nook, getting lost in the place I call home.

"We can do this, okay? I can't promise the past won't drag itself up, but I promise never to doubt your love for me."

"Ditto."

Slowly, I unbutton the top of his shirt, sliding my hand against his chest and allowing it to rest on his heart. With every beat, I know it beats for me, *for us.*

"So, what now?" he asks, stroking my hair as we both sit quietly on the couch with our thoughts.

"Food, shower, then anal."

Lex shakes his head, laughter escaping him.

"I'm hoping this sticks, and it's not just pregnancy hormones?"

I tilt my head, caressing his chin with my hand. "Something tells me it's not pregnancy hormones, Mr. Edwards. I think you've hit the jackpot."

"What a lucky man I am," he says with a cocky grin.

"The luckiest in the world."

TWENTY-EIGHT

LEX

The moment that text appeared on my screen, I knew I had to haul some serious ass back to the apartment.

My heart's thumping out of my chest, my breaths barely able to escape as I desperately try to stop Charlotte from having to see any of this. I open the text message again, and it definitely is Roxy with dark brown hair, not her usual bleached blonde, one wrist handcuffed to my bed, she's barely dressed with her legs spread open as she fingers herself.

> **UNKNOWN NUMBER**
>
> You wanna taste this again, Lex? Every finger has been in my cunt. Come and get it, baby.

I hate that word, it screams 'whore.' I clench my phone, the grip so forceful I can feel it dig into the palm of my hand. The fucking bitch, who does she think she is, and how on earth did she get in!

The elevator is irritatingly slow, and the moment the

doors open, I run up to the main bedroom. Roxy is lying on my bed with a smug look on her face as BJ is consoling Charlotte. Even as her husband, there's no getting through to Charlotte. The pain she's experiencing is impossible to ignore, her eyes glassy and her posture sunken. BJ holding onto her is questioning my trust, but right now I don't have a leg to stand on. The damage of my colorful past is sitting right there on my bed.

Charlotte walks away without saying a word. I pull her to me, needing her so desperately, looking for a sign, any sign that she isn't leaving me. She can barely look me in the eye, but then she says the words calming me the hell down —she isn't leaving me. I breathe a huge sigh of relief until she mentions *him*.

It rips through me, the blades slicing me slowly. The cuts are deep, they are starting to bleed. Inside, I'm screaming, the pain so unbearable and the heat, the burning sensation is crawling throughout my skin until finally the doors close behind her, and I'm left with nothing.

All that turns into rage as I stomp back to the room. Without any words, I uncuff Roxy and drag her off the bed. She kicks and screams, calling me every dirty name possible, but I don't care. I push her into the elevator and press the button to the lobby. When the doors open, everyone turns to look as I pull her arm and push her out of the building and onto the street. Standing there, barely dressed, she curses my name loud enough that across the street people turn, but I simply walk away.

I ride the elevator back upstairs. The first thing I need to do is change my security code and call a locksmith, but suddenly I stop, realizing this place holds nothing for me. This isn't my home, that's why I was so reluctant to come back here. This place is a reminder of how I was institutionalized for the last few years. How I was drowning in my own mistakes without a lifejacket to save me.

Pulling my phone out, I call Kate, briefly explaining what happened. She isn't surprised and also gives me a lecture on my past behavior. Normally, she wouldn't have had the balls to say shit like that to me, but more so in this moment, I need a friend rather than an employee. I give her instructions to put the penthouse on the market. I'm saying goodbye to another piece of my past.

My vision is blurred as I hear a noise. I have had several drinks trying to erase the memory of the dickhead fucking my Charlotte in what is our home in New York. I close my eyes, willing the torture to stop.

Suddenly, I feel her beside me as she sits down. The silence falls over the room, and she is quick to break it. Charlotte sounds cold, her tone stiff. I've grown accustom to this trait as it's her defensive-lawyer voice. Somewhere in the middle of her words, she slowly slips, and the true Charlotte reveals herself by telling this lame story about college.

The corners of my mouth curl involuntarily, my shoulders moving as I struggle to hold in small fits of laughter bubbling to the surface. Here I am thinking Charlotte is some sex demon with a sordid past, just to be reminded that it's so far from the truth. Her double-groping session at a drunken frat party is her closest encounter to a *ménage à trois.* It's laughable, but somewhere in my insane reasoning, the images find their way back, and I blurt out the pain she caused me.

She doesn't deny it. Do I honestly believe she is telling lies? And so, it's done. Parts of our past are brought to the surface once again, and no matter what happens, no matter what we say, every part of me still wants every part of her.

We hit a hurdle but together, we jumped and made it to the other side.

London turns out to be a blessing and a curse. The whole Roxy thing put a massive dampener on the end leg of our so-called honeymoon. The positive being able to restructure the London office which means I will no longer need to be here.

I'm back to being a red-blooded American.

Life in New York is busy with Kate and me running the office. Our staff count is larger than London, and business booms. I manage to keep my hours down, wanting to spend as much alone time as possible with Charlotte before the baby comes. It means learning the art of delegation, something I've struggled with my whole life, but with Kate, I can trust her.

She proves to be exactly what I need and never once lets me down.

We are still living in Charlotte's apartment much to my annoyance, however, I'm only tolerating this because bigger things are on the horizon. With life being chaotic combined with our last argument when looking at places to buy, it's been placed on the backburner but for a very good reason.

I'd been reluctant to broach the subject with Charlotte about a possible move to the West Coast. It's been in the pipeline for a few years, but I had recently been approached by a head executive of one of the top production companies in LA looking for an investor. But I know Charlotte loves Manhattan, her career and most importantly—her friends. Her whole life is here, and a part of me doesn't want to cause additional stress because of the baby.

"Yay, Kate's here. She better have brought that Chinese take-out or you're toast, Edwards."

Charlotte makes her way to the front door. Instead of their usual hug, Kate bends down and rubs Charlotte's stomach. With Charlotte in her second trimester, her stomach is beginning to bulge, and her tits are fucking amazing. By far the best part of pregnancy.

"So, what are we celebrating?" Charlotte asks Kate while unscrewing the cork off a bottle of wine.

Kate glances at me, surprised I haven't mentioned anything. "Well, I've been promoted."

Charlotte immediately turns my way with a curious stare. "Congratulations! To what?"

Here we go.

Five... four... three... two... one...

"Director of the New York office..." Kate pauses, her eyes warning me now is the time to reveal the reason why.

"But wait a minute, then what will Lex do?"

"I would be busy with other projects on the West Coast..."

I wait bravely for the ball to drop.

"I'm a little confused here, so please pass me the last eggroll so I can get this right." Kate hands her the last eggroll, which she munches on. "When you say 'West Coast,' do you mean us or you?"

"Us, Charlotte. I wanted to speak to you about this earlier, but the deal was only sealed this afternoon. Dreamteam Studios needs an investor, and I've wanted to get into production for a long time. They are located in LA."

"So, we will need to move to LA? And when?" she questions rather calmly.

"Yes, we will need to move to LA, and probably after

the baby is born. Look, Charlotte, I know it's a lot to take in, your practice is here, and so are your friends... it's just—"

"It is a lot to take in, and I wish you would have spoken to me about it when it first came up," she clips, narrowing her eyes with annoyance. "Yes, I will miss my friends, and as for my practice, well, Nikki and I are looking at expanding anyway."

"Wait, you mean you want to go?"

"It'll be nice to start fresh, and Manhattan is too crowded to raise a baby. I just have one condition," she demands, keeping her expression stern.

"What's that?" I ask.

"Oh, not a condition for you but for Kate." Charlotte grins playfully.

Kate looks at me, shrugging her shoulders in confusion. "Err... what's that?"

"That I get custody of Eric."

We all laugh. Yes, even me. Eric has entertained me with his sick humor on more than one occasion, and if it makes Charlotte happy, then I'm happy.

"But I get him on the holidays," Kate argues.

"Deal."

They shake on it, and I can't be happier that soon we will start a new life in LA. With my nerves disappearing, I realize I should have been honest from the start. I need to give Charlotte the respect she deserves, and there's no more hiding behind my own insecurities.

Planning to move to LA is a huge task in of itself. I find myself flying back and forth with the paranoia Charlotte will give birth at any moment. She's only in her thirty-second week, but I can't shake the worry, so I have my mom stay with her every time I have to fly out. Charlotte doesn't complain. They can talk babies all day, and as much as I love my baby, an hour-long conversation discussing diaper genies is tedious.

Charlotte is busy scouting houses on the internet, and after a whirlwind trip to LA, we find a house nestled in the Hollywood Hills we both instantly fall in love with. It's a Spanish-style home, full of character and plenty of space. Our neighbors are big-shot celebrities, but Miss Charming won them over, discussing once again—diaper genies. That's my cue to leave. I busily inspect the home and put in an offer. It will be home as soon as the baby is born, and we are able to fly over.

Charlotte finds herself busy with Nikki, planning out the new LA practice. Eric, as predicted, is eager to move out to Hollywood, his constant texts begging me to use my connections and locate where Matthew McConaughey lives. I keep reminding him that I won't be the one to bail him out of jail should he violate the restraining order I have no doubt will be placed against him.

Mason & Romano already has a client base, mainly their clients from New York who have moved to the West Coast. Between that and being heavily pregnant, I warn Charlotte to slow down.

"If I slow down now, then it'll be all downhill from here," she complains.

"Charlotte, having a baby is not going downhill," I say, trying to ease her fear.

"Well, of course, you would say that, you don't have a giant head coming out of your vagina!"

And the worst part of the third trimester is the mood swings. One minute she's counting down the days to finally holding the baby, and the next she is talking about going downhill. I know, I know, I shouldn't complain. I should be sympathetic since I'm not the one who has to physically go through this.

Then there is the *sex*.

It's becoming difficult.

Charlotte has never looked more beautiful, and my desire for her only intensifies, but much like a box of assorted candy, I don't know what I'm getting. I make a move, and she's riding me faster than a bucking bull, but then, I make another move, and she recoils and complains that my cock is too big and full of sperm, and it's what got her in this 'fat' state to begin with.

Hormones, Lex... blame the hormones.

The sex has become challenging as her stomach grows, and doggy style has fast become a favorite. I'm not complaining, just taking whatever I can.

Late one Friday night, Charlotte, Eric, Kate, and I are in our apartment packing up boxes. The three of them decide to rent *Magic Mike*, much to my disapproval. At what point they actually think I need or even want to watch men strip on stage is beyond me.

"Okay, listen, I'm heading out to Rocky's. I need to hang out with testosterone because Eric, you've really let the team down," I complain.

"Lex, I'm not on Team Pussy. I'm Team Wang. Look, I'm even wearing my Team Wang shirt!" He unzips his jacket, and there it is in bold for the whole world to see.

I kiss Charlotte goodbye and head out to Rocky's. Nikki and Will are in Jersey visiting Nikki's mom, so I'm not surprised one bit when I arrive, and Rocky is watching porn. The moans and groans can be heard down the hallway, the idiot even has it on surround sound.

"You better not be hard," I warn him.

"Nah, I jerked off already. This is just the after show." He grins.

And so, we sit there watching porn until Elijah arrives. He doesn't look himself, and Rocky suggests he watch some girl-on-girl action to liven up his mood. I'm not sure if it works, but he manages to piss Rocky off by talking throughout the whole thing. According to Rocky, porn must be watched in silence.

Halfway through the movie, *Whores'R'Us*, I receive a text from Charlotte.

> **Charlotte**
>
> So you need to come home RIGHT now. I love you baby but seriously Magic Mike has flooded the channels if you know what I mean.

I have to laugh, the old Lex would have been a jealous prick reading that, but somehow, I've loosened up over the past few months, probably because she's my wife and carrying my baby. I don't need any more reassurance than that.

I text her back saying I'll be home soon to take care of the problem, and Rocky is more than happy to see us leave. He has changed movies and is now watching *Ass-ablanca*. He warns us his dick is out of control, and unless we want to watch him jerk off, we need to leave immediately.

Elijah and I are out of there so fast, you can hear Rocky's zipper.

Outside the apartment block, Elijah is still quiet, and I know something's off. He asks me to join him for coffee, and as much as I need horny Charlotte, something tells me Elijah needs me more. I send her a text saying I'm going to be a little bit late and not to fall asleep. She doesn't respond, so I assume it means she probably already has.

As we order our coffees, Elijah nervously plays with the sugar packets until he finds the courage to speak.

"The cancer is back."

I place my steaming hot coffee down with a slight tremble, trying to figure out if I heard him right. His deadly silence indicates I did. "How? And where?"

He pauses then states, "Prostate, again. I was told it was contained, and the chemo worked, but my test last week shows abnormal cells, and well, it's back."

"Does Adriana know?"

"No. I haven't told her yet. She's been doing IVF treatment, and she's under a lot of stress."

"Elijah, I don't think trying for a baby is best right now. What if..."

Shit! I want to retract the words.

I didn't mean for it to come out so morbid, but why the hell are they even thinking about starting a family now?

"I know, and I'm not sure how to bring this up."

"Listen, if you need my help..."

My phone startles me. It's Charlotte. I hit reject knowing she will understand.

"There is this clinic in Australia. They have advanced chemo treatments, but there is a year-long waiting list."

"Elijah, of course. Text me the details, and I'll get on it ASAP, but listen, you really need to tell Adriana as well as Mom and Dad."

The phone rings again. My mind isn't thinking straight, so I hit reject. Elijah's cancer is the worst possible news right now, and I can't shake how ill and sad I feel. I only have to look at Elijah to remember what he's going through is a million times worse.

"Thanks, brother. Can you believe this? Someone up there has it in for me." Elijah sighs.

"We'll get through this. We did it once, and we can do it again."

As I say the words, my phone vibrates.

"Someone really wants your attention." He laughs.

I pull out my phone and read the text, my heart leaping out of my mouth.

CHARLOTTE

ANSWER YOUR FUCKING PHONE MY WATER JUST BROKE!

It's showtime.

Fuck, I'm not ready.

I'm going to be a *father*.

Me, Lex Edwards, has to take care of a baby. *What the hell do I know about babies?*

"Lex, are you okay? You look... pale."

"The baby... it's coming."

Elijah's eyes widen as he stands, throwing some bills onto the table.

"In the words of Rocky, let's get the hell out of here, dude."

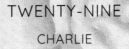

TWENTY-NINE

CHARLIE

I t starts off as your typical Friday night.

I'm watching a movie with Eric and Kate. It's our third *Magic Mike* night, the first two being screenings at the cinema. We have our buffet of fried chicken, pizza, Mexican, and desserts sitting on the coffee table in front of us. In support of my pregnant state, we all drink mocktails, but I swear Eric's has the stench of vodka seeping through it. When I ask him if that's a flask in his pants or is he just happy to see me, he replies with "both."

With Nikki and Will away at her mom's, Lex left us to go to Rocky's, no doubt to watch porn. Nikki once told me that every time they are gone, the boxes of tissues somehow disappeared from their apartment.

The image instantly needs erasing from my mind.

So, watching extremely hot men dance on stage is a sure way to get the fire started below. I'm surprised when I feel how soaked my panties are. Geez, pregnancy hormones are seriously out of control. I text Lex to get his ass back home because if I am this wet, he sure as hell needs to take care of it.

It's somewhere toward the end where I begin to feel uncomfortable. My third trimester has been smooth sailing so far, and I still have weeks before this baby will make its grand entrance. I can't quite understand exactly why, and embarrassed with my panty predicament, I'm not sure how to explain it to Eric and Kate.

Yeah, okay, Matt Bomer dressed as Ken does things down below which should be illegal, but nevertheless, it's just a movie, and again, have you seen my husband? I'm not one to hold my thoughts in, but this is highly embarrassing, so in typical Eric fashion, I blurt it out, "Right, I'm so soaked right now, I swear a tsunami just flooded my channels."

Eric chokes on his burrito. "God, Charlie, do you need a TENA? Is it Channing in that combat outfit?"

Kate pipes in, "Oh, I bet it was Mickey Rourke."

"Hate to break it to you guys, but I don't know. It's weird. I mean, yeah, they are all hot, but I wasn't horny looking at them. Maybe my vagina has expanded, and I can no longer feel horny?"

"Wait. Your vagina expands?" Eric asked.

"Eric, did you not learn this in high school? How else does the baby come out?" Kate questions.

"Kate, how many times do I need to tell you that I'm not a vagina expert? The whole thing scares me like paranormal activity."

"How is a vagina related to paranormal activity?" Both Kate and I are barely able to hold in the laughter. However, I can't ignore the slight stomach ache I get from eating another burrito. Seriously, like every time I eat a jalapeno.

"Well, for starters, there's mucus and periods," Eric points out.

"Okay, this conversation is so done. I need to get

changed, plus my stomach is really hurting from the food." I stand up to hear Kate and Eric gasp.

I quickly turn around, both of them pale white with stunned expressions on their faces.

"Umm, Ch-Charlie..." Kate stutters. "I think your water broke."

Eric yelps, "*See!* Paranormal activity!"

I try to focus on his hand, the warmth, the way his perfectly-shaped fingers look. Trying my best to ignore they are white, the blood drains as I squeeze onto them for dear life. My mind is racing and lost in my thoughts, I try to think of anything I can besides the fact that I'm only thirty-six weeks, and this baby is coming.

Doctors and nurses come in and out of the room, their words all lost on me. Lex, on the other hand, asks questions in his medical jargon, the doctors surprised with his knowledge. When they leave, he talks to me, but I'm scared to listen. The fear of losing our baby is ripping me apart.

"Charlotte, please look at me," he begs.

If I look, I will cry. The tears sit on the edge of my eyelids, ready to stream down my face.

"Everything will be okay. Please, look at me."

I muster up every muscle in my body to move to face him. The second my eyes meet his, the floodgates open. He pulls me into his embrace as much as he can without cords from the machine being tangled up and kisses the tears on my face.

"Please listen to me."

I nod, forcing myself to listen.

"The baby is breech, but the heartbeat is perfect. Your

blood pressure has spiked, and if it doesn't come down in the next twenty-four hours, they may need to do a cesarean."

"Cut me open?" my voice quivers.

"Yes, but it's only a small incision, and I'll be in the operating room with you. You won't feel any pain, maybe just some pressure."

I listen intently, trying to garner any of the calmness that Lex feels.

"Twenty-four hours?"

"Yes. And don't worry, I will be here the whole time, and outside you have a hoard of visitors waiting if you're up for it."

I hold onto his hand tighter, wanting to savor what is quite possibly our final moment alone as husband and wife before we are officially parents.

My eyelids feel heavy. I struggle to keep them open amid the sounds of panic around me. My heart starts to beat fast, the wave of panic followed by nausea setting in. In the distance, I hear my name being called, a familiar voice. I focus on this voice, something about it I just can't decipher. I hear it again. Now, I shut my eyes tight, and every ounce of me is trying to focus on this voice.

"Sweet baby girl... everything will be okay... hush baby girl."

My body jerks, and my eyes open rapidly. The voice...

It's my grandmother.

Lex looks panicked, and even with all the chaos in the room, this serenity envelops me because I have an angel watching over me—two angels. One that can be heard but not seen, and the one that sits holding my hand beside me eagerly waiting.

"The baby needs to come out now, Charlotte. We need to go the operating room," Lex says softly.

I smile, unafraid of what lay ahead.

We are safe.

We are protected.

At exactly 2:46 a.m., Amelia Grace Edwards is born. Her tiny screams echo through the operating room causing everyone to cheer. Around me, the hospital staff is hovering, and the nurse takes away the baby as they clean her up. It feels like hours later when Lex walks over to me, his face beaming with pride as he places our daughter against my face.

"Say hello to Mommy."

The second her face touches mine, I become complete. Her precious skin is so soft as I run my lips over her cheeks. She is tiny and perfect. There are no other words to describe her.

With my vision clouded, I turn to look at Lex. A single tear falls down his face only to be swallowed by the gigantic smile consuming him.

"She is perfect... just like you," he murmurs.

"Just like her daddy."

The nurse comes over and explains Amelia needs to be taken to the NICU because she is premature. I don't argue, nor does Lex. The second she's taken away, I feel the loss. *Okay, Charlie, this is your maternal side kicking in. Just get used to it because life has changed forever.*

The days seem a blur. I'm beyond exhausted and trying my best to recover. Thankfully, my vagina is still intact from the cesarean and not looking like a battered lasagna—you can thank Eric for that analogy—but I still feel disabled.

My body aches, painful in different areas, and overall, I feel weak. It takes me a day to get up and pee on my own.

Thank the Lord for a catheter. By day two, I feel incredibly gross and ready for a shower.

A simple task like showering is a huge effort. It takes the nurse and Lex to help me. Apparently, my legs decide they can no longer function.

When she leaves us to tend to another mother, I cry in Lex's arms, overwhelmed by the exhaustion and state of my body. What makes it worse is my fear of seeing the wound. The nurse, thankfully, changes my bandages without me seeing a single thing, but Lex, on the other hand, hovers over her, which she seems to take offense at. Yes, she is like sixty and immune to his looks, unlike the candy stripers who wear their slutty outfits. I swear they visited me more times than any other patient in here. It might have also been the reason why Rocky visits me every day, without Nikki.

I want to say Amelia is the most well-behaved baby in the world, and we are blessed. *Wrong.*

She won't latch on. The nurses give me tutorials on breastfeeding, and, frustrated, I wind up crying every time. She screams through the night when other babies sleep. I'm drained both physically and emotionally. Both my boobs and I cry every time she does.

When Lex arrives in the morning with fresh bagels, I cry again.

He's quick to take Amelia, and in his arms she remains silent for hours on end. In fact, she remains silent for Emily, as well, and everyone else who visits. It's in those moments alone with me that she turns into a monster baby and finds her voice. I find solace in one of the nurses. She sits down with me and explains the changes in my body, and why I'm a blubbering mess every two seconds. It's getting beyond ridiculous.

Amelia cries, I cry.

My orange juice spills over my blanket, I cry.

The button fails to work on my bed, I cry.

I'm tired of crying.

"Charlie, you are normal. I was like this, too. You wouldn't be normal if you aren't like this," Nikki says as she rocks Amelia back and forth.

"I don't remember you being like this..."

"That's because I held it in, which made it worse because I suffered post-partum depression."

The memory triggers. "I remember now. Nikki, this feels so hard. Physically, I can barely walk. My boobs have turned into watermelons on steroids, and Amelia won't stop crying."

And there go the tears again.

"Charlie, you need to rest, relax, and let Lex help you as much as possible. And, of course, me."

"Okay, I hear you, what I'm feeling is all normal. I'm just saying it's no walk in the park, and those stupid Lamaze classes and books did not prepare me for this."

"They focus on the before *not* the after. Give it a week, and things will get better. Plus, you'll get your mojo back." She winked.

"The last thing I can think about right now is sex. Besides, don't you have to wait six weeks anyway?"

"Yes, you do. I'm not saying you should have sex, what I'm saying is don't be surprised when you're at home and your hormones do a number on you, and all you can think about is hopping on Lex's dick."

"Don't be silly. Don't judge me by your own slutty standards."

"Bets are on, Charlie. I give you three days tops before you're blowing him like a trumpet in an orchestra."

"Honestly, Nikki... ridiculous thought."

"Where's my niece?"

Adriana decides to make an impromptu visit. It can't have been worse timing because we have been home less than twenty-four hours, and Nikki won her bet. I'm as horny as a teenage boy. It's so left field, totally catches me by surprise when I see Lex in his wife-beater and gray sweats standing in the kitchen making dinner. I'm ready to blow his brains out when we hear a knock on the door.

Fuck off!

Adriana immediately pulls Amelia out of her bassinet and sits on the couch, cooing and singing lullabies.

"I'm pregnant," she says quietly.

Shocked, I look over. "You're pregnant? The IVF worked?"

She nods with this enormous smile on her face. "Yes, but I haven't told Elijah yet."

I lean over and hug her because this is crazy awesome! Cousins so close in age. It can't be more perfect!

Lex walks into the room carrying dinner. Adriana breaks the news to him but warns him first that Elijah doesn't know. His face pales, putting shame to ghosts. It's impossible not to notice how he almost drops the plates. This isn't at all like him, especially since Elijah and Adriana are married, and having a family holds importance for them.

"Lex, why aren't you happy?" Adriana questions, looking rather annoyed.

"I just think you should have told your husband first."

"Lex, he's in Australia for that art promo convention. I want to tell him in person."

Lex remains quiet. I don't want to pry right now, but something is definitely wrong. He must have realized how transparent he is and quickly hugs his sister, offering his congratulations, but the more I watch them closely the more I know there's more to this.

Adriana stays for a few hours, asking question after question about pregnancy. When I can't stop yawning, she announces she will head home even though both Lex and I offer for her to stay.

The moment she closes the door behind her, the words practically fall off my tongue.

"Why are you upset that she's pregnant?"

His posture changes, and he appears defeated as he rubs his face with his hands. "Elijah's cancer has returned."

It takes me a moment for the words to sink in. *Cancer?* Adriana never mentions the cancer nor does it seem to cross her mind as she joyfully told us the news about the pregnancy.

"It's back?"

Lex stands and walks over to Amelia's bassinet. She's sleeping, but for some reason, he picks her up and holds onto her. He rubs his nose along her face almost as if he needs a distraction while we speak.

"Stage three, we think. He's in Australia being treated."

"Huh... wha..." I can't form any words, my stomach riddles with nausea at the news. "Why didn't Adriana say anything to me... and she's pregnant?"

Again, Lex buries his face into Amelia's hair. I don't quite understand what the hell I'm missing.

"She doesn't know. Elijah wants this treatment first. He doesn't want to stress Adriana out while they are doing IVF."

"Why would he want to have a baby if he can quite possibly die?" I bellow.

"Charlotte," Lex warns.

"No, Lex, why didn't you knock any sense into him?" Unable to stand quickly, I remain seated with my arms folded beneath my chest. A fresh swell of anger rises within me over the stupid decision they've made to bring a child into this world right now. "At least convince him to tell Adriana so she won't be so baby crazy."

"Because, Charlie... he has recovered from cancer before. He won't die, okay... he *will* be just fine." His words don't convince me, and I doubt they convince him.

We sit in silence, holding onto Amelia as if our lives depend on it. Mixed emotions run through my mind, and despite barely sleeping the past week after the birth, my mind refuses to shut down.

I pray Lex is right, that he can prove me wrong, but something greater tells me we need a miracle. I feel its forces and know that only one person can confirm my fears.

Late at night, I reach for my phone as Lex falls asleep with Amelia in his arms. Finding her number in my contacts, I hit call and make my way to the kitchen. It rings, and just before I'm about to hang up, she answers, "Charlie?"

"Mom, I need your help."

"*Corazon,* what's wrong?"

"I need you to do a reading, Mom. I need some answers..."

THIRTY

LEX

There is this feeling that words can't describe the moment your child cries for the very first time.

The sound rings in the dawn of a new life, new beginnings, and the world is once again blessed with another angel. The adoration I feel for this little girl has consumed me all in one touch. I'm not good with babies, or children for that matter, but somehow, when you are handed your baby for the first time, life just falls into place.

Amelia is perfect in every way as I hold her, carefully counting all her fingers and toes. Of course, she's tiny and wrinkly, so it's impossible to figure out who she looks like. Everything about her is so small and delicate that I struggle with this fear of breaking her. She quiets down enough for me to bring her angelic face toward my lips. I know that women talk about how amazing babies smell, but I never understood that until this moment. Amelia Grace is Daddy's little girl, and she has only been in this world for less than a minute.

I can't be any prouder to call Charlotte my wife than at this moment. She has gathered her strength and faced the unknown. I'm so proud of her and forever grateful she carried our beautiful child, and now she's living, breathing, and ours to cherish for a lifetime.

It all seems like a whirlwind. The constant stream of visitors, the sleepless nights, but through it all, we are finding our feet. Life has completely changed. I'm no longer putting in ridiculous hours in the office, and Kate has taken over most of my work and is learning the ropes. We have a few days left in New York before we head to LA. Our apartment is pretty much packed, and Kate is going to sublet it from us. Charlotte is spending a few hours in the office, having meetings with Nikki and Tate planning out the new office in LA, which is due to open in the next few months once Charlotte is settled.

On the days when Charlotte has things to do, I relish in the opportunity to stay home and spend time with Amelia. Okay, so I have turned into one of those soft dads, but I swear I can look at her perfect face all day. Most of the time, she simply lies in the crook of my arm, and I manage to conquer the art of typing emails with one hand. My favorite thing to do is feed her. It's our special bonding time. She takes to the bottle well, but secretly I think she prefers the breast.

Who fucking doesn't?

Charlotte's tits—my fucking God, they are massive. I know I'm busy with work and moving, but fuck me sideways, I'm a walking boner around her. Six weeks was supposed to be the minimum healing time. Even from my medical days, I know that. It was somewhere in the second week Charlotte became a ravenous horn dog and caught me by surprise one night.

.   .   .

A warm sensation wrapped around my cock. Mmm, what is that? Fuck, it feels good. Sex dreams are the next best thing when you can't have real sex. As the sensations intensified, I reached under the blanket and felt her soft hair... but it was real?

I opened my eyes, and even in the darkness, I saw her movements. Fuck. Wow.

"Charlotte," I murmured, sliding my hands in her hair as I moved her head, pushing it deeper.

She stopped for a moment, gliding her hand from my shaft and moving slowly. "I can't wait, Lex, I'm going insane not touching you."

"Do you even know how much of a turn-on it is to wake up with you sucking my cock?"

No more words were said. It took only a few more strokes along with her mouth taking me all in, and I was done, seeing fucking stars because that was how good my wife gave head.

It's all about blowjobs in this household, but hey, who am I to complain? We're both desperate to fuck, and because we can't, it made it all the worse. Every night we tried other things. I rubbed her clit and made her come. Some titty-fucking, but that was one big fucking mess with all the milk squirting everywhere. Then, it was all back door.

Okay, yeah, I know, we do it often, but this week it had been three times.

Like I said, it's a full moon or something because we're both animals.

We officially caved on the fifth week. *What's one week, right?*

I was rearing to go. Well, until Charlotte said we had to

use condoms because she hadn't figured out what to do yet in preventing her from getting knocked up.

Fucking raincoats on my dick felt all kinds of wrong.

We used it once, and then I told her I was not wearing that shit again, and I'd rather pull out. Of course, Miss Cautious said that was a joke. I couldn't pull out if my life depended on it.

Okay, so she has me there.

I told her to see Dad and have him give her the mini-pill since she's breastfeeding.

She proceeded to tell me that was wrong on so many levels.

I didn't fucking care, I just wanted to fuck my wife and blow inside her like the real man I am. Right, that sounded like something Rocky might say. Next, I'll be calling everyone *dude*.

The day before we were due to fly out to LA, Adriana invited us over for dinner. Adriana had no choice but to tell Elijah over the phone she was pregnant since he was in Australia for two months.

He returned two weeks ago, and unfortunately, I hadn't had the chance to see him yet.

Charlotte was still upset Adriana had no idea about the cancer returning, and I kept reminding her that it was Elijah's decision to keep it a secret, not ours.

We drive over to Brooklyn to have dinner with them, and I warn Charlotte repeatedly not to mention anything to Adriana.

"Lex, have you any idea what it's like keeping secrets from Adriana? I didn't like it all those years ago, and I sure as hell don't feel comfortable doing it now. I'm not sure our friendship will survive it again."

Elijah opens the door, and much to my surprise, he

looks well. I pat him on the back as Charlotte goes to hug him, maybe for a bit too long, and the last thing I want is for Adriana to be suspicious.

We walk into the kitchen where Adriana has laid out dinner for us. She's cooked my favorite pot roast, just like Mom's. I'm sure going to miss having her so close by.

She rambles on about the baby and surprises us with some news. "So, I'm a little further along than we expected. It turns out I'm five months already."

"Totally explains the belly. See, I told you it isn't all the donuts you are eating." Charlotte chuckles.

"And we also found out the sex of the baby..."

Charlotte and I wait in anticipation.

"It's a boy!" Adriana squeals

Charlotte jumps up and hugs her, then moves on to Elijah. I congratulate them both, but there's something off about the stiffness in Elijah's body when I hug him. I pull away and search his face, looking for something, but he simply smiles. Maybe I'm overreacting. Surely, if the treatment didn't work, he'd have told me.

Dinner is delicious, and I thank Adriana. She's quick to point out that there's still dessert to come. We leave the ladies in the kitchen and head to the balcony to talk.

"So, the chemo worked? You look well."

Elijah manages a smile. "All is good."

"Did they catch it all?"

"Clean bill of health."

Our conversation is interrupted when Adriana calls us in for dessert. She gives us a farewell speech and even cries. Why? I have no idea. She is flying out next week to see us.

We say our goodbyes, and finally, it's time to start a new life on the West Coast.

"That better not be Eric again," I complain as I roll over Charlotte and purposely throw her phone to the foot of our bed.

"That might have been important!"

"Doing yoga on the beach, when really I know you two are hanging out and waiting for Matthew McConaughey to stroll on past, is *not* important."

She opens her mouth, but I place my palm over it. With my free hand, I slide her nightie up and move inside her. Her gasps are trapped as I cover her mouth, our morning ritual coming along nicely until that familiar scream rips through the baby monitor.

One word—*cockblocker*.

"One more minute... please," I beg.

Charlotte pulls out the big guns, and in one hot minute, she does that thing to my earlobe causing me to explode in the midst of the chaos. She kisses my lips gently before pushing me off her to attend to Amelia.

"How you can come with her crying is beyond me." Charlotte shakes her head.

"It's called my-wife-is-too-damn-hot and my-dick-has-his-own-agenda.'"

She laughs before leaving the room. I grab her phone and read the text. Low and behold, it's Eric. I reply to him.

LEX

> Charlotte was doing yoga all over my cock. Sorry, rain check?

I let out a laugh and hit send. It takes him seconds to reply as I watch the bubble appear on the screen.

ERIC

> I don't know whether to be grossed out or turned on. Damn you Edwards and your hogging wang! It's been a selfish bastard recently. I need my BFF back!

Charlotte walks in carrying Amelia. I immediately grab her from Charlotte's arms and am met with the biggest gummy smile. At four months, she has gotten chubbier and is starting to smile. Her eyes meet ours, and I know she recognizes us already, hence, why we moved her into her own room. Don't get me wrong, I miss having her close by, but having a child's eyes on you while you're trying to pump your wife is a massive killjoy.

The moment we realized she stares at us from her cradle, we knew it was time for her to sleep in the nursery. It's the room next to ours, so Charlotte stops fretting but insists we still need a baby monitor.

According to everyone, she looks just like me. Yeah, the eyes are a dead giveaway. Charlotte will throw in her at-least-we-know-she's-yours banter. That joke lasts ten seconds before I remind her that it could have easily not been.

"Don't tell me you've been riling Eric up again?" Charlotte complains as she takes Amelia off me and latches her onto her breast to feed.

"But it's fun," I whine, trying not to get worked up again because her beautiful tits are screaming 'look at me, look at me.'

"You aren't the one who needs to listen to him all day. Thank God, we are flat out with three new clients this week. If it weren't for that, your ass would be his target, and I don't mean that in a flattering way."

"Fuck, Charlotte, stop talking about Eric and my ass. Let's talk about yours," I tease.

"I will if you stop riling him up."

I let out a sigh and ask her what her plans are for the day. "Amelia and I have playgroup this morning, then after lunch, your mom will take her for a few hours while I head into the office."

My mom and dad decided they can't live more than five minutes away from Amelia. The day they told me they bought a house the next suburb over, I wasn't surprised. Charlotte's elated because my mother and her get along like a house on fire. As far as my dad, it makes no difference. He still travels across South America, helping families who require medical help. Adriana is the one left behind, but after much persuasion, they decide to move out to LA, so they will be closer when the baby comes.

I hop into the shower, get changed, and kiss my girls, ready to head into the office. Dreamteam Studios turns out to be a highly successful venture. I find myself getting involved in movie productions, castings, you name it. When Eric got wind of what I'm doing, he begged me to let him tag along. I allowed it only because he was nagging me like a two-dollar whore. According to Charlotte, Eric's sex life is like a roaring fire in LA compared to the dwindling one back in New York. The moment I heard Eric was blowing some Hollywood A-lister, I warned Charlotte details like that need to remain between the two of them to avoid media scrutiny.

Working without Kate as my assistant has been rather difficult. The thing about Kate is that she is intelligent and has the brains to be more than just an assistant to a CEO. She is thriving in New York, and with the office running well, she still manages to fly to LA every few weeks. The trips over are classified as a business expense, but they are because she and Charlotte miss each other.

Days like that, I know Kate won't report in to work, but I don't care. She is one of the godmothers to our daughter and spoils her rotten on every visit.

And so, it means I'm on the hunt for an assistant again. Kate has scoured through the resumes, conducted phone interviews, and is due to fly in next week so she can interview them face to face with me.

When it comes to hiring, I leave it to Kate. Kate knows exactly how difficult I am to work for and my expectations. I have confidence she will only allow me to sit in on interviews with the top candidates. This new assistant has big shoes to fill. Eric, on occasion, will drop hints about how great it would be if we work together. I tell him he belongs to Charlotte, and even if I wanted him, he would be waiting in line after Kate, who said she was next when Charlotte retires. Fat chance, Charlotte loves her job *and Eric*.

My desk is piled up with manuscripts, and I'm about to read through them when my phone rings.

"Lex, it's me. Listen, we may need to delay the move. Elijah's not feeling well, and I'm as huge as a beached whale."

"Adriana, what's wrong with him?" The concern in my voice is a dead give-away. *Calm the fuck down.*

"He's been feeling off lately. Probably a nasty virus, and he hasn't been eating particularly well. A few of his students had the same bug."

"Okay, listen, let me arrange for movers to take care of everything. Just get yourself on the next flight over here, okay?"

"Lex, I don't think Elijah is well enough to fly." She

sounds stressed and it's the last thing I want for her in her current condition.

"Adriana, please listen to me... I'd feel better if you were here with us. Please," I beg.

"Okay, Lex, just text me all the details."

"Thank you. I love you, Adriana."

I don't know what comes over me, but inside, the feeling of something unpleasant hovers on the horizon. My stomach becomes crampy, almost pained. The weight inside my chest becomes heavy and uncomfortable.

"Hey, love you, too, big bro. See you soon, okay?"

Once she hangs up the phone, the panic sets it. He told me he was well, his exact words were that he had a clean bill of health, but something tells me I was naïve to believe it.

I open my browser and find the invoice for the clinic where he was treated in Australia. I haven't paid attention to the amount when it hit my statement months ago, but now I notice it's oddly low. I dial the number on the invoice and get through to the receptionist. She's reluctant to put me through to the treating specialist, but several threats later, I am put through.

I'm straight to the point and ask him what the hell is going on.

"Mr. Edwards, I really can't discuss this matter with you," the specialist informs me.

"I don't need to remind you who I am. I paid for this, and I demand answers."

"Again, Mr. Edwards, this is confidential."

Fucking hell. I know these fuckers need funding. Great, use that to bribe him.

"I know for a fact you are trying to receive funding for

your new center in Sydney. I will be more than happy to assist if you give me what I'm looking for."

There is dead silence.

"What exactly do you want to know, Mr. Edwards?"

"Why is this bill for Elijah Evans's treatment so low? I know the chemo treatment is pricey."

More silence.

"Mr. Evans refused the treatment."

What did he just say?

"I-I don't understand. Why on earth would he do that?"

He lets out a sigh. "Mr. Evans refused the treatment because the cancer is quite aggressive."

"Wh... What do you mean?" I stammer.

"It's stage four. He has maybe a year to live. He wants to enjoy what time he has left."

The phone slips out of my hands, the voice echoing as it calls out through the speaker, "Mr. Edwards, are you there?"

"I'm here..."

Those are the last words I speak to him before hanging up the phone like I am on auto-pilot.

I no longer feel in control of what the fuck the universe is trying to do to our lives. There is no plan. How can there be a plan when Elijah no longer fights to live? I want to reach out to Charlotte, but I don't want her to carry the burden with her. For hours, I sit staring at my screen, trying to figure out what the hell it is I need to do until the answer that was there all along presents itself.

I call my dad.

With heavy crackling on the line, he answers. I demand he come home straight away. It's a family crisis, and when times like this occur, we all need to be together to get through it.

Family, it's all we have at this moment.

We sit in my parents' living room waiting for Adriana and Elijah to show up. Eric's taking care of Amelia for the night. I thought it was best that she isn't here. She may be too young to have any clue as to what's going on, but I don't want any negative energy around her. I told Charlotte what I had discovered, and as I predicted, she's upset and has been crying for days along with my mother. She rambles on about something her mother read in her tarot cards, but I'm quick to shut her down, angry with her for seeking help from a woman who, in my eyes, is full of shit.

My father tries his best to remain strong, but I can see it has aged him. For the past few days, we spend hours locked in his den, trying to find any treatment that will cure Elijah, but deep inside, we know it's a lost cause. Only a miracle can save him and the power of prayer to God almighty.

The important thing, he keeps reminding us is that we have to remain strong for Adriana. Elijah still hasn't breathed a word to her, and she is gullible enough to believe it's a nasty virus consuming him.

Elijah knows why we called this intervention, and the moment he walks into the room, I know we don't have long. He looks gaunt, especially standing next to Adriana, who's in her third trimester. The healthy glow is missing from his face, his eyes are deeply sunken, and only a hint of color remains in them. His hair has thinned, but he's shaved his head, the excuse being the summer heat.

"Sweetie." My mom calls Adriana to take a seat beside her. I know how much my mom is hurting as she turns to look at me, a silent, desperate plea to prepare ourselves for the worst.

"Can we make this quick? Elijah isn't feeling the best." Adriana allows my mom to hold onto her as they sit side by side on the couch.

"Adriana..." My dad glances over to Elijah, terrified of what is about to happen, knowing he has to tell the woman he loves who is carrying his baby she will soon be alone. The thought alone makes me almost violently ill.

Remain strong, Lex. Adriana needs you.

"Adriana," Elijah kneels in front and whispers so softly we can barely hear the words. "I lied to you. It's not a virus... the cancer is back."

Adriana raises her head to look at Elijah, then back at all of us. She lets out a small laugh followed by an even louder one. We remain quiet until she realizes we aren't laughing along with her.

"Wh... What do you mean the cancer is back? Is this some sort of sick joke? What is the date? Is it April Fools or something? Wait... am I being punked? That's it, right?"

"Adriana..." I mumble, scared to look into her eyes.

"Lex, you hate practical jokes. Tell me it's a joke... a sick, twisted, cruel joke?"

With my face sullen, I try to maintain eye contact with her, so she understands this is no joke. I watch as her face morphs into disbelief, and abruptly, she turns her focus back to Elijah.

"Stage four, Adriana. It's too late," Elijah explains, his voice monotone.

The blood drains from her face as his words sink in. Her body recoils, her hands automatically flying to her stomach, the trembling starting.

"What do you mean, 'too late'?" she yells.

"Adriana, baby girl, stage four means he has only a few months to live." My dad finds the voice Elijah has finally lost.

"*You're lying!* Charlie... please tell me they are lying? This is some sort of cruel joke you're playing."

Charlotte's face is covered in tears. I reach out and hold onto her hand, which is shaking uncontrollably.

"Adriana, I'm so sorry, I have no words," Charlotte cries out.

Adriana stands, unsteady on her feet.

My mom follows quickly to hold onto her.

"We are having a baby. In one month, this baby comes into this world, and you are telling me you only have months to live?"

"Adriana, I didn't want to jeopardize the health of the baby." Elijah's voice is barely audible.

"*What's the fucking point? The baby won't have a father!*"

The sobs intensify in the room, my mom and Charlotte unable to hide the pain unfolding before us.

Adriana stands still, not shedding one tear until Elijah joins her and holds onto her, both of them falling to the floor as they cry in each other's arms.

THIRTY-ONE
ELIJAH

Amazing Grace, how sweet the sound
That saved a wretch like me
I once was lost, but now am found
Was blind but now I see

My dearest Adriana,

I walk away from this earth into the light with God's guidance, which has given me the strength I need to allow myself the peace my body deserves.

My love will forever live in our beautiful baby boy, Andy. He is eternally blessed, and I promise to watch over both of you and keep harm and nightmares away.

Love never dies, Adriana. It may move onto a place that you can't see but believe me when I promise you that it's all around you.

It will never stop, and when you feel alone, I want you to know that my love will forever embrace you.

My life may have not been long in years, but it was fulfilled in more ways than I ever thought possible. The moment I laid my eyes upon you at the football field on that hot summer night when you were just seventeen years old, I knew you were my soul mate, the woman to complete me and make my dreams come true.

In so many ways, Adriana, you made me feel alive, and the biggest gift you have given me was bringing our son into this world.

I may have only held Andy for a few days, but he is my son, and his beating heart, his first breaths were the reason that I could die an incredibly happy and content man.

Adriana, my love, promise me that you will continue life with our son. Give him every opportunity that he deserves. Let him grow into a fine, honorable man. Let him find his own path and understand the unity of a family.

I know you will never stop loving me, but know that you have my blessing to find someone who will love you and take care of you. I can't say he'll love you as much as I do, as I doubt there is anyone who has the ability to love you like I do and have done for so long. But please, find someone that will be the father Andy deserves. Don't deny him this because you are scared, Adriana.

Anytime you miss me, just look into Andy's eyes. I am there staring right back at you.

Forever with you,

Elijah

THIRTY-TWO

CHARLIE

Ten days after Andrew Elijah Evans was born, we lost Elijah.

The doctors had warned us he had only days to live, but somehow, he managed to beat the odds and was able to witness the birth of his son. No matter how much we prepared ourselves for it, we couldn't nullify the pain when he was finally gone. He had deteriorated over the past few months, his quality of life brutally robbed from him.

His family and friends buried him as the sweet, delicate sound of 'Amazing Grace' was sung in the background. Lex sat beside Adriana, never letting go of her, and Adriana sat there, stone-cold frozen. She didn't shed a tear, nor did it seem she blinked an eye. She is like a sister to me, yet at a time when I knew she needed me the most, I had no idea how to help her. The pain I felt when I lost my grandmother and Alexander can't even compare to losing your husband, and to add to that, being left with a newborn child.

I try my best to talk to her, but she shuts down every time, closing off from everyone except *Lex*.

People pay their last respects as Emily cradles Andy in her arms, rocking him to sleep. Andrew holds his head up as the patriarch of our family. He knows exactly what to say and what needs to be done. Little did I know at the time how much it would impact our family. It's impossible ever to imagine walking in these shoes unless your feet are the ones firmly in them, barely taking steps, unsure of why you are being punished by having lost such a beautiful soul.

I wait for Adriana's breakdown, but it never comes. Instead, Adriana climbs into a very dark place, one I'm all too familiar with. We constantly worry with every second that goes by because deep down inside, we know we can't lose her. As every new parent knows, a newborn baby is hard at the best of times, but we can see Adriana withdraw in herself and she's closing off from us.

Emily moves in with her and takes care of Andy full-time. I visit every day just to give Emily a break. Nikki and Kate fly down often to help me with Amelia and work. The stress is taking its toll on all of us, but we continue to pray somehow, someway, that Adriana will wake up from the nightmare and realize Andy needs her too.

The tornado of grief sweeps her away, and much to my sadness, it takes Lex along with her.

Lex withdraws from our family, and I constantly find myself alone. Adjusting to life in LA is hard enough without having a teething baby who's beginning to crawl all over the place. Between taking care of Amelia and the occasional hours I put in at the office, I'm barely holding on.

But time passes by, and life as we know it has changed forever.

The enormity of my marriage falling apart is hidden behind the grief and chaos of events consuming us since the moment Elijah passed. The realization came a few week-ends ago when Nikki and Kate flew in to spend some time with me. Of course, Eric, not wanting to be left out, has joined us for lunch.

"You've done a lot with the place, Charlie," Kate says, eyeing the frames on the wall.

"Just keeping busy, you know?"

It isn't a lie—how I wish it was.

I find myself twiddling my thumbs, waiting for Lex to come home. I can even count the times he's been home in the past two weeks. Nikki knows me well enough to know what's happening. One look at me, and she knows I'm falling apart.

"Charlie, if you want to keep busy, you should check out the fresh meat at that new hot club on Sunset Boulevard," Eric chimes in as he takes a sip of his mimosa.

"Fresh meat? Thanks to you, I can no longer enjoy a good bratwurst," Kate complains.

"I only referred to Karl as a bratwurst once... you know, that German dog-walking guy."

"Wait... who the hell is the German dog-walking guy?" Nikki interrupts.

I let out a laugh, a momentary welcomed distraction from all my worries as I sit around my friends, enjoying, just for a moment, how things used to be. But like always, a moment of happiness will always be overshadowed by the chain wrapped around my neck dragging me down.

"Do you not read my status updates? Honestly, Nikki... even Rocky knows about Karl!"

"Eric, I don't have time to troll Facebook like you and my husband. So, explain... in proper English, please, not Eric English."

"Okay, so one of our clients, a well-known actress, has a dog walker. She owns three Shih Tzus and two Bulldogs.

Karl refers to them as *Bullshits*..." Eric roars at his own joke, and Kate and I soon follow. I have to admit it's hilarious.

"So, anyway, Karl gets paid to walk her dogs every day. He just moved here from Germany, land of the sausage, and well... I blew him in the pool house while the dogs were taking dumps all over her newly manicured lawns."

Kate bursts out laughing, accidentally knocking over her water. I stand to grab some paper towels, barely able to control my own laughter for a moment.

"Eric, I don't even know where to begin with this story. So, I'm guessing the reference to the bratwurst is because he is thick and juicy?" Nikki licks her lips, shooting one of her seductive looks at Kate and me. I roll my eyes at her. For someone who has so much sex, I swear she acts like a deprived sixteen-year-old boy.

"I guess you could say that... too bad it's served with a side of sauerkraut." Eric pinches his nose.

Kate bangs her fist on the table, almost falling off her chair while Nikki, who is normally immune to Eric's hilarity, breaks down laughing, and I just sit there enjoying my friends until a tear slides down my cheek. I'm a tough person, and I rarely break down, but this is my marriage in crisis.

Nikki is the first to notice. "Charlie, tell us what the hell is happening?"

She moves her chair closer and places her arms around me. Nervously, I play with the bands on my finger. The metal feels like it's constricting my blood flow, and I yearn to take them off.

"I don't know what the hell is going on in my marriage," I blurt out.

Eric and Kate remain still.

Eric being the first one to open his non-filtered mouth. "Do you think Lex is having an affair?"

"*Eric!*" Kate and Nikki screech in unison.

"No, it's okay, guys. Of course, it's crossed my mind. When your husband barely looks at you let alone touches you, that's automatically the first thing you think," I mumble.

"Well, okay, let's think about this for a sec. Kate, wouldn't you know what he's up to?" Eric knowingly asks the question, raising the topic of Montana Black, Lex's new assistant. I ranted on several occasions about how perky she is, and when I say perky, I don't just mean her personality. Eric Facebook stalks her and digs up whatever information he can. Nothing exciting, of course. Bottom line is that she's spending more time with my husband than I am.

When I married Lex, I realized I had to find a way to restrain my jealousy because other people's actions are not something I can control. Women make crude comments about him online and even in his presence. But at the end of the day, he chose to marry and love me.

Past tense, it feels like.

I have no idea how he feels about me now, but 'love' is something he's not willingly showing me, more so the exact opposite.

"No... I don't see his schedule anymore. I mean, I could if I really need to. Is that what you want me to do? I can hack into Montana's schedule?" Kate worried, grabs her phone and begins typing a message.

"No, no, of course not. Listen, I'm probably just being paranoid. I'm sure it will sort itself out," I say, not entirely sure who I'm trying to convince, them or me. The word 'affair' is ugly. I should know, after all, I was labeled a home-wrecker many moons ago.

Is this karma being a fucking bitch?
Has she finally found my address?

"Girl... when was the last time he fucked you?" Nikki is straight to the point.

I shuffle my feet. It isn't that I don't know, it's because I know exactly when it was, and it is killing me. Every night, I lay in our bed, and sleep has become an afterthought. His scent is sprayed all over our sheets, and the torture of lying beside someone who holds so much contempt is enough to shatter any confidence I had.

And the desire he once had lacing his eyes each time they devoured me has been replaced by darkness.

"Hmm... two months ago... the day before Elijah passed away." My voice is barely above a whisper.

I'm waiting for a look of shock from my friends, but instead, each one of them places their hands on mine. I look up as my eyes cloud with tears.

"You'll get through this, you have us. Don't ever forget that." The three of them smile as I place my other hand on top of theirs.

It's exactly what I needed to hear right now.

Lex calls occasionally to say he will be home late from work, but he's rarely home before midnight. He succumbs to his old ways, buries himself in his work, and spends the little time he has free with Adriana and Andy.

It breaks me. Each day it hurts more and more. I try to keep my mind busy, but without him, I'm slowly dying inside. The insomnia sets in. I'm out of my mind trying to save my marriage. Things haven't improved, if anything, they are getting worse. I struggle to find a moment alone with him without Amelia around us constantly distracting him from any kind of conversation. Emily knows Lex has reverted to what she calls 'post-Charlie' days, and on a whim, takes Amelia for the night, knowing Lex will be home in an hour.

The hour ticks by and nothing. I know I need a distraction, so I sit at the dining table with some briefs I need to work on. Two hours later, I hear the car pull in the driveway. My heart beats intensely as I wait for him to enter the house. Strong-willed Charlie decides to fly the coop the second I lay eyes on my husband. Despite our relationship taking a turn for the worst, I want him so badly.

I ache for him to look at me, for his emerald green eyes to feast on me the way they used to. On several occasions, I have to take matters into my own hands because that's how fucking desperate I have become. Of course, it's when I am in the shower, and every single time I wish he would enter and fuck the living daylights out of me, but that never happens.

"Where's Amelia?" his voice is flat. *Great, no "Hello, how are you?"*

"Staying over at your mom's. Lex, we need to talk."

"You sent her over there, so we could talk?"

"No, your mother wanted to take her for the night to give me a break. In case you haven't noticed, it's been a struggle trying to juggle Amelia, work, and everything else going on."

"YOU *think it's a struggle?*" He lets out a laugh, but it's cold and snarky. "How about *you* put yourself in Adriana's shoes for a moment and then tell me if *you* are still *struggling.*"

What the fuck?

He has no idea who he's messing with.

I was born to fucking argue, and I've even got a degree in it. This is what the extent of our communication has become as of late, and I'm sick and tired of arguing with a man who's supposed to love me for better or for worse.

"Don't you dare compare me to Adriana. Her pain is the worst pain imaginable, and I wouldn't wish it on my worst enemy, but I'll tell you what comes a very close second to that, shall I? Your husband going AWOL, not fucking touching you for two fucking months! Not even able to look you in the eye or hold a civil conversation."

There, I'd said it—done! *Take that, you asshole!*

"Wow, and here I thought marriage was about love, not sex," he answers sarcastically.

"Really, Lex? You want to turn back into Asshole Lex? Well, don't think I'll be sticking around to welcome that bastard back home." With my chin held high, I grab my briefs and head for our room, slamming the door behind me. My muscles are quivering, the speed in which my pulse is racing impossible to ignore. I'm livid. The fucking jerk has the nerve to turn everything back onto me.

I grab my phone and text Eric that I need to go somewhere and drink. Within moments, he suggests a bar we can meet at on Melrose.

Inside my closet, I change into a pair of black jeans, a very slinky white top with an open back, and my strappy gold pumps to complement the outfit. Stopping by my vanity, I can't help but notice how much weight I've lost from all the stress. I dab on some lip gloss and tousle my hair which I had let out. Not satisfied with the dark circles under my eyes, I apply some foundation and pull out the mascara.

As I make my way back to the kitchen, I search for my keys.

"Where the fuck do you think you're going?" He leans

with his back on the countertop, arms crossed with a smug look on his face.

The worst part is I still hope he will grab me, bend me over, and fuck me into the middle of next week. I hate my fucking *cooch* for betraying me on so many levels. On a side note, I know I look hot, and I purposely wear this top because it makes the ladies look like they are parading for a Miss America beauty pageant. *Oh, and because I know it will get some sort of reaction from him.*

"Out. No point staying here."

"Wearing that?" he blurts out.

"I don't need your permission to wear anything. Besides, not sure why you'd care since anything involving me doesn't seem to matter to you anymore."

Where the fuck are my keys? I open each drawer looking for them to come up empty-handed.

"So, you don't care that every guy walking past you will fucking look at your tits bouncing out of that top?"

"Does it look like I care? You seem to be confusing me with someone who actually gives a shit. Anyway, it's a bar, so get over it," I shoot back.

"You are *not* going to a bar." His tone is tense, muscles protruding as he stands across from me trying to intimidate me with his tall stature and fierce glare. I can see he is struggling with that jealous streak of his. Serves him fucking right!

"Lex, you obviously don't care what I do. You're lucky I even told you this much because apparently, I have no business knowing why you come home late every night, so you can think what you want. If you think I'm going to try and fuck every dick in that bar, then great. Maybe that will pull you out of this sham that is called our marriage."

I spot the keys, and dammit if they are sitting on the

countertop behind him. Fuck, fuck, fuckity fuck! I have no choice but to walk over to him and reach behind him.

I can do this—stay strong.

He motions his head to where the keys are sitting and looks over at me. There is a brief, albeit fleeting look of the old Lex there before it's gone again.

I take a deep breath and walk over. I lean around him, only inches apart for the keys. For a split second, I linger, inhaling his aftershave which seems a little too fresh for my liking. My warped mind immediately jumps to the conclusion that he would only have re-applied it because he had to cover a smell, and what smell would you need to cover? *The smell of a woman.*

With my emotions battered and ego bruised, I pull away, but his hand grips firmly around my arm, slightly hurting me. My eyes almost close, desperate for any touch, heedless of its intention. The touch is causing a wave of desire within me, ferociously crashing against my morals.

"You are my wife, and you don't need to degrade yourself in front of strangers."

Oh, he did not just fucking say that!

I tear my arm away from his grip, fury building inside my chest.

"So, I'm a slut now? And here I was thinking I was just a bored, horny housewife looking to get laid tonight."

I walk to the back door and open it, followed by a 'very dramatic' slamming it shut. I can't get out of there fast enough, the anger swelling within me causing an outrage of emotions.

Eric, being my lifesaver, meets me at a non-gay club much to my surprise. His reasoning is that he'd had enough of the bitchiness and wants to score with some confused straight guy.

The bar is packed, and I feel extremely old. Not that it was hopping with all young folks, but because I feel over-dressed. Apparently, showing your ass cheeks is a prerequisite these days.

I fill Eric in on all the details about what happened at home, and he's quick to tell me that Lex will probably be here in five minutes, dragging my body to the back room to claim his property. Of course, that doesn't happen, and so the drinking games begin. Some people we become friends with in LA join us, and I am having a blast and pushing the past few months aside until Lex sends me a text.

LEX

Choose your next move very carefully and remember the band on your finger.

Is he fucking serious? With several shots of vodka running through my veins, I find the courage to say how I really feel. To say the words eating me up inside despite the band on my finger.

ME

It doesn't stop you.

LEX

I'm warning you Charlie. Remember who you belong to.

ME

Lol, so I'm Charlie tonight? I'll remember that Alex. Leopards don't change their spots.

By throwing his past back in his face, I light the match ready to play with fire. His callous use of my name *Charlie* brings to the surface the anger we both feel. The difference is he is fucking up here, not me.

Beside me, a guy is standing awfully close to the point
he has bumped my arm several times, apologizing profusely.
Each time, I smile and tell him not to worry about it. So, he
looks at my chest a few times, but I brush it off as a single
guy's behavior and turn my attention back to Eric until my
phone vibrates again.

LEX

> You are my wife, so tell the fucktard who is
> trying to grope your tits to back the fuck off
> or I will fuck him up more than you can
> imagine.

My heart picks up a beat. So, he is here watching me
from somewhere in the room because he just can't help
himself. I shove my phone back in my pocket, ignoring his
last comment. Purposely, I turn to face the guy and start up
a conversation. He's nice, offering to buy me a drink, then
asks if I want to dance.

Sure, what do I have to lose?

My husband is gone.

My marriage has ended.

The music is blaring as a local band plays Bon Jovi,
settling for a rendition of 'Always.' Around me, the crowd
sings loudly, swaying their glasses of liquor in the air
without a care in the world.

Eric is the loudest, the diva excels on karaoke nights
with his over-dramatic expressions and attempts at high
notes. The guy beside me pulls me onto the dance floor,
wrapping his arm around my waist.

We sway along, but despite the need to get Lex back for
his hurtful words, everything about this feels wrong.

But Lex doesn't care.

He no longer loves me.

I place my hand on the guy's shoulder, leaning in to whisper in his ear, "I need a drink."

Pulling away, I walk back toward the bar where Eric has stopped singing and is on his phone trying to type a text. Biting his lip, he lifts his head drawing his eyebrows as he notices me.

"We need to go, Charlie, like now."

I laugh, it is only the beginning of the night, and I have no plans to go back to an empty house. This is very unlike Eric to want to leave early unless Lex texted him.

Of course.

"You know what? You can go. I'm perfectly fine here, plus..." I point to the guy walking back toward me, "... I've got a new friend to hang out with. If Lex is that worried, he would have dragged me home by now. So, if you'll excuse me, I'd like to get another drink."

I call for the bartender, and when he comes over, I order a tray of shots for the folks around me.

One.

Two.

Three.

Throwing them back, I begin to feel better about my newfound freedom with the desperate need to dance. The room begins to spin, the music fades away. My body erupts into laughter until my feet give away, and I fall into a pair of arms.

I mumble words, something about being 'married' and 'pussy' until the cold air graces my face, and all I can see is *black.*

THIRTY-THREE

LEX

She still sits in the same spot I left her in last night, against the windowpane staring out to the backyard. The plate of food I left beside her remains untouched.

The house is eerily quiet, my mother has taken Andy for a few days to give Adriana some time to sleep, but she doesn't.

The same nightmare plays over and over in my head, the screams that echoed down the hospital hall as the monitor beeps increased in pitch, and the doctors rushed in, the sign he was finally gone.

When his casket was lowered into the ground, I held onto my sister who stood perfectly still. I knew I was losing her too, the grief insurmountable, and not once did she speak nor did she shed a tear. She was catatonic. It frightened me that the once-bright future ahead was now unknown. I prayed every night she would pull out of this coma. *I couldn't lose my sister*. She's my blood, my family, and I wanted to shield her from the pain. I wanted the old, annoying Adriana back, faults and all. I wanted her to tell me ridiculous jokes only to laugh before she reaches the punchline, the kind only she finds funny.

Most importantly, I want her to be a mother to this little miracle who defied all odds to make it into this world. If I were honest, that's what hurt me the most—watching her son grow more and more each day. To witness him not being embraced by his own mother. It wasn't her fault—she had to deal with this in her own way. She lost the love of her life, and I couldn't conceptualize her pain, not in a million years. Nor do I wish it upon me, and with this decided, I do the unthinkable, I find myself pulling away from Charlotte.

At the funeral, Charlotte placed her hand on my forearm, and I felt my body instantly recoil. She pulled away, the hurt in her eyes cutting me deep.

It's my way of dealing with the grief, I'm crippled inside, and love becomes a foreign concept.

Why do we love when in the end, it's taken from us, and we are left to die a slow death?

I spend every moment I can in the office, desperate for a distraction. If I wasn't there, I was at Adriana's house, trying to bring her back to life. I spend the mornings with Amelia, the guilt eating away at me of not being home sharing the responsibility of our daughter, but distance makes the pain hurt less. Charlotte tries to bring it up a few times, but I simply walk away from the conversation. She knows not to touch me, and therefore, our conversations become limited to Amelia and the talk of the weather.

After a while, Adriana slowly starts to come around, but all around her the memories are a painful reminder of what she's lost. While we see improvement, the breakdowns quickly accompany it. It's almost like she refuses to move on with her life. My mother is at her wit's end, afraid of her daughter doing something drastic, and my father finally suggests she get some professional help. I know Charlotte visits Adriana almost daily, and those are the times I rush home to get changed and make sure I'm gone before she returns.

The sounds of the traffic echo in the background as I sit in my office alone. It's well into the night, what time, I have no idea. The dim light of the lamp is the only thing illuminating the room. My bourbon sits on my desk, enticing me with its ability to erase the nightmare I'm living.

Last night got the better of me, and for that reason alone, I know I can't see her tonight. When I see Charlotte dressed in those skinny, ass-cupping jeans and that slinky top—*that top*—my weakness engulfs me and my inability to fight off the side of me that wants her, the side so desperately needing to be buried in her, means I have to make her loathe me.

I'm surprised to find Amelia isn't home as I want nothing more than to be smothered by her. In turn, my anger redirects to Charlotte. I know she wants to talk, our marriage right now is a complete train wreck. I know full well it's my fault, but I do what I have to do to protect myself.

The words I say have the intent of hurting her because I feel myself caving. She's beyond furious, and when she leaves the kitchen, I thought she would lock herself in our room. I had no inkling whatsoever she would come out dressed in that top, her tits on full show. *Has it been that long since I have touched them?* My body is betraying me, my cock throbbing at the sight of her, and yet, I allow the jealousy and rage to fight off any desire I feel. She's justifiably livid at my venomous outburst, and in typical Charlotte fashion, she doesn't back down. She goes at me and matches me toe to toe, and fuck me, if that isn't the hottest thing ever.

She searches frantically for the keys, and the second I spot them behind me, I know it's inevitable what will happen next. I could easily push them away, but the masochistic side of me waits for her to come near me. The overpowering scent of her skin lingers in the air, enough for me to inhale it, and all my senses in that moment weaken.

She lingers, and I know I can have her right there, *all of her,* but those tortured voices in my head tell me to back off. If I give in now, the pain will be much worse later.

I don't want to feel pain.

I don't want to lose her.

I don't want to love her.

Words hurt, sometimes more than sticks and stones.

And tonight, I speak those words.

After she slams the door in my face, the jealous side of me knows I have no choice but to go to the bar. She will get drunk, and she's angry at me, and I'm talking steam-coming-out-of-her-ears angry. Any guy with a fucking dick will want in her pussy, and *that* side of me still needs to control her.

I find myself a stool at the far end of the bar, camou-flaged by others who surround me, and thankfully, my height gives me the advantage I need. My eyes fixate on her there on the dance floor, and just as I suspected, all dicks are trying to get their filthy hands on what's mine. The fury forces me to pull out my phone and text her. I can see her respond, and unlike the Charlotte who is my wife, she laughs it off, only to rub herself up against some bleached-blond fucker who places his hands on her *ass*.

Acting on impulse, I move toward the dance floor until I feel a hand press up against my chest.

It's Eric.

"Move the fuck away, Eric," I grit.

"Lex, let her be." His voice is calm.

"Let her be? She's going to be dragged to the back alley and get fucked by that fucker. She's my fucking wife!"

"Give her some credit, you aren't such a saint yourself," he shoots back.

"What's that supposed to mean?"

"It means that Charlie wouldn't be all up on that guy's dick if she didn't think you are screwing Montana Black."

"Montana? Sh... She's my assistant," I stammer.

What the fuck is this about?

"Yeah, well, that hasn't stopped Montana before. Look, I promise you Charlie will come home, vows intact. Just let her have this night."

"No, Eric... Look!" I point to her, the guy burying his head into her neck. I push Eric aside, but he's quick to grab my forearm, forcing me to stop for a second.

"Okay, I'll break it up, but for the record, you're a jerk. You are hurting my best friend. If you must take her home, then wait until I get another shot in her, and she passes out." Eric walks onto the dance floor as Charlotte is walking back to the bar. He whispers in her ear only her for to laugh it off. The fucker, annoyed with the interruption, tries to pull her away from Eric, but she resists. *Thank fucking God.*

I stay at the bar watching her like a hunter. As promised, another few shots down, and she can barely walk. Eric motions for me to come over and just in time as she stumbles into my arms. The weight of her body is as light as a feather, the contact unbearable as again I struggle to fight off any urges which stir.

With her eyes glazed over, she attempts to focus on my face. "Oh, look, it's my so-called husband. Did you manage to pry yourself away from Montana's pussy to come see your wife dance?" she slurs her words as she speaks, losing balance, and I swiftly grab her arm to stop her from falling over.

Eric tries to talk, but she tells him to shut up. "No, Eric... if my husband is fucking someone else, then why shouldn't I? I need to get laid, too, you know... it's been like forever, and if my own husband doesn't want to fuck me, then I should find someone who will!" She tries to wiggle herself out of my grip, but my strength overpowers her.

We drive home in silence as she falls asleep instantly. I carry her into the house and lay her on our bed. I stand over her, watching her sleep, her shallow breaths making soft sounds, her chest slowly rising and falling in harmony.

Tonight is too much. I let my guard down and know if I were going to allow myself to give in to my weaknesses, now would be the perfect time.

I remove her shoes and place them on the floor. Next, I unzip her jeans, knowing these will be a struggle to get off. Somehow, I manage to slide them off without her waking up. Her slinky top is much easier. I tug on the strings allowing it to fall gracefully. Her tits are impossible to ignore, and clenching my jaw, I struggle to finish my task.

What's that again? *Undress her? Fuck her?*

I try to ignore the anger starting to rise, knowing she isn't wearing a bra tonight. Who the fuck does she think she is? *Don't use the word, Edwards... don't you dare call your wife that name.*

As I continue to watch her, my cock pulsates, pressing hard against my jeans. The ache is unbearable as I fight back the urge to reach out and touch her. *The loss, Lex... remember how painful it is to lose someone.* The rational side of me already jumped ship hours ago as without even thinking, I slide her black lacy thong off. I can smell how wet she is. It overpowers me in a way which makes me so weak, any willpower I have left will be unable to reason with me at this moment.

You are weak, pathetic in all forms.

The chances of her waking up will be slim to none. She drank enough for her to pass out until morning. She is incredibly beautiful. How can I deny myself this beautiful woman? I place my hand on her thigh and that *jolt* electrifies me in every way possible, there's absolutely no way I'm turning back now. I spread her legs enough so I can see her lips glistening in the pale light. She's fucking soaked.

I kneel in front of her as she lays before me, legs spread open, and I lean in, inhaling her sexual scent, allowing it to drive me to insanity where all I can think about is how much I need to taste her. My body tenses knowing I'm not strong enough to resist. Moving forward only inches away from her pussy, I stick my tongue out waiting in anticipation until it touches her clit, and I'm ready to convulse.

I move my hand to my cock and begin stroking myself slowly, unable to ignore the pre-cum which oozes out of the tip. I rub it all along my shaft, allowing it to lubricate me as I continue to stroke myself. I'm lost, gently licking every inch of her pussy like it's the first time, all the while hoping she will remain asleep.

She stirs slightly, and I pull away knowing I can't risk her waking up. I position her legs so I can see her wide open as I move forward, my cock nestling at the entrance.

Don't fucking do it, Lex.

Just once, fuck her one more time.

The pain if you lose her will break you.

You have already broken her, just fuck her.

The voices won't stop, my mind betraying me, and so I

stroke faster, every stroke bringing me closer. I grip tighter with the familiar feeling rising from my belly, arching my back, remaining focused on her wet pussy and then, I feel the rush and allow the cum to spray all over her. My body jerks from the intensity of the orgasm, and tiredness takes over.

Like a thief in the night, I don't allow myself to sleep beside her tonight. Instead, I sleep on the couch, making sure I'm gone before the crack of dawn.

Without Kate as my assistant, I go through a stream of interns until I settle on Montana. She's twenty-three and moved here a few months ago from Florida. She's excellent at her job, clear competition for Kate. She brings ideas to the table, works long hours without a single complaint, and does nothing but go above and beyond her job duties.

On an impromptu visit, Rocky was quick to notice her looks. He constantly texts as to what she's wearing, or does her perky tits do that bouncy thing they do when she walks. He's a perverted motherfucker, and I tell him that every day. I didn't hire her because of her looks. Yes, she's stunning. She is short, reaching only my shoulders. Yes, I do know that because we have stood beside each other in the elevator. She has tanned skin and jet-black hair. Her blue eyes stand out against her dark features, and, okay, like I said, she is stunning, but she's twenty-three, and I'm fucking married. End of story.

It never occurred to me she would be such a threat to Charlotte until Eric mentioned it that night in the club, and Charlotte's drunken rant only confirmed it. For a minute, I'm surprised she hasn't mentioned it earlier. After all,

Charlotte's a vocal I-am-woman-hear-me-roar type of chick. Then I remember communication no longer exists in our marriage.

It has been two weeks since the club incident, and I'm needed in the London office to tie up some loose ends. Montana drops some not-so-subtle hints about accompanying me on the trip, but I know if she did, my marriage would be officially over. Not because I have no sense of control, but because Charlotte will never speak to me again.

Part of me does care, I just have a shitty way of showing it.

Two weeks fly by, and every few days I call Charlotte to see how Amelia is. Her tone is always flat. We speak about Amelia, and that's it. There are no *I love you, I miss you,* no dirty texts, or video-call sessions. I don't know why I expect Charlotte to say the words when I haven't given her any reason to.

I arrived back in LA late last night and know Charlotte has her black-tie gala tomorrow for her firm. Montana's the one to mention it to me, reminding me of its importance to Charlotte.

Of course, I said I would go. I'm her husband, right? We still need to keep up appearances for everyone.

Montana sits opposite me at my desk, surrounded by mountains of scripts which need reading. With this production company I invested in, we need some massive deals to turn business around. So far, things are progressing nicely, just not as fast as I want.

"I think that's all the contracts signed. I'll have the producer and directors in for a meeting, Mr. Edwards."

"We did it. Thank you, Montana, for staying back."

"I wanted to close this deal as much as you did. Oh, wow, it is late!"

I glance at my watch, it's just after ten in the evening.

"Say, why don't we get out of here? There is this club downtown, and there's this act I've been meaning to show you. He would be great for a few talk shows we have. Plus, he is my brother," she adds.

"Club?"

"Yeah, it's the current *'it'* place." She laughs, tossing her hair over her shoulders. "C'mon, we've worked so hard this past month pulling these all-nighters. Let's loosen up, a few drinks won't hurt."

I search her face, her eyes fixate on mine. What is that look? I have been so absorbed in my grief that I haven't noticed her blouse buttoned down low, her long legs crossed in a very short skirt, the garters slightly peeking out below.

Fuck, Lex, turn away.

Eric and Charlotte can't be right about this one.

With a smile, I agree to go. Why? Because I'm a fucking douche, but I'm also a control freak and rarely, and I mean rarely, will I do anything out of my control, except for the night I ate out Charlotte's pussy when she was passed out. Seriously, Lex, you are letting your thoughts go there when you have this leggy twenty-three-year-old practically laying it all out like an all-you-can-eat buffet.

Montana asks to hop into my car since she prefers to have a few drinks. We spend most of the drive talking about work, nothing personal because the last thing she needs to know is my marriage is falling apart.

We arrive shortly after, and Montana's right, the club is busy and has been labeled the current *'it'* place. The young crowds dance seductively to the beats, it is skin-on-skin dancing at this joint. It really makes me feel old, but not to be an egotistical bastard, I could have any one of these girls in here, just like Charlotte could have had any in that bar. *Great, you had to go there, Lex!*

"There he is!" Montana yells over the music.

A young guy, mid-twenties maybe, walks our way. He has jet-black hair and the same tanned skin as Montana, so I assume they are related. He has a tattoo on the side of his neck which I can't make out in the dim light.

"Mr. Edwards, this is Jett Black, my one and only brother."

He holds out his hand, and I shake it.

"Montana can't stop raving on about you," I say, politely.

"Well, what are baby sisters for? Will you stay and listen to my set?"

"Sure," I reassure him.

He pats my shoulder before kissing Montana on the cheek. We stand at the bar and have a few drinks. By the fourth, I feel myself relaxing.

"So, Jett is your only brother?" I ask Montana, breaking the code of not allowing myself to get to know any employee on a personal level.

"Yep, and I have three sisters. There's my older sister, Carolina, then Jett, then my sisters, Dakota and Indiana. They are twins, a little older than me."

I laugh as I take a sip of my drink. "So how did Jett escape your parents' patriotic love for naming all their children after US states?"

She giggles, placing her hand on my hand. "I tell you what, Mr. Edwards—"

I interrupt her. "Lex, you can call me Lex."

What the hell am I doing?

She loses her train of thought for a moment searching my face for something, licking her lips.

S*hit, kill me now.*

"Well, let me tell you this, Lex. Jett escaped our naming ritual because apparently, he was born with jet-black hair... but the funniest, yet grossest part of the story my father would tell us is that the moment Jett came out, the doctor congratulated my parents and mentioned his thick black hair and quote 'for a second there I didn't know if that was his head or your bush, Mrs. Black'... *I know, right?*" She laughs immensely.

I join her, impossible not to laugh at a ridiculous story like that.

"It was the eighties... bushes were in then. At least that's what my mother says," she points out.

Right. Fuck. Are we talking about Montana's distaste for pubic hair, which can only mean she's sporting a Brazilian? Rocky would be in fucking heaven if I even mentioned this conversation to him. Seriously, I need to cleanse my thoughts because they are bordering on extremely unhealthy, let alone, inappropriate.

We sit in silence enjoying the music until Montana stands up and pulls my hand with her. "C'mon, Mr. Edwards. Sorry, I mean *Lex,* let's dance."

"Montana, call me Lex, especially in here."

"So, you're off duty as my boss, then?"

"I'm off duty as your boss."

"Then we better dance," she teases.

She pulls me onto the dance floor and moves her body a little too close to mine. The dance floor is packed, almost everybody crammed into the small area. I try my best to ignore her body mere inches away from mine, but the bourbon is setting in, and I haven't gotten laid in God knows how long. *Your own fault, Edwards.*

Jett Black comes on stage, the guitar strumming at a

slow beat as he begins to sing a song he wrote, according to Montana. It is called 'Afraid.'

No one has ever made me feel, the things you make me feel
Girl when I'm with you I struggle to breath
Your power has a hold of me
And I'm frightened of this spell you cast over me
So I hurt you because I'm frightened
I push you away because I'm scared
I do it because I love you
I do it because I hate you
I don't know how to be with you
Without being afraid of losing you

I listen to the lyrics. It's spot on to every emotion I have felt the past few months. I'm terrified of losing Charlotte, yet I push her away. Even in our darkest moments, she has a hold over me, and that frightens me, makes me scared to love her the way she deserves to be loved.

Lost in my own pessimistic thoughts, I don't notice Montana moving in closer. Her body brushes against mine, and I scream at my brain not to let my cock get hard, but being a fucking piece of shit, it does not listen to me. She knows as she continues to put pressure on it, which in turn makes it worse.

I lean in and whisper in her ear, "I think I should take you home, Montana."

Her eyes find mine, and perhaps she misinterprets my meaning. *Yeah, good one, Lex, you didn't need to deliver it in your seductive my-cock-is-throbbing tone.*

She says goodbye to her brother, and I wave to him as we head out the back door.

In the car, there is an awkward silence. Shit, Edwards, seriously, think of something to keep the conversation going, otherwise, your dick will start talking, and that is the last thing you need.

"So, how long have you lived here in LA?"

Great, that's all you can come up with?

"About six months now. My brother lives here and just signed a major recording contract. Mom is back in Florida, and Dad lives in Hawaii."

"Divorced?"

"Yeah, around the time I was ten, I think."

"So, you live here alone?"

"I have a roommate, but she's not home if that's what you're asking."

Shit! I wasn't asking that. *What the fuck is wrong with me?* Honestly, you might think my brain would be smart enough to realize where this conversation is heading.

Instead, I remain quiet until she asks me to pull over at her condo. I don't know why, but I turn off the engine, almost like I'm on autopilot.

"Thanks for tonight, Montana." I continue to stare out the front window avoiding her gaze.

"It doesn't have to be over, Lex." The palm of her hand rests on my thigh, slowly moving up until it's sitting firmly on my dick. *Fuck!*

"Montana," I warn.

She tells me to be quiet, and I place my hand on top of hers to remove it, but instead, she tightens her grip on my cock.

Fuck! Push her away now!

I don't know how long I sit there, it could be seconds or minutes.

My head is a scattered mess, and my body is numb, knowing this is wrong. She pulls my hand toward her, directing it under her dress and places it firmly on her bare pussy.

Jesus fucking Christ, do something, Edwards.

I pull away.

Images of Charlotte flash through my mind faster than a bullet train.

I can't do this.

I still love my wife.

I still want my wife.

I just don't know how to fix the damage I have caused.

"Montana, you know I can't do this. You are beautiful, but I'm married."

She shuffles her body a little closer. "Lex, I know you're married, not necessarily happy. This can be a one-time thing, I promise. No strings attached. You wouldn't be so hard if you didn't want me."

Where the hell is my voice, the stupid motherfucker runs into its panic room and locks the door behind it.

She takes my silence as a yes and moves my hand back toward her, this time pushing my finger against her clit until I abruptly pull away.

"Montana, no... I love my wife. Despite what's going on, it will only ever be Charlotte."

I pull all hands away, starting the engine, waiting for her to exit.

"I... I... I'm sorry," she stammers.

"Listen, it's late. I need to get home."

Montana opens the car door and climbs out, and she leans in one more time. "Mr. Edwards, I don't know what came over me. I hope this doesn't change our working arrangement."

"We can talk about this tomorrow." I remain still until the door closes.

When I arrive home, I jump into the shower and scrub my body vigorously, attempting to wash away tonight's events. I know there's no chance in hell I can continue working with Montana, and fuck if I haven't just opened myself up for a lawsuit.

Great! You can get your wife to represent you in a sexual harassment claim.

I climb into bed that night, knowing Charlotte hears me. I need her at this moment more than ever, but as I look at the clock, I know my coming home at two forty-five will not be well received.

With her back turned toward me, she moves slightly.

"Where were you?" she whispers with a slight tremble in her voice.

"Work."

"At this hour?"

"Meetings, sorry. I should have called."

I yank the sheet over to my side, annoyed she claims most of it. Thinking this conversation is over, I get myself comfortable.

"You should have called, Lex. Despite everything going on between us, I was worried about you."

"Well, don't be. And frankly, I'm tired, so good night."

I turn over with my back facing her. Despite the hour, I stare into the night unable to sleep until beside me, I hear a small sob. Unsure of what to say or do, I ignore the pang in my heart and close my eyes, wishing this nightmare away.

We are broken.

Just how much, I have no clue just yet.

THIRTY-FOUR

CHARLIE

The club incident happened over a month ago now, and nothing has changed.

Lex flew to London for two weeks, only returning yesterday. I've yet to see him, the only reason I know he landed was the ever-so-warm text simply stating, *landed*.

I keep myself busy with the black and white gala our firm is hosting in conjunction with a cancer charity. Nikki and Eric came up with the idea, and by some miracle, they managed to get Adriana involved.

Adriana is far from being her normal self, but slowly, she's starting to function as a human being again. She's been over twice this week, so Andy and Amelia can play. We chat briefly, and she even eats some lunch, a huge step forward in my eyes as her thin frame worries me.

The realization that life will never be the same is the biggest hurdle our family is struggling to come to terms with. Whenever I can, I try to help lessen the burden for Adriana, but all it does is mask my own pain.

My own family, as I know it, has fallen apart, and

nothing I say or do seems to fix it. Work and Amelia are all I focus on. I don't have a choice in the matter. Work demands don't stop because my marriage is failing, and opening a new office brings on a new type of workload forcing me to hire more staff.

And, of course, my daughter is my world needing the most attention. Amelia deserves a mother, and that's what I concentrate on being despite her father being a complete and utter asshole.

Rocky and Nikki have planned to fly in tomorrow with Will. I welcome the presence of more family praying they will help me make some tough decisions weighing heavily on my mind.

Thankfully, Emily being the fantastic woman she is, offers to babysit all the kids tomorrow night, so we can enjoy the event.

The saddest part to all of this, I have to send Lex an invite via his new assistant, Montana.

Don't even get me fucking started on that.

I lay in bed, wide awake, listening to the sound of my breathing. It's slow, almost stopping momentarily, followed by a tightness inside my chest. I turn to face the clock noticing it's just after two in the morning. Lights hover over the window, the engine of a car turning off.

Lex never called or texted to say he would be late. Instead, I worry, but more so, my insecurity drives me to madness. My imagination conjures up multiple scenarios, all involving a certain assistant.

I close my eyes, pretending to be asleep as he crawls into bed. I'm surprised he chose to even sleep beside me, given he has opted for our guest room on more than one occasion.

As he settles, I ask him of his whereabouts, not

surprised he chooses to make up some excuse about meetings. Rather than arguing, I express my worry only for him to respond by being a complete asshole. He turns over with his back toward me, switching the lamp off, and with every morsel in my body, I hold back the tears.

This moment cements what our marriage has become. And in the dark of the night, the truth unfolds, and I have nothing left in me to fight. There is only one way to carry on, and only one way to stop the hurt and pain killing me slowly, I have to serve him with divorce papers.

For the sake of our daughter, I can't allow our toxic marriage to affect how we raise her in this world.

I wake the next morning to find him at the breakfast table with Amelia sitting in her highchair. They are laughing, and I can't help but notice how happy he is, his eyes sparkling again, but the moment he sees me standing in the doorway, his demeanor changes. He becomes cold and distant. If I knew what I had done, then this would be easier to deal with, but like every time we have been in the same room, the sharp knife is stabbing me every which way I turn, the bleeding impossible to stop.

"I have the black-tie event tonight for my firm. Will you still be able to make it?"

"I said I would, didn't I?" he responds coldly.

Refusing to entertain his behavior toward me, I work in silence, void of emotion as I pack my things for the day. Emily offers to take Amelia early as there will be no chance for me to stop at all.

With Amelia resting on my hip as I carry her, I lace her bag over my shoulder, grabbing my keys without a goodbye.

The drive to Emily's house is only fifteen minutes, and during that time, I crank the radio up without disturbing Amelia and immerse myself in the music until they switch to a ballad, forcing me to turn it off. I don't need a reminder on love, nor the cruel reality when someone breaks your heart.

"Here's my girl!" Emily removes her from the car, carrying her in her arms with a proud smile.

"Everything is in her bag. I'll pick her up first thing tomorrow morning."

"Charlie," Emily says, her smile disappearing. "I can take her for longer to give you time."

I shake my head, pursing my lips.

"I don't need time, Emily, what I need is a husband."

Emily knows well enough not to continue this conversation with me. It isn't just me Lex hurt with his actions. His parents are feeling the blow of them as well.

I kiss Amelia goodbye before jumping back into the car and making the tedious trip to the office.

The day flies by rather quickly, and I find myself on my feet. Last-minute details need confirming, and the party planner has some catering issue which I make her sort out. Eric's excitement becomes rather annoying, reading out the guest list to me as celebrities accept their invites. Our tables are completely sold out, and although I should be proud of this achievement, inside I am dead.

With an hour to go before I have to head home to meet a stylist and change, I sit at my computer staring at the document.

For the past few weeks, I have lived in denial, replaying our entire marriage in my head to understand exactly where it went wrong. Ultimately, Elijah's death had a ripple effect, but it's one thing not to have intimacy in a marriage and another to be looked at by your own husband with defiance like this is somehow all my fault.

This quickly turns into anger.

Lex continues to act like a jerk, and no matter what I do, it's never right. My emotion turns heavy with blame, rage, and cynically dissecting events in our marriage.

I suppress my anger which leads to hostile and vindictive decisions like the night at the bar. We were both hurting but for two different reasons, and our relationship turned into a complete disconnect.

I love Lex and always will, but this pain is unbearable, and for the sake of our daughter, a decision needs to be made.

Saving the document onto the server, I shut down and head home to get ready for tonight.

Standing in front of the mirror, I gaze at my reflection. The dress I'm wearing is black, couture Dior, stunningly beautiful with a bustier top and ethereal skirt.

The stylist works wonders with my hair and makeup, using a dramatic ruby red lipstick to accentuate my lips. My hair is curled and styled toward the side, showcasing the Tiffany pendant Lex gave me.

Touching the pendant with my fingertips, I swallow the giant lump inside my throat, willing the hurt to disappear if only for tonight. Aside from my wedding band, I don't need a reminder of a time in my life when he promised me the world. And so, I remove the necklace and replace it with a diamond heirloom my grandmother gave me before she passed away.

The event starts in one hour, and his tux still hangs waiting for him to come home. His phone rings out several times when I tried to call, but he doesn't text or call me back, so I leave with a heavy heart, trying to make sense of how I can put on a façade tonight without everyone thinking something is wrong.

"Charlie!" Eric calls out, his sun-kissed tan looking fabulous against his tux.

"Hey, E." I manage to smile.

"He's not with you, is he?"

I shake my head, mustering up the strength to remain calm and levelheaded while I greet our guests. Tonight means so much, and a lot is riding on its success, and it must be my only focus, not my absent husband.

"Well, I need to meet me a man tonight. Charlie, my sex life is drier than the Sahara Desert."

"Eric, I thought you were seeing that actor... the one who's in that soapy?"

"Yeah, well, kinda. Turns out soap actors are drama queens."

"You don't say?" I laugh, enjoying his dramatic realization.

Nikki makes her entrance with Rocky who immediately walks to the bar. I ask her what's wrong, and she rambles on about how he's complaining he has blue balls. Like he can talk. I have a blue fucking vagina from no sex in months. I hit up my rabbit any moment I have alone time. Good old faithful bunny hasn't been used for over a year, and suddenly, it's rabbit season.

I mingle in the crowd, saying hello and doing the social thing, but in body, my mind is elsewhere. I lie through my teeth when asked about Lex. Thank God, I'm a lawyer and know the art of showing no emotion. I'm on my fifth champagne when a familiar voice calls my name. I turn around, and it's none other than Julian Baker.

"Julian?"

He stands before me, and I'd be lying if I said he has no

effect on me whatsoever. He hasn't changed one bit, his looks on par with the ever-so-dashing Christian Bale. Maybe his hair is cut a little shorter, his chiseled jaw freshly shaven, and he smells so fucking amazing, my blue vagina may just have skipped a beat. The tuxedo on him is sexy. God, it's like a blast from the past knocking the wind out of me.

"If it isn't the gorgeous Charlie Mason."

"Edwards... Charlie Edwards," I correct him.

Yeah, but for how much longer? *Stop right there, Charlie.*

"Right, of course. So, tell me, gorgeous, how have you been?"

Fuck, did I slightly melt at him calling me gorgeous? No, you didn't, Charlie, you are just mad at your husband.

"Good. And you? Are you still living in New York?"

"No, I moved to LA not long ago."

Oh.

We chat about his move, and surprisingly, it feels just like old times. We laugh about life in general, and not once does he ask about Lex. Thank God. And maybe it's my paranoia, but he's standing awfully close. I don't push him away, welcoming the feeling of being wanted. There's always a place for Julian, but tonight his importance has stepped up a notch.

"Dance with me, gorgeous."

"Julian... I don't think it's such a good idea."

"Why? Your husband didn't care enough to attend this event and celebrate this milestone of yours. Why can't an old friend celebrate with you?"

"Because we were more than just friends, Julian."

He holds out his hand, and reluctantly, I take it. There's

something comforting and familiar about his touch, something I crave so desperately, intimacy.

Our bodies become flush, and inside his arms, we dance slowly to 'If It's Over,' the song setting the mood. We remain quiet for a few minutes, just enjoying the moment. I know I'm playing with fire here—I mean I was going to marry this guy. I'd planned to have kids with this man. I did things to him in the bedroom that could only be described as ferociously kinky. I need to back away now before it's too late, the voices in my head are screaming at me.

But Lex doesn't love you anymore, Charlie.

It's over.

It is almost like he knows, pulling me in closer and whispering, "Gorgeous, I've missed you."

With a pained stare, my body is in turmoil, fighting off past memories of a time when this man gave me the world. The second my eyes close, unwillingly, I breathe in his scent and question my choices. I'm at a loss of what to do, my head telling me to run with my vows still intact, but the hurt Charlie, the one yearning for her husband who pushes her away, is enjoying this moment with this unbelievably sexy man who once called me his.

"I should have fought harder for you. I let him win."

"It wasn't a game, Julian."

"But he won."

"Did he?"

Fuck, I didn't mean for that to come out. I'm hurting, wanting Lex to feel the same way. I want him to feel the pain of giving up on our marriage, on us. Julian will always be the dark cloud hanging over Lex's ego, and perhaps, that alone pushes my senses to a place of irrationality.

"Gorgeous, I still love you."

Julian's stare is boring into me, causing a wave of emotions only adding to my confused state. He says the words every part of me wants to hear, the weight of his intention resting on my shoulders inducing a tightness in my chest.

But I crave to hear these words from my husband.

"Tell me you still feel the same," he begs me with his eyes.

"Julian... I do still love you, but I'm not *in* love with you, and certainly not in the way you deserve to be loved. You can't erase the past, and for a while, we were happy."

"And now... leave him, Charlie. He doesn't deserve you."

"Maybe he doesn't, Julian, but I made a commitment. I made vows... I carried his child. I can't just let go of that."

Julian remains quiet, his lips only inches from mine, and I know that if I don't do something drastic at this moment, my marriage will be officially over. I move my head sideways and gently rest it on his shoulder. We continue to dance, our bodies so close that I'm heavily ignoring his hard cock pressed up against me. *Like seriously, fucking kill me now.*

My mind wanders to a future with Julian. How easy it would be to have a rational man by my side without the tainted past and trauma which hovers over my marriage. It would be easy and nice.

But he is not Lex.

He isn't the father of my child.

And he will never own my heart the same way.

My stare moves toward the bar, and I see Lex standing there watching me intently, but this time his stare is of pure rage, the shade of his eyes dark and vengeful. It's the same stare he gave me the moment he saw my engagement ring the first time we ran into each other at the restaurant—wide eyes, his neck muscles straining against his skin. His arms are folded flat against his chest, intimidating me with his controlling stance.

"Julian, I need to go..."

"Gorgeous, please stay. I need this," he pleas, his hands wrapped tight around my waist refusing to let me go.

I reach down, removing them. "I can't... I love him, Julian."

"Don't... please, just stay."

I pull away as he holds onto my hand before I reluctantly let go.

With every step I take, my heart buries itself deeper into my chest. In true Lex style, his words will be callous and hurtful, sealing the fate of our marriage. I have never felt so alone despite being surrounded by family, friends, and colleagues. This journey to free myself from a man who no longer loves me will be the start to endless suffering, but perhaps, endless suffering in solitude is better than it being in the flesh every time you wake up.

"You're late."

"Does it matter?" he growls, nostrils flaring as his eyes widen. "Old habits die hard."

"They certainly do, don't they, Lex?"

He takes a swig of his bourbon, then grabs my wrist, pulling me toward the exit. I drag my heels, begging him to stop as I'm on the verge of tripping, but he doesn't listen. Instead, he leads me down the path of the garden until we find ourselves in the parking lot. I recognize his car immediately, parked in the dark corner.

"Let go of me!"

He refuses to listen as he just stands, his eyes flashing with molten rage.

"What, Lex? Now you're jealous? Tell me, does it hurt?

Does it hurt to know that someone else wants me? Does it hurt that for a moment it made me come alive, another man's words made me feel alive? The same man you hate with every fiber of your being?"

"Charlotte..." he bellows.

"What? You gave up on *us*... our marriage is on the verge of over, and I don't even know why!" I throw my hands in the air, frustrated he chooses to have this conversation tonight. "You won't fucking talk to me... you don't even want to see my face."

He pulls a piece of paper out of his pocket, and I recognize it immediately.

"Tell me what the fuck this is?" he yells.

"You can read," I say calmly.

"You want a fucking divorce?"

I clutch my stomach, bowing my head, willing the pain piercing every inch of me just to stop. This isn't the life we planned, and I refuse to settle for anything else.

"Lex, I can't do this anymore. It's killing me."

His nostrils flare like a bull ready to attack. In a quick move, he pushes me onto the hood of the car, the metal touching my skin as the shock stills my breath.

With force, his lips crash onto mine, and I try with strength to push him away. He deserves to be pushed away, but I miss him so much. I don't know what this means, but right in this moment, do I care? For a moment, he is mine again, and I'll take it while I can.

Lex pulls away, and I sit up struggling to catch my breath.

His eyes, that stare.

I wait for what seems like forever.

Is this it? Are we finally over?

He turns me around in a split second and pushes me

back onto the hood. I let out a small whimper, the force scares me. It feels wrong on so many levels. I should feel degraded, but I'm so far from it. He's my husband for crying out loud.

The sound of his belt clicks, and without warning, he rams into me. I bite my lip attempting to muffle my moans. I'm not sure if he takes this as an invitation, but he does it harder. I cry tears, a mixture of happy and sad, feeling the salty liquid run down my face because I miss him in every way possible. It's pleasure and pain all rolled into one fucked-up ball.

"You belong to me, Charlotte. Do you understand? Every inch of this body belongs to me. I'm your husband. I own you."

I struggle, the ache in my belly forming. I'm close, the build-up is quick, and I know if he speaks again, I will come undone.

He leans over and pulls me in harder and faster, his pleas driving us both to an explosive finish.

"Mine..." he cries out. "You are my wife, Charlotte..."

And then we are done.

Somewhere in our heated moment, he pulls away.

I can't do this.

I miss him so much and having this moment, having a chance to feel him again, I just know I can't go back to the way he treated me. I miss being loved and desired.

I miss being his entire world.

"Lex... I can't do this anymore. Please just let me go," I beg, shaking my head.

"You can't leave me!" he cries, running his hands through his hair in desperation. "I saw him, I saw you look at him."

"Julian is—"

"It's my fault. All this is my fault. I was terrified, Charlotte, of losing you the way Adriana lost Elijah. Her pain... it's unfathomable. So, I did the only thing I know how... I pulled away. Distancing myself from you because I was terrified that if I continued to be this happy, the hurt would kill me if anything happened to you. I would die a slow, excruciating death just like Adriana."

"You're my husband," I sob, my body shuddering. "You've hurt me beyond comprehension, but I can't imagine life without you. You've left me no choice."

"I can't begin to tell you how sorry I am. I didn't know how to deal with this. I was so angry, at everyone, at the whole world."

"The grief, Lex, swallowed all of us."

The truth hurts more than anything, and no matter what, we can't erase the pain we all feel over losing Elijah.

He wraps his arms around me, burrowing his face into my neck, but I pull away, desperate for distance as anger sweeps through me like a gust of wind, now remnants after the wildest of storms. I can't deny the hurt, but I refuse to give him back so easily what he wants.

All of me.

"You got what you wanted, Lex, you needed to fuck me, and it's done."

"What do you mean I got what I wanted? Charlotte, I—"

I raise my hand toward his face, shutting down his plea before it even begins. He expressed his feelings, showed some sort of remorse for his actions, but I need time to process, not throw myself back at him like everything is somehow now okay.

"I need to go back inside," I tell him, unable to look into his eyes as my gaze wanders over the ground. "You might have unloaded your baggage, but mine is still packed and ready to leave."

"No..." he bellows, shaking his head while running his fingers through his hair in obvious denial of what we have become. "You cannot leave me! I *won't* sign those papers."

"I need time, okay? You can't just ambush me tonight, of all nights, after months of treating me this way and expect me to fall back into your arms like all is right in the world. You want to fix what you broke? Then don't push me."

I turn around, taking steps away from him as my chest tightens from the overwhelming emotions all brought on by his presence. So easily, I could have fallen into his arms and pretend like this never happened. But I want him to feel *my* pain, understand what it means to be in a marriage. To respect your partner, through sickness and in health, even if that is comprised due to someone else in your family.

"Are you going back inside to be with him?"

The despair is his tone halts my movement. Jealousy is a curse so powerful it can tear even the strongest of people apart. It's relentless in its fight for attention, cunning like no other in manipulating your thoughts into scenarios your imagination conjures up with sometimes no substance. And I know Lex all too well. His thoughts are misplaced because he sees Julian as a threat, rather than having faith in me despite my earlier admittance when I told him that Julian may have been an easier choice, but easy doesn't mean it's right.

Easy doesn't validate what the heart wants.

What my soul *needs*.

Refusing to turn around, I keep my back toward him. "Goodbye, Lex."

I don't validate his question, nor give him another spiel

on love or vows. Instead, I continue my walk back into the
ballroom to finish what I came here for.

After a quick restroom stop to fix my hair and makeup,
which make me look presentable again and not like a train
wreck of a wife who just got fucked by her screwed-up
husband, I make the rounds talking with as many people as
I can.

Shortly after, I call our team onto the stage to make a
speech, mainly to thank everyone for attending.

"On behalf of myself, my partner, Nicole Romano, and
our team, we thank you for joining us this evening to raise
money for this great cause."

A round of applause erupts, and despite my resistance
to speak in front of such a loud crowd, the outcome
outweighs my own insecurities. As my eyes wander across
the room with a gracious smile, they stop at Lex, who's
standing beside Adriana. Despite our earlier fight and his
desperate plea for me to not leave him, there is a different
expression on his face. Almost proud if I care to be honest.

I remember, a few months back, as our business began
to grow here in L.A., Lex warned me of my attention
needing to be redirected to other areas, hence hiring more
staff. I recall asking him questions, and it led to discussing
his presence in the business world. The more he spoke, the
more I became fascinated with his alter ego, Lex Edwards—
billionaire mogul. His confidence is never misplaced, and
when it comes to conventions, summits, or anything
involving public speaking—he is an absolute natural.

At this moment, in front of a few hundred guests, I beg
some of his confidence to rub off on me. Taking a deep
breath, I find the strength to get through this. If I can handle
everything life has thrown at me up until this moment, I can
handle this one speech.

"Three months ago, our firm was approached by Marjorie Adams, community leader, at a women's shelter downtown. Marjorie is an integral member of the community and has devoted years to rebuilding families."

Marjorie is sitting at the table in front, encouraging me with her warm smile as do the team surrounding her.

"Both Nicole and I did not understand the severity of problems that existed at the shelter. However, with countless hours spent on-site, spending our time with families forced to seek housing at the shelter, we slowly began to grasp the enormity of the situation.

"The message is clear... our shelters are not only giving broken families a place to sleep and eat, but are also giving them hope. Children are educated, mothers are taught how to take care of their families. And so, our team at Mason and Romano are pleased to announce your contribution tonight will help Marjorie and her team continue to devote their time to those in need, and expand the premises to cater to more families in need."

The crowd stands, raising their hands in applause. With a proud smile, I welcome the support. We, as a team, have done an amazing job, and this boost will provide the shelter with help for those in need. Aside from the free legal services we offer the women on-site, this extra financial aid will boost help in so many more ways.

Nikki makes a small speech, thanking everyone before we step off the stage and allow the festivities to continue.

"You guys did it," Rocky cheers, embracing me tightly, almost to the point of suffocation.

"We still have some hard work ahead, but this will give us the financial backing to do so."

Marjorie joins us, wrapping her arms around me for a

tight hug. "Charlie, you've done amazing things for our families."

I pull away, smiling as I watch tears glass over her eyes. "Hey, no tears. Come Monday, we've got a lot more work to do, okay?"

She nods, willing a small laugh before saying goodbye.

The night carries on with guests dancing and mingling.

Eric tries to chat to every celebrity he can lay his hands on, and a few times I see his phone come out for his much-needed 'selfie' collection.

Adriana calls it a night, tired from her first child-free outing in months. I thank her again, hugging her goodbye before reminding her of our lunch next week.

It's evident Julian disappeared after our dance, and I knew well enough to close the book on that chapter of my life. As much as I wanted to make sure he was okay after my blatant rejection, some things are better left unsaid.

The clock has just ticked after midnight, and now the exhaustion is seeping in as my limbs begin to feel like lead weights.

"We're heading over to Melrose to continue drinks. You coming?" Eric asks, busily texting on his phone while half paying attention to me.

"You know what... you go have fun. I'm tired, and—"

"And your husband is waiting for you." Eric nods toward the bar, where Lex is talking with Marjorie.

I thought she had left earlier, but with curiosity growing, I walk over, wanting to know why he's still here.

"My dear, I know, I know... I said I was leaving an hour ago, but your lovely husband has been a pleasure to talk to."

I force a smile. The words 'lovely' and 'husband' should never be in the same sentence, especially when you're married to Lex Edwards.

Marjorie says goodbye again, leaving the two of us standing here alone. I'm not at all surprised he's still here. Lex is probably keeping tabs on Julian because his ego can't take the hit.

"I'm heading home. Come with me, please?"

Letting out a sigh, I turn to face where Eric is standing with Rocky. Their conversation is animated, and Nikki is standing with them, arms crossed while rolling her eyes. No doubt Eric and Rocky are planning something adventurous for tonight, of which Nikki doesn't approve.

"Um... sure."

With my clutch in hand, I wave goodbye to Nikki, who purses her lips in return. She knows what's been going on, and Lex has made it onto her naughty list, and he's currently sitting right at the top in red marker and a gold star.

I walk beside Lex toward his car. Both of us remain silent, which is exactly what I need. Exhaustion has hit at an all-time high, and I'm grateful Lex has chosen not to bring up anything, especially Julian, and has allowed me the solitude I crave.

When we reach the car, the memories of Lex taking me on the hood flashes before me. Not wanting to throw my body into turmoil, I do my best to shake it off. Nothing good will come of me giving him what he wants right now.

The car ride is quiet, only the soft melodies of Lex's music humming through the speakers is keeping me awake. He always had great taste in music, and I welcome the tunes of Coldplay as we drive home from a long night.

With Amelia staying over at Emily's, the reality of being alone with Lex will be a true testament to my willpower. It would be easy to ask Lex to come to bed, make sweet love to him, and listen to him promise me this will never happen again, but stubborn Charlie wants to think, alone.

"So..." He drops his keys on the countertop, removing his bow tie and unbuttoning the top of his shirt.

Yeah, I'm not immune to his sex appeal. So, I purposely turn away trying frantically to ignore its magnetic force.

"Amelia is at Mom's?"

"Yes." It's all I manage, not being sure which of Lex's personalities is about to emerge.

He nods his head, raising his eyes to meet mine. "Do you want me to sleep in the guest room?"

"It's your house, Lex, just as much as mine," I say, defeated. "I'm going to bed. Goodnight." I begin to walk out of the kitchen until Lex calls my name, prompting me to stop and turn around.

"I'm proud of you... for what you're doing to help Marjorie. It takes a lot of strength and willpower to fight for what's right and when it comes to family. You're the strongest advocate any mother or child could ask for. You're a warrior, Charlotte, and you deserve to know that." Lex walks past me, leaving me with those words.

Lex heads off to sleep in the guestroom while I lay wide awake unable to clear my thoughts. Lex's words run on repeat...

"You're a warrior Charlotte, and you deserve to know that."

I'd never considered myself a warrior. I've fought many battles alone, but only because I had no choice. And now, I'm married, yet the person I should be standing with, in the frontline, is sleeping in our guest room. Countless nights over the past few months I've laid in this bed alone.

The only difference now—I'm controlling the situation.

It's all on me.

A blessing and a curse.

I've managed to sleep a few hours despite my predicament. Before picking up Amelia, I decide to shower, change, and get some work done. With my breakfast and coffee sitting beside me in my home office, I'm interrupted as Lex knocks on the door. My gaze lifts, to see him dressed in a pair of jeans, a white tee, and sneakers. *How this man goes from tuxedo to sneakers and still looks like Adonis is beyond me.*

"Working?" he asks, keeping his distance.

"Yeah," I huff, slipping my glasses off. "These numbers are... frustrating, to say the least."

"Do you mind if I take a look?"

I push the papers toward him, wrapping my hands around the hot mug of coffee and taking a much-needed sip. Perhaps I've been overanalyzing, or my brain is tired from crunching numbers. Either way, I feel like I'm getting nowhere.

"Suggestion?"

"Go for it."

"If Marjorie can move the budget toward this column, you'll see a rise in losses. However, if you look over here, the return on investment will increase."

I carefully look over the numbers and his direction. Lex is right. Marjorie and her team need to find a way to sustain the everyday running of the shelter and still pay rent despite the increase because of greedy investors. The plan is to raise enough money to be able to purchase the land, plus renovate the building to make it more accommodating and functional.

"That makes sense. A lot of sense..." I trail off. "I'm going to work on this now before I pick up Amelia."

"I was thinking of picking her up. You know... spend

some time with her, plus give you some hours to work?"

I raise my eyes to meet his, offering him a smile. "I'd appreciate that. Thank you."

I present the numbers to Marjorie and her team. She nods her head, agreeing all the while appearing somewhat relieved. The shelter runs on sponsored funding, with many of their staff volunteers. Any penny saved will make a difference to the future of the shelter.

"You're an angel sent from above, Charlie."

My lips curve upward, welcoming the compliment, yet I am quick to remember it had been Lex's intelligence, not all mine.

"Actually, you can thank my husband. He's the brains behind numbers."

"As I've said before, you've got yourself a good man. He loves you very much."

Unsure of what to say, I express a "Thank you" for her kind words.

"You know, he reminds me of my Clifford before he passed," she says, reminiscing fondly. "Marriage is never easy... you've got to work hard *all* the time. We make mistakes, sometimes we hurt, but with the right love, it will burn into your soul forever."

Unable to hold back a smile, I thank her again before saying goodbye and walking out of the office. As I step past the small communal room, there's a teenage boy sitting at an old piano. Marjorie's son donated the piano to the shelter when they discovered many women could play. It wasn't fancy, nor grand, but it looks good enough for this boy to run his fingers along the keys and play the tune.

A girl who appears to be the same age sits beside him. They both laugh, a joke between them I can't quite hear, from where I am standing. At the same time, their faces brighten, grinning like two teenagers on the verge of falling in love. The boy nudges her shoulder with his own, playfully, before he rests his fingers on the keys again and begins playing a tune.

Each note becomes familiar, and like a blast from the past, it's the same song Lex played the day we sat at the piano together for the first time. I'm drawn back to Charlie from high school—young, naïve, and unfamiliar with the power of love. I'd fallen in love with Alexander Edwards, all of him, despite his marital circumstances. I had been foolish enough at that time to think we would never break, yet my innocence led me to believe our love would last forever.

And this will never change.

There is no choice but to start the journey of healing our marriage. We aren't completely broken, just bent over something we are both struggling to navigate through. And despite it all, the pain and suffering, keeping Lex away at an arm's length because of my own fears, will only hurt us more right now.

We are a family.

It isn't just about Lex and me either, Amelia also deserves my complete and utter devotion in joining Lex by trying to make us whole again.

I drive through the streets at record speed until Dreamteam Studios is directly in front of me. Parking my car, I run toward the entrance, almost out of breath as the receptionist greets me. I haven't been on-site for months and have no idea who she is, surprised to see Lex has hired a brunette for once.

"Can I help you?"

"I'm here to see Lex."

"I'm sorry." Her fake smile irritates me so much, along with the way she stares at my attire.

I would let her know I'm wearing Valentino, but my fashion choice is of no importance right now.

"You'll need an appointment."

Frustrated, I shake my head. "I'm his wife. Now, tell me where he is, or I'll hunt him down myself."

The receptionist is taken aback by my threat but slowly connects the dots in her air-filled head.

"He's in an important meeting in Boardroom A. You can't interrupt him... there's a strict no interruption rule. He will fire me if you go in there!"

Screw that rule.

I'll make sure he doesn't fire her.

My Louboutin heels click on the porcelain tiles, searching the nameplates on the doors until I see Board-room A. There's a glass wall, and Lex is sitting at the head of the table appearing uninterested while an older gentleman is talking. Lex's jacket is removed and hanging on the back of his chair, he's wearing his vest and tie, and looks dashing as the ever-so-powerful CEO.

With his body leaning back in his chair, his expression appears conflicted with his phone in his hand. His eyes wander to the screen, then his fingers are typing rapidly, only to press his lips together in a slight grimace before pressing send.

Seconds later, my phone vibrates in my purse.

LEX

> I love you, Charlotte. Forever. Always. I'll wait as long as you need me to.

His words evoke the emotions I've forced myself to

bury. I had grown accustomed to impatient, demanding, and controlling Lex, but I can see his repent for the mistakes he's made.

I open the door wide, every face in the room glances my way, and with my heart beating incredibly fast, I ignore everyone beside Lex.

With a concerned expression, he immediately rises from his chair, his neck muscles straining as he walks over to where I am standing. "Charlotte, is everything okay?"

"Yes, no... I need to speak with you," I rush out.

Lex excuses himself before closing the door behind us, grabbing my hand, he walks me toward his office. Once the door is closed, he let's me go and asks, "What's wrong?"

I bury my head in his chest, welcoming his quick embrace while allowing the suppressed emotions to run free, sobbing loudly as the weight of our actions has come to the surface.

"I love you," I cry, swallowing the lump inside my throat. "It hurts, but I love you."

Raising his hands, he cups my cheeks, forcing our gaze to meet, and almost like a chameleon, I swear, even in the darkest of times, his eyes morph into emerald green.

Just like always, they blanket me with love and warmth, but still, there's a part of me that's scared to allow him access to all of my heart if the only purpose is to break me until there's nothing left.

You have to learn to trust him, Charlie.

Love will never survive without it.

"If I have to spend my entire life earning your forgiveness, I will do just that. I can't... we can't be apart. I cannot let you go."

"I don't want you to let me go. We promised it was ride

or die. I'm standing here, breathing, alive, and want to give our family a second chance to become one again."

Lex closes his eyes, almost as if a weight has been lifted off his shoulders, only to open them again moments later. "Charlotte Edwards, I love you."

He places his mouth on mine, teasing me with a slow and soft kiss, igniting the fire within my belly and comforting me in the way words never can. I refuse to regret my actions or wish the past away, understanding the purpose of the journey is to strengthen our bond.

And in this one kiss, I now know I'm on the right path.

"How long until you're off duty?" I whisper, pushing my hand through his hair and relishing in the soft strands falling between my fingers.

Lex grins, running his nose against mine before letting me go. "Give me fifteen minutes, and I'm all yours."

"You're all mine or... I'm all yours?" I tease.

Pausing at the door, he lifts his gaze to meet mine. With a cocky grin, Lex tilts his head slightly then bites his bottom lip. "As long as I'm inside you, take it any which way you please."

And that's what we do, all night until the sun rises, my husband makes love to me. Devouring every inch of me, in our bed, in our home.

Thankfully, Adriana offered to take Amelia, which came as a surprise as well as convenient for us. Of course, I couldn't refuse. We needed some bonding time without the biggest cockblocker crying in her crib in the room beside us.

In the morning, I awake with his body curled into me. My phone beeps. I reach over, but Lex grabs my hand and places it on his cock. It's throbbing, and it only means one thing.

I don't have time to even finish that thought. He slides

inside me, and I moan, my body sore and tender from being ravaged on the car and the all-night sweet loving.

"I can't get enough of this, Charlotte. Being inside of you... my beautiful wife."

We come in sync, out of breath. I lean back, unable to move my muscles.

"Go ahead, you can check your phone now." He chuckles.

"I forgot... whoever it is can wait."

"I bet he can't."

"Lex..."

"If that phone beeps in the next minute, I get to fuck this pretty little ass of yours right now."

"And if you're wrong?" *Please don't be wrong!*

The phone beeps.

"Show me the text," he demands.

I grab my phone and slide the screen, two texts in a row, and they're from *Eric*.

ERIC

OMG Charlie, Matthew McConaughey is working out at Venice Beach! Meet me there in ten minutes.

Hurry up woman! My wank bank is in need of a refill!

"Looks like you won, Mr. Edwards, *what a shame...*"

"If you weren't soaking wet again, I would somehow think you were trying to weasel your way out of this. Now shut the fuck up and bring your beautiful ass here."

And in the morning sunshine in the light of day, he takes me in our bed, *again*.

THIRTY-FIVE

LEX

I sit at my desk, watching the clock, unable to move a muscle.

Charlotte has called me several times, and being the dick I am, I let it go to voicemail. I don't know how to handle what happened last night. This morning was bad enough as I swear I looked guilty of having my finger near someone else's pussy.

Today, I offered Montana a job at another company I invested in, which she gladly accepted. Her ego is bruised, and thankfully she's mature enough not to take this further because she holds the cards that can destroy me.

The phone rings again, and I glance at the caller ID. *Nikki.*

"What do you want?" I answer, defeated.

"Act however you want to act, Edwards, but I'm warning you that you are on the verge of losing your wife."

Honestly, women and their overly dramatic emotions. Nikki always has to voice her opinion when it comes to Charlotte's and my relationship.

"Nikki, I'll be right there, okay? I'm just leaving."

"So, tell me, Lex, is Montana worth losing your family over?"

"You don't know what you're talking about..." I trail off.

"Right, I have no idea what I'm talking about. That's why today I found divorce papers drawn up by Charlie on our server."

I freeze, my body stiffening at the use of the word 'divorce.' Nikki is causing unnecessary drama. Charlotte will never leave me.

"That's right. You don't believe me?" She almost laughs. "Check your email."

I hear a ping and quickly open the email, the attachment sitting in front of me titled 'Edwards vs. Edwards.' My heart sinks to the lowest pit possible. I have royally fucked everything up and have no idea how to fix anything. With a wave of nausea threatening me, my stomach hardens as reality begins to set in.

"I'll take your silence to mean you had no idea," she deadpans.

I'm speechless. I don't want her to leave me. *Why would she leave me?* Yes, I'd made life impossible for her, but we agreed to this unity until death has us to part. Listen to yourself, you've fucked her up and trying to place blame on her now. *You narcissist piece of shit, Edwards.*

"I'm warning you now, Edwards, so listen to me real good. I don't know what you're doing or who you're doing, but you might want to rethink your actions because as you sit there wallowing in self-pity, a certain journalist is here at the gala, and I can tell you now that your wife seems to be enjoying his company."

The fucking scumbag.

A wave of fury crashes through me at the thought of

him trying to win her back. I panic, needing to get out of here.

"Nikki, please promise me you won't let her do anything," I plea, desperately.

She remains quiet.

I can hear whispers in the background.

"I've got my eye on her. You just better be on your way here because it looks like your competition is this close to winning his girl back."

I hang up the call quickly and dash out to my car. I speed home, then rush inside and quickly change into my tux. As I race back to the car and drive off, I'm lucky not to get pulled over for what I am clocking. I drive up the long, winding driveway, frustrated that the parking lot is full, but luckily, I find a spot in a dark corner.

I enter through the side entrance, not wanting to be noticed, but Rocky has me on radar. Nikki is across the room, talking with Kate, eyeing me with caution.

"Dude, seriously, what the fuck is going on? Are you banging Montana? You're a fucking mess. I swear that chick looks nice and tight... but fuck you if you are 'cause I love Charlie like a sister."

"Rocky... I'm not, okay? In fact, she is no longer my assistant."

"All right, what happened? She sucked your dick, is that it?"

"Listen—"

"Dude." His tone softens. "I know you wouldn't do that to Charlie. I mean, purposely fuck around, but you gotta fix your marriage. Whatever the hell is bugging you, fix it now because if you look over there..." he points to the dance floor where Charlotte is in Julian's embrace, her head resting comfortably on his shoulder, "... you are gonna lose your woman forever." He pats me on the back before walking away.

The temperature in the room is rising, my blood pressure ready to blow as I remain fixated on how she is dancing with him. He whispers words in her ear, my heart beating out of my fucking chest. I'm trapped in my own mistakes, bleeding profusely, yet I'm the one holding the knife, tearing us apart.

She's parading my weakness in front of me and the world, the one thing I can't control no matter how hard I try. Julian Baker will forever be the man who proposed marriage first to Charlotte, who offered her a life when I didn't. He's touched her in ways only I should have fucking touched her. And despite it all, they will always have that bond, and nothing I do will ever change that.

Charlotte is my fucking wife, yet I stand absolutely paralyzed with anger until her eyes search the room and focus on me.

Don't leave me, Charlotte.

I love you, baby.

Don't listen to him, I'm good for you.

I watch her pull away from him. I watch as he grasps onto her for dear life without a doubt making promises to give her everything I haven't because I'm a fucking selfish dickhead ambushed by my own insecurities.

She walks over, and it's impossible to be immune to her beauty as she stands before me in a strapless black evening dress that hugs her body in all the right places, the places I want to roll my tongue over.

Hold onto her, Edwards.

Don't let him steal her from you.

Charlotte says the words that need to be said after I allow my emotions to ravage her with accusations. Knowing

I'm completely out of control, I pull her along to the exit, needing to get out of there and get her alone. I need answers. I need her to know she's mine, I'm finally finding my balls and putting up a fight, hoping it's not too late, and I haven't lost her forever.

The desperation has consumed me. I pull her forcefully, pushing her onto the hood of my car taking back what has been mine all along. I need to claim what belongs to me, it conquers all rational thought, and I know I'm hurting her. I know she is crying, yet the minute my cock buries itself within her, I'm falling into a beautiful abyss, one full of light, blinding me, yet calming my senses all at the same time. It's only a few thrusts, but my body has ignited into a roaring flame, and I can only hold out for so long before it's all over.

I remind her again who she belongs to, and even in her pleas, I feel her body sink into me. Her walls tighten, and knowing my beautiful wife will explode all over my cock within seconds is enough to slam into her one more time until my walls shatter, and every single nerve is overcome by a pleasurable finish.

In the cool of the night, I gulp in the fresh air, trying to calm my racing heart. I reluctantly pull away, and then she tells me she can no longer do this.

"Please let me go..." she begs.

We planned our future, our lives as one. We brought a child into this world and talked about expanding our family again one day.

With my heart broken and in despair, I beg her to stay with me.

I'm a fucking idiot. I have the best thing in the world and almost lost it, caught up in my old greedy and selfish ways.

And I thought she would forgive me, but instead, she walked away.

She asked for time, but time to me meant more reasoning to leave our marriage. I panicked, saying words, bringing up Julian, until she disappeared back into the ballroom and I'm left to stand on my own.

For once, I allowed my jealousy and controlling nature to take a back seat. Charlotte made herself perfectly clear and in order to gain her trust, I need not to push her.

I kept my distance towards the back of the room, watching her as she spoke so confidently. I was so damn proud of her, amazed by her talent and strength, making the effort to tell her that when we got back home.

I slept in the guest room, despite my body craving her touch. In the morning when I woke, I'm surprised to find her working. I knew her well enough to know her need to bury herself in work is to distract from my presence. So again, I didn't push just offered to help with numbers. Trying my best not to control the situation as I do every day in the office, I offer some suggestions which she welcomed with gratitude.

As hard it was, I left her to work and spent the day with Amelia. I took her to the park, then a long walk along the beach as she slept in her pram. By the time we got home, it was the usual routine of dinner, bath time then bed.

The same night, I slept in the guestroom not wanting to force myself on Charlotte.

When Monday rolled around, I was knee deep in mundane discussions about budget restraints with shooting locations. No matter what I did, my mind wandered to Charlotte. I needed her to know how much I loved her but every text I wrote, came out wrong. For the last hour, I had typed, then deleted multiple texts. And then something pulled me, like a magnetic force so great and with just one tap, I finally hit send.

The second I laid eyes on her inside my boardroom, I'm riddled with worry until she told me she loved me.

It was exactly what I needed to hear.

I look back now and remember how close I was to losing my family. How easy it was to make promises in front of God, your family, and friends, only to forget them in desperate times. Charlotte and I made a pact that day, we would remain true and honest in good times and bad. For the sake of our daughter, we both owe it to our family.

We also agree we need to be honest about what happened when we were apart. This, I know, will not go down well, and there's a chance Charlotte will not speak to me ever again, but I rely heavily on our faith and trust that somehow, we can push the darkness behind us.

"We said we'd do this," she reminds me.

"I know," I respond.

I don't know what's worse, telling her that my finger was on Montana's pussy for a brief second, or what she is going to tell me about Julian. My insecurity and anger are mixed into a bag of fucked- up emotions, drying my throat as we sit across from each other ready to unleash.

"Are you ready?" she sounds nervous.

"Yes."

We sit in a hotel room, Charlotte's idea of not tainting our house with any bad conversations or memories. We left Amelia with my mom because both of us have no idea how this is going to go down. I'm hoping what she is about to tell me isn't so bad, and we can just be done with it so I can spend the night inside her.

"You first," she says

"No, you."

"Rock, paper, scissors." She holds out her hand, and we shake until we both get scissors. *How ironic,* I think. *Stabbed in the heart, it's an omen.* On our second attempt, she beat me.

Fuck.

Charlotte sits still, crossed-legged at one end of the bed staring at me. I think about complimenting her on her choice of blouse which will look nice on the floor but decide against it.

"You're doing that lawyer thing you do in court. It's freaking me out and turning me on."

"It's my coping mechanism because somehow, I don't think I'm going to like what I hear and don't try turning on the charm."

I take a deep breath, and with my eyes never leaving hers, I tell her everything that happened the night with Montana. When I finally finish, I wait in silence for her reaction. I expect her fist in my face, not for her to hurt me with words.

"I'll tell you what happened with Julian. He reminded me of how good we were together. He asked me to leave you, and I thought about it. I remembered how once upon a time my body craved him and gave into him, and there he stood, right next to me, offering to love me the way I deserved to be loved, and I thought about it, Lex. I thought about giving myself to him that night."

The stabs are sharp, each one of them cutting through the scars that are finally healing, ripping them open. My body tenses, my adrenaline spikes, and my throat goes dry unable to say what I need to say.

How the fuck can she want another man!

I don't know what's worse, my physical indiscretion or her emotional one. They are on par. We were both hurting because of what we did to each other. It didn't make it better that she didn't touch him, it fucking hurt like mother-fucking hell that she had a moment of wanting him for the rest of her life.

"It's done, Lex. Now, tell me how strong our marriage is?" Her eyes fixate on mine. I can see she is praying we can get through this and restore all faith in humanity. We've gotten this far, defeated the odds, and our love should be able to stand any test of time.

"You're a bitch for wanting him."

"You're a cunt for touching her."

"I hate that word," I grit.

"Used sparingly, for occasions like this," she rebuts.

Emotionally exhausted, I want the book closed on this. We've lost so much time, torn apart by grief over the last few months, and I want more than anything to forget we were almost over.

"So, what happens now, Charlotte?"

I want her, and I need her at this moment. My eyes penetrate hers, attempting to cast that so-called spell she claims I do every time I look at her. *C'mon, eyes, you can do it, make her see the light.*

"Now, we fuck harder than we have ever fucked each other in our lives. I need to claim you just as much as you need to claim me. You got me?"

I put on a huge grin. Despite this mess I created, my fucking girl makes me smile. Best yet, I get to fuck her so hard and mark her as mine again.

"I got you... and I'm never letting go of you. *Obsessed together forever.*"

"*Obsessed together forever.*"

She winks.

EPILOGUE
CHARLIE

It's Christmas Eve, and this year we are fortunate enough to celebrate with our family as well as with friends. Rocky, Nikki, and Will flew in early and are staying with us. I couldn't have been happier. I missed Will so much. He has grown so tall and is at that age where hugs are awkward according to him. He has matured beyond his years, but deep down inside, he's still that little boy who captured my heart many moons ago.

Kate and Emma also fly over but chose to stay with Eric. What the three of them get up to is beyond me. They are deemed the three musketeers, with their shenanigans always the talk of the town. Rocky whines like a left-out schoolgirl every time they go out, and, eventually, Nikki gives in. Hours later, the four of them will plaster their buffoonery all over Facebook, the visit to the Playboy Mansion being the best one yet.

Somehow, I always get stuck with the shitty stick. I stand there in the kitchen, preparing dinner for everyone, including Dad and Debbie, who have driven down to spend time with Amelia. My mom's traveling across Europe with

my sister, a much-needed bonding session I suggested after
my mother came clean about her past. I still remember the
night it happened, a month ago when she came to visit us.

*"Tell me, Mom, what did your dark angel do to you that has
made you so bitter about love?"*

*She placed her hand over her heart, and with her other,
she reached out to me for support. "He came into town one
day. He was beautiful like a knight in shining armor. I was
seventeen, I knew nothing about love, but I knew enough to
know that my heart only wanted him."*

*Her eyes scanned my face, waiting for judgment. "He
promised me things... the world, and I allowed him to take
me in the woods that night. He promised he would love me
and be gentle, he always promised he would, but that night
he hurt me, took my innocence on the dirty, cold floor. I
begged him to stop. I told him if he loved me, he wouldn't
hurt me. He didn't listen... he took me, then left me there,
crying, and I never saw him again."*

*I was shocked at the revelation. It all made sense why she
warned me of this creature. Her dark angel, the big bad wolf,
had robbed her of her innocence.*

"Mi corazon... Please don't hate me..."

*"Mom," I reassured her, squeezing her hand tight. "I
don't hate you."*

"Melanie..." she trailed off.

*What about my sister? I watched my mom's eyes as the
secret lay within, and it was there written all over her face.*

*"It was too late. He left me and implanted his seed. How
could I ever forget him?" Her voice now trembling.*

*Daddy, my heart bled for him. He loved Melanie so
much.*

"Does Dad know?" My voice was high-pitched, the air not flowing quickly enough.

"He knew that this man had a hold of me. Deep down inside, I know he does, but he always loved Melanie the same as you."

"Go to her, Mom, go release the demon that has ravaged you. You've been carrying this burden for too long. Set it free, and I promise you he won't haunt you anymore."

She nodded, smiling before caressing my cheek. "I was wrong, Corazon. He's not your dark angel."

I let out a small laugh "Oh, he is, Mom, the only difference is he knows who's got him by the balls if he ever pulled a stunt like that."

Amid her tears, she let out a laugh and began the journey to setting her demons free.

I'm knee-deep, or should I say fist-deep in turkey and cranberries when I hear a noise beside me. I look up and find Adriana standing by the kitchen bench. I muster up a smile, and lean over to hug her tight, careful not to smear anything on her beautiful white dress.

"I didn't think you would come," I murmured.

She smiles, it still pains her, but it's a smile. "Someone has to help you out in the kitchen because the lazy-ass crowd in the living room is playing Twister."

"Again?"

"It's down to Rocky and Eric."

"This never ends well—" I am interrupted as Rocky yells out, "Dude, your fucking dick is in my face!"

Adriana laughs. It's the first laugh I have heard since Elijah passed away. She has the most beautiful smile, and what right does God have taking away the one thing that brings it out?

Not now, Charlie, be strong for Adriana.

"I'm glad you're here. We'll get through this. As a family, I promise you that."

"I know, Charlie. Elijah told me we would."

We hug each other again before carrying the starters into the living room. As I suspected, Rocky and Eric's position put gay porn to shame. I burst out laughing as the spinner requests Eric to move his left foot, which causes him to collapse onto Rocky's face.

"Fuck, Eric! You did that on purpose," Rocky yells, pushing Eric off him.

The entire room bursts into laughter, ending the Twister game.

Emily suggests we sing some Christmas carols to celebrate, and Lex asks Amelia if she wants to play with him. She nods and holds his hand as he places her on the piano stool. Andy wants in on the action, and monkey crawls his way over, begging Lex to lift him. He does with ease. If anyone has a piece of Lex's heart, it's Andy.

"Any requests?" Emily asks.

"Yeah, I have one..." Adriana speaks up.

A hush falls over the room.

Andrew automatically moves to Adriana placing his arm around her.

"I'm okay, Dad. Elijah is here, I can feel him."

Adriana looks at Lex. He knows his sister well enough and turns around and starts playing. She starts singing as she moves her way over to Andy.

Silent night, holy night

All is calm, all is bright
'Round yon virgin Mother and Child
Holy infant so tender and mild
Sleep in heavenly peace
Sleep in heavenly peace

I can't help it as a tear slides down my face. Eric and Emma move my way and link their arms with mine.

We continue to sing until the clock strikes midnight. We make our way throughout the room, hugging each other and wishing everyone a Merry Christmas. As I reach Lex and a sleepy Amelia, I whisper in his ear for him to follow me down the hall. He hands Amelia over to Kate who takes her with open arms, and I watch as Lex's face lights up. The dirty bastard probably thinks I'm going to give him a hand job or something.

"Close your eyes," I request, excitedly.

"Will you be naked when I open them?" He shuts his eyes.

"Yeah, sure... with my dad here, you psychopath. Okay... you can open them."

I watch his reaction as he stands in our guest room, admiring the shiny new drum set which sits in the middle of the floor.

"Are you kidding me? I always wanted a drum set!" He has the biggest smile on his face, running over to the seat and settling himself in. He grabs the sticks and does a beat, much to my surprise since he doesn't play. This man is a fucking musical prodigy.

"I know... I remember, *Alex*."

His eyes met mine, and I'm surprised he doesn't recoil when I call him that.

"You called me Alex," he whispers.

"There's a huge part of me that still sees him in you. If you look close enough, he's still there."

"Charlotte, I... don't know what to say to that."

"You do, but you don't have to say it."

"You miss him?" I can hear the trepidation in his voice like a lost little boy finding his way home.

"I don't need to miss him. I've been staring at him for the past two years."

It's hard to explain what I see, almost like a burden has been lifted from his shoulders.

He finds himself again.

He finds his true identity.

"Thank you, baby, I love it, and I love you." He stands and walks back over to me, leaning in to kiss my lips.

"You want your present now?" he asks enthusiastically.

I nod. He pulls a long black velvet box out of his pocket. Lex has a massive thing for jewelry, so I'm not surprised that he spoils me again. I carefully open the box, but much to my shock, I find a pregnancy stick sitting inside.

"What's this?" I ask, barely able to get my words out.

"You're pregnant."

The words don't register. *I'm what?*

"Read my lips, Charlotte. You're pregnant."

I'm astounded. The test is new, so I haven't actually done one. *How on earth would he think I'm pregnant?*

"I know you so well, Charlotte. I've studied every inch of your body over the years. The slightest change, and I can see it. *You're pregnant.* I promise you with all of me that you are carrying another baby inside of you."

Without a word, I pull him to our nearest bathroom and

close the door behind us. I'm not late, at least I don't think I am. I'm not nauseous. Nothing at all has changed.

I pee on the stick as he watches me with an amused look on his face. I carefully place it on the countertop and wait. "Are you sure about this?" I ask, nervous.

"Never been so sure about anything in my life."

It's time. I walk over with nerves of steel and open my eyes, the two blue lines staring me in the face.

"Holy shit, I'm pregnant!" I jump into his arms as he swings me around. "This is the best Christmas present ever!" With the biggest grin on his face, he kisses me deeply, and I wrap my arms around his neck.

"Can we tell everyone tonight, please?" he begs.

I nod. That's what family is for, to celebrate the good times and to hold your hand at the worst. Sometimes it's the family we are born into, and sometimes it is the family we make for ourselves. I'm lucky enough to have both, and I thank the Lord every day that I'm blessed with such a gift.

We make our way back outside where everyone stands around the tree. Before we make the announcement, Lex wants to show off his outside Christmas decorations. He has become Clark Griswold with an unhealthy obsession of having the best lights on the street. Everyone makes their way outside as we stand on the lawn while Lex flips the switch.

The whole house illuminates as everyone gushes like watching fireworks on the 4th of July.

It's breathtaking.

There's something about Christmas lights that brings out the inner child in each of us. The lights are shining so bright, the warmth rushing over me, the spirit alive as we all admire the work that Lex has done. I turn to look at Lex carrying Amelia in one arm and Andy in the other. Both of them are wide awake, enjoying the spectacle and babbling in baby talk as they point to the moving reindeers that Lex installed on our roof.

He turns to look my way and mouths the words 'I love you.' I mouth the words back, then rest my head against his arm.

Amelia tugs on my sleeve. "Momma, looky," she babbles, turning my face to look at the lights.

Adriana comes up beside me and holds onto me tightly. Her smile is gracious as she focuses on the house, then moves her eyes to the stars above.

I don't know how I spotted it, but there on the ground in front of me lays a white feather. I reach down and pick it up handing it to Adriana. She leans across to Andy and hands it to him.

"See, Andy, I told you Daddy was here."

There are angels all around us. Sometimes we can see them and other times we can't. If you look carefully, all around us there are clues. There are some that are placed on this earth as a gift from God, and there are some that are around to protect us from harm and evil.

And then there is mine, my dark angel.

He does everything my mother said he will do, and one other thing she doesn't know he's capable of—*he loves me.* He gave me not just one, but two angels of our very own.

They say there is a light at the end of every tunnel, but they never tell you how long the tunnel is. Sometimes, we stand looking into the dark with the hint of light peeking its way through, and sometimes, we stand looking into the tunnel with only darkness surrounding us.

Things happen for a reason, good or bad. We never truly understand why, instead, we live in a world of regret, focusing on what can never be changed—the past. Sometimes when we are lost in our current happiness, it dawns on us that without mistakes, without regret, we wouldn't be where we are today.

Once upon a time, I was afraid of the dark. I lived a life trapped in my mistakes. I questioned why I was forced to look into the darkness. Now here I stand, strong, with an understanding that all I have endured made me who I am today. It made me understand the strength and power of love. It made me understand that life may hand you bananas, but sometimes you just need to beat the odds and somehow figure out how to make lemonade.

There will always be darkness in the world we live in, but how we survive is measured by the love that surrounds us. I know that no matter what happened in the past, what will happen in the future, there is and will only ever be one man who has my heart, one man whose love has no bounds.

Alexander Matthew Edwards.

My husband, my soul mate, my forever.

CHASING HER

A Stalker Romance
The Dark Love Series
Book 3

BLURB

I hear his words echo in my head.
The voice telling me to leave her alone.
The threat to end my life should I dare go near her.

Julian Baker had it all. Stunning good looks, wealth,
intelligence, and the girl. To everyone around him, he was
Mr. Perfect.

Fate was never on his side, and much like a domino effect,
his life starts to spiral out of control. Behind the mask lies a
broken man, haunted by his tragic past. In a bid to forget, he
finds himself desperately trying to hold on to someone who
is equally unattainable, Charlotte Edwards.

In a last-ditch effort to save himself, Julian reaches out for help, but the universe has other plans when someone completely unexpected walks into his life, and an unlikely friendship is formed.

His enemy's sister—Adriana Evans.

ALSO BY KAT T. MASEN

The Dark Love Series

Featuring Lex & Charlie

Chasing Love: A Billionaire Love Triangle

Chasing Us: A Second Chance Love Triangle

Chasing Her: A Stalker Romance

Chasing Him: A Forbidden Second Chance Romance

Chasing Fate: An Enemies-to-Lovers Romance

Chasing Heartbreak: A Friends-to-Lovers Romance

Lex: A Companion Novella

The Forbidden Love Series

(The Dark Love Series Second Generation)

Featuring Amelia Edwards

The Trouble With Love: An Age Gap Romance

The Trouble With Us: A Second Chance Love Triangle

The Trouble With Him: A Secret Pregnancy Romance

The Trouble With Her: A Friends-to-Lovers Romance

The Trouble With Fate: An Enemies-to-Lovers Romance

The Secret Love Series

(The Dark Love Series Second Generation)

Featuring Alexandra Edwards

Craving Love: An Age Gap Romance

Craving Us: A Second Chance Romance

Also by Kat T. Masen

The Office Rival: An Enemies-to-Lovers Romance

The Marriage Rival: An Office Romance

Bad Boy Player: A Brother's Best Friend Romance

Roomie Wars Box Set (Books 1 to 3): Friends-to-Lovers Series

ABOUT THE AUTHOR

Kat T. Masen is a USA Today Bestselling Author from Sydney, Australia. Her passion is writing angsty love triangles involving forbidden men like besties older brother.

She is also the founder of the Books Ever After store, Books By The Bridge Author Events, and spends way too much time on Tik Tok creating videos for her #1 Amazon bestseller Chasing Love.

Oh...and she's a total boy mom.
1 husband, 4 boys, and a needy pug.

Download free bonus content, purchase signed paperbacks & bookish merchandise.
Visit: **www.kattmasen.com**